Table of Contents

Economic Production

1

Mastering the Art of Economic Production, Empowering Your Prosperity

Fouad Sabry is the former Regional Head of Business Development for Applications at Hewlett Packard (HP) for Southern Europe, Middle East, and Africa. Fouad has received his Bachelor of Science (B.Sc.) of Computer Systems and Automatic Control, dual master's degrees, Master of Business Administration (MBA) and Master of Management in Information Technology (MMIT), from University of Melbourne (MoU) in Australia. Fouad has more than 25 years of experience in Information and Communication Technologies (ICT), working in local, regional, and international companies, such as Vodafone and International Business Machines (IBM). Currently, Fouad is an entrepreneur, author, futurist, focused on Emerging Technologies, and Industry Solutions, and founder of one billion knowledge (1BK) community.

One Billion Knowledge

Economic Production

Mastering the Art of Economic Production, Empowering Your Prosperity

Fouad Sabry

Copyright

Economic Production © 2023 by Fouad Sabry. All Rights Reserved.

"Economic Production" is your gateway to understanding the engine that powers our world. This book demystifies complex economic concepts, making them accessible and relevant. Whether you're a student, professional, or curious mind, it equips you to make informed decisions and contribute to economic growth. Unlock the secrets of prosperity – grab your copy today!

Economic Production: Unlocking the Engines of Prosperity

In a world driven by the complexities of modern economics, understanding the heartbeat of our economies-production-is the key to unlocking a world of opportunity, influence, and informed decision-making. "Economic Production" is your gateway to this captivating realm. It is an indispensable resource that demystifies the intricacies of economic production, unveiling its profound impact on our daily lives, businesses, and governments. From the food on your plate to the gadgets you use, from the jobs that define your career to the policies that govern your nation, production is the force behind it all.

At the heart of this exploration is the recognition that economic production is more than just an academic concept-it's the pulse of our societies, the catalyst of prosperity, and the source of transformation. This book offers an immersive experience that brings the subject to life, revealing how production drives economies, shapes our choices, and influences our world.

Foundations of Prosperity

The journey begins with a comprehensive look at the foundations of economic production. You'll dive into the factors of production, unravel the complex relationships that underlie economic growth, and discover the pivotal role that production plays in shaping the world. The knowledge you gain in these foundational chapters serves as your compass, guiding you through the intricate landscapes of economics.

Demystifying Economic Theories

Economics, often regarded as a complex and daunting field, is made accessible through this book. We have distilled intricate theories into clear and engaging narratives, ensuring that readers of all backgrounds can embark on a journey of enlightenment. You will find economic theories brought to life, such as the laws of supply and demand, the impact of technological advancements, and the interplay of factors that drive production.

A Global Perspective

"Production knows no borders," and this book takes a global approach. It reveals the interconnectivity of economies, the shared challenges that transcend national boundaries, and the opportunities that stem from international collaboration. As you explore the global nature of production, you'll gain a deeper appreciation for the forces that drive international trade, cooperation, and economic development.

Real-World Application

"Economic Production" goes beyond theory, offering a bridge between academic knowledge and practical understanding. It invites you to engage with the real-world implications of production in your personal and professional life. You'll discover how production shapes industries, influences businesses, and impacts your everyday decisions as a consumer and citizen.

Empowerment Through Knowledge

The true power of this book lies in its capacity to empower. Whether you're a student embarking on an academic journey, a business leader making strategic choices, a policymaker crafting the future, or a curious individual eager to navigate the complexities of the economic world, the knowledge you gain here empowers you. It equips you to make informed decisions, contribute to economic progress, and understand the forces that drive our world.

An Invitation to Explore and Engage

"Economic Production" is not just a textbook; it's an invitation to become an active participant in the world of economics. It is an opportunity to unlock your potential as an informed and engaged decision-maker. You are invited to immerse yourself in the intricate world of production, question established paradigms, and explore the dynamic forces that shape our economies and societies.

The world of economics need not be limited to experts and scholars; it's a realm for everyone who wishes to be a more informed, engaged citizen. Whether you're an aspiring economist, a professional seeking mastery, or a curious mind eager to understand the forces that shape your world, this book welcomes you to embark on an intellectual journey, to embrace knowledge, and to become a catalyst for change.

In "Economic Production," you hold the key to unraveling the mysteries of economic prosperity. It's an invitation to explore, to question, and to engage in a dialogue that shapes our economic future. We invite you to unlock the secrets of economic production, to empower your future, and to embrace the knowledge that will empower you to make a difference in the world of economics.

Empower Your Future. Unlock the Secrets of Economic Production. Grab Your Copy Today!

Dedication

This book, "Economic Production," is dedicated to the inquisitive minds and passionate individuals who seek to unravel the mysteries of the economic world. It is dedicated to those who believe in the transformative power of knowledge and its potential to shape our lives, our communities, and the broader global landscape. Whether you are a student beginning your academic journey, a seasoned economist honing your expertise, or a curious reader eager to explore the intricacies of economic production, this book is dedicated to you.

We dedicate this book to the countless educators who have dedicated their lives to imparting the wisdom of economics. Your guidance and mentorship have ignited the flame of curiosity in generations of students. This book serves as a tribute to your unwavering commitment to nurturing the next generation of economists and thought leaders.

To the researchers and scholars who have devoted their careers to advancing the frontiers of economic knowledge, this book is dedicated to you. Your tireless efforts to explore, question, and innovate have enriched our understanding of production in economics. We honor your contributions and seek to build upon the foundation you have laid.

This dedication extends to the policymakers and practitioners who use economic insights to shape our world. Your decisions and actions have a profound impact on the lives of countless individuals. This book is dedicated to providing you with the knowledge and tools to make informed choices that promote economic growth and social welfare.

Lastly, we dedicate this book to the curious minds who may not yet be fully aware of the fascinating world of economics. It is our hope that this book will serve as an inviting gateway to the subject of economic production, sparking your interest and inspiring you to explore further. We believe that a better understanding of economics can empower individuals to make informed decisions, foster economic progress, and contribute to a more prosperous and equitable world.

In dedicating this book to each of you, we acknowledge the vital role you play in the pursuit of knowledge and the advancement of our collective understanding of economics. We hope this dedication resonates with you and invites you to join us on an enlightening journey through the intricate and captivating world of economic production.

Epigraph

In the grand tapestry of economic life, production stands as the warp and weft that weaves the fabric of prosperity and progress. It is the driving force behind the creation of goods and services, the generation of wealth, and the enhancement of human well-being. The words of Adam Smith, often regarded as the father of modern economics, serve as an apt epigraph to our exploration of "Economic Production":

"To found a great empire for the sole purpose of raising up a people of customers may at first sight appear a project fit only for a nation of shopkeepers. It is, however, a project altogether unfit for a nation of shopkeepers, but extremely fit for a nation whose government is influenced by shopkeepers."

These words resonate with the profound influence of production on the course of nations. Production is not merely a matter of material output; it is a cornerstone of economic policy and societal growth. Adam Smith's wisdom reminds us that the intricate interplay between production, government, and commerce shapes the destiny of nations, laying the foundation for the discussion that follows.

As we embark on this journey, we draw inspiration from the renowned economist John Maynard Keynes:

"Capitalism is the astounding belief that the most wickedest of men will do the most wickedest of things for the greatest good of everyone."

Keynes's words encapsulate the complexity of the economic production landscape. They challenge us to critically examine the dynamics of capitalism, human behavior, and the broader pursuit of economic prosperity. Our exploration of economic production delves into the forces and mechanisms that govern these interactions, offering valuable insights for readers seeking a deeper understanding of the economic world.

Lastly, the words of Nobel laureate Paul Samuelson offer a guiding light for our endeavor:

"Every good cause is worth some inefficiency."

In a world where efficiency and productivity often take center stage, Samuelson's insight serves as a reminder of the importance of balance and purpose in economic endeavors. Our exploration of economic production is underpinned by the understanding that the pursuit of economic prosperity must be coupled with a commitment to the greater good. As we delve into the intricacies of production, we aim to shed light on the path toward balanced and purposeful economic growth.

This book set the stage for a comprehensive journey through the world of economic production, reminding us of the influential voices and profound insights that have shaped our understanding of this vital subject. We invite you to join us in this exploration, as we delve into the complex tapestry of "Economic Production" and unveil the threads that bind together economies and societies.

Foreword

Welcome to "Economic Production," a book that unlocks the mysteries of a subject that shapes our world, influences economies, and impacts lives on a global scale. In this thought-provoking journey, we invite you to explore the dynamic interplay between production and economics, revealing the critical role it plays in our daily existence. Whether you are an aspiring economist, a seasoned professional, or simply a curious mind, this book promises to enrich your understanding of the economic forces that drive our world.

Economic production is the heartbeat of human civilization. It represents the transformation of resources, both human and material, into the goods and services that fuel our societies. From the foods we eat to the smartphones we use, from the services we enjoy to the infrastructure that supports our lives, production is the backbone of our modern existence. This book offers a unique perspective, taking you on a journey behind the scenes of the economic engine that powers our world.

Our exploration begins with a deep dive into the fundamental principles of production. We dissect the components of production, from the factors of production to the mechanisms that drive it forward. In the chapters that follow, we unearth the secrets of economic growth, productivity, and the intricate forces that influence the dynamics of modern economies.

"Production is not an end in itself, but a means to the satisfaction of human wants." This statement by renowned economist Alfred Marshall epitomizes the essence of our journey. As we delve into the complexities of economic production, we invite you to reflect on how these processes impact the well-being of individuals, communities, and nations. Our book provides a bridge between theory and real-world application, making it a valuable resource for students, professionals, and anyone eager to understand the dynamics of economic production.

Economics is often described as the "dismal science," but in these pages, we aim to illuminate the subject with clarity, relevance, and a touch of excitement. We have striven to make this book not only informative but engaging, helping you unlock the insights needed to navigate the complex world of production. We are confident that the knowledge you gain here will empower you to make informed decisions, contribute to economic progress, and develop a deeper appreciation for the intricacies of our interconnected world.

Whether you are a student embarking on your academic journey, a professional seeking to deepen your expertise, or simply someone intrigued by the forces that shape our lives, "Economic Production" has been crafted with you in mind. We believe that the key to making informed choices in our complex world lies in understanding the production processes that underpin it. We hope this book will inspire you to explore, question, and engage in the dialogue surrounding economic production, and we invite you to join us on this enlightening journey through the intricate world of "Economic Production."

Preface

Welcome to "Economic Production," a journey into the dynamic world of economic forces that shape our lives. This book is a testament to the belief that economic production is not merely an academic subject; it's the lifeblood of our societies, influencing every facet of our existence. Our preface is an invitation to embark on an intellectual adventure, to explore the intricacies of production, and to gain the knowledge needed to navigate the complex world of economics with confidence.

At its core, this book is a celebration of the power of knowledge. We believe that understanding the principles that govern production is the key to making informed choices in our personal and professional lives. "Economic Production" serves as a beacon for those eager to gain insight into how our world works and to make a positive impact on it.

Economics has often been viewed as a daunting and inaccessible field, but our preface offers reassurance that this book is designed to demystify complex concepts. We have taken great care to present economic theories and principles in a way that is engaging, relatable, and, most importantly, understandable. Whether you're new to economics or an experienced professional, this book bridges the gap between theory and practice, enabling readers of all backgrounds to join the conversation on economic production.

Our journey begins with an exploration of the fundamentals, where we dissect the essential components of production, from the factors that drive it to the mechanisms that make it thrive. As you turn the pages, you'll come to understand the intricate web of choices, processes, and influences that shape economic production, allowing you to unravel the mysteries of our economic world.

We've also taken a global perspective, acknowledging that in today's interconnected world, production knows no borders. The book delves into international trade, economic cooperation, and the shared challenges and opportunities that drive the global economy. Our aim is to inspire a broader understanding of the forces that shape the economic landscape, highlighting the significance of international collaboration in today's world.

"Economic Production" is more than a book; it's an invitation. It's an invitation to explore, to question, and to engage in a dialogue that shapes our economic future. It's an invitation to become an active participant in the world of economics, whether you're a student, a business leader, a policymaker, or simply an informed citizen. We invite you to unlock the secrets of economic production and empower your future.

Thank you for choosing "Economic Production." We hope this preface resonates with your curiosity and inspires you to join us on a journey of enlightenment. Together, we will explore the intricate world of production, understand the dynamics of our economic lives, and embark on a quest to make informed decisions that contribute to the well-being of individuals, communities, and nations.

Empower Your Future. Unlock the Secrets of Economic Production. Grab Your Copy Today!

Acknowledgements

In embarking on the journey to delve deep into the complex world of economic production, we stand on the shoulders of many giants, whose wisdom, guidance, and support have been instrumental in the creation of this book. Their unwavering commitment to the pursuit of knowledge and their dedication to the field of economics have inspired us at every step of this endeavor.

We would like to express our profound gratitude to the numerous economists, scholars, and experts whose tireless research and scholarly contributions have paved the way for the exploration of production in economics. Your valuable insights have been instrumental in shaping the content of this book, and your enduring commitment to advancing the field of economic production serves as an inspiration to us all.

Our deepest appreciation goes to the dedicated educators and mentors who have tirelessly shared their knowledge and wisdom with countless students, sparking an enduring passion for economics. It is your commitment to fostering the growth of the next generation of economists that has provided the foundation upon which this book is built.

The generous support of our colleagues and peers within the academic community has been instrumental in shaping the ideas presented in this work. Your intellectual exchange, critical feedback, and shared enthusiasm for the subject have contributed significantly to the book's depth and breadth, and we are truly grateful for your collaboration.

We extend our heartfelt thanks to the readers who are about to embark on this educational journey. Your curiosity and thirst for knowledge are what drive us to share our insights and discoveries on the intricate subject of economic production. We hope that the knowledge and perspectives you gain from this book will not only inform your understanding of economics but also empower you to contribute to the ongoing discourse in this field.

Last but not least, we are immensely grateful to our families and loved ones who have provided unwavering support throughout this challenging and rewarding process. Your encouragement, patience, and understanding have been the bedrock upon which this work has been constructed. We hope that this book serves as a testament to the value of economic production and the remarkable individuals who have made it possible. Thank you all for your indispensable contributions, and we hope that this book proves to be a valuable resource in your journey to unravel the intricacies of economic production.

Introduction

Welcome to "Economic Production," a journey through the beating heart of modern economies. In this introductory chapter, we invite you to embark on a captivating exploration of a subject that influences our daily choices, underpins economic policies, and shapes the world as we know it. Whether you're a student on a quest for knowledge, a professional seeking to master the intricacies of production, or a curious mind eager to understand the economic forces that drive our lives, this book is your ticket to unveiling the mysteries of economic production.

At its core, economic production is the process by which societies transform resources into the goods and services that sustain our livelihoods. It is the engine of economic growth and the driving force behind the creation of wealth. As you delve into the pages of this book, you'll gain a profound appreciation for the vital role of production in our daily existence and in the broader context of global economies.

Our journey begins with an examination of the foundations of economic production. We'll explore the factors of production, the mechanisms that drive it forward, and the significance of production as the nucleus of economic growth. You'll come to understand how the choices made in the realm of production ripple through the fabric of society, affecting the prices of goods and services, the allocation of resources, and the prosperity of nations.

We've designed this book to be more than a theoretical guide; it's a bridge between academic knowledge and real-world understanding. Economic theory can often be daunting, but our goal is to simplify complex concepts and provide you with practical insights. Whether you are new to economics or well-versed in the subject, you'll find that our approach breaks down the barriers to comprehension, empowering you to engage confidently with the world of production.

As you turn the pages, you'll not only uncover the secrets of economic production but also gain a global perspective. Our interconnected world relies on the exchange of goods and services between nations, and production is central to this international dance. You'll come to appreciate the shared challenges and opportunities that transcend borders, enriching your understanding of the forces that shape our interconnected global landscape.

At the heart of "Economic Production" lies an invitation: an invitation to become an informed decision-maker in your personal and professional life. The knowledge you'll acquire here will equip you to make choices that contribute to the well-being of individuals, communities, and nations. It will empower you to participate in the ongoing dialogue of economic discourse and to influence the forces that drive our world.

Whether you're a student, a business leader, a policymaker, or simply a citizen eager to engage with the world of economics, this book is your resource for unlocking the insights needed to make a difference. We hope that this introduction piques your curiosity and inspires you to join us on an enlightening journey through the intricate world of "Economic Production." It's an invitation to explore, to question, and to engage in a dialogue that shapes our economic future. We are excited to have you as our companion on this intellectual voyage.

Editorial Reviews

"Production is not the application of tools to materials, but logic to work." — Peter Drucker

"The real wealth of a nation is its people. And the purpose of development is to create an enabling environment for people to enjoy long, healthy, and creative lives. This simple but powerful truth is too often forgotten in the pursuit of material and financial wealth." — Mahbub ul Haq

"To achieve real prosperity, we must strive for economic growth that is both sustainable and more equitable. To do that, we have to invest in people – particularly their education and health." — Gro Harlem Brundtland

"Economic growth without social progress lets the great majority of people remain in poverty, while a privileged few reap the benefits of rising abundance." — John F. Kennedy

"All wealth is the product of labor." — John Locke

"Production is the only answer to economic progress." — Ayn Rand

"The essence of wealth is to allow a person more free time." — John Maynard Keynes

"The best way to predict the future is to create it." — Peter Drucker

"The power to create wealth is the power to create happiness." — Ayn Rand

"The production of too many useful things results in too many useless people." — Karl Marx

Prologue

Imagine a world where the essentials of life are produced in abundance, where innovation thrives, and economic prosperity knows no bounds. Picture a society where individuals have the tools to make informed decisions, businesses flourish, and nations prosper. In this vision of a flourishing world, economic production stands as the lighthouse guiding the way. Welcome to "Economic Production," where we embark on a quest to uncover the secrets of this vital subject and empower you with the knowledge to navigate the intricate landscapes of economics.

Our prologue serves as the gateway to a captivating journey that transcends the boundaries of academic theory and delves deep into the practical realities of the world. It's an invitation to understand how the choices we make, the products we consume, and the policies we advocate are intimately connected to the concept of production. In this prologue, we offer you a glimpse of the intricate web of forces that shape our economic world and empower you to become an active participant in it.

Economic production is not merely a topic of study; it's the cornerstone of our modern existence. It is the process by which we transform resources into the goods and services that fuel our lives. From the crops that nourish us to the cars we drive, from the homes we inhabit to the digital technologies we rely on, production is the engine that powers it all. By exploring the principles and mechanisms of production, you gain the insights needed to appreciate its profound influence on our world.

This prologue is an invitation to make economics more approachable, more engaging, and more relevant to your life. We demystify complex theories and present them in a clear and relatable manner. Whether you are a student embarking on your academic journey, a professional seeking to deepen your expertise, or simply an individual curious about the forces that shape your world, this book aims to bridge the gap between academic knowledge and practical understanding.

We envision a world where everyone can be an informed decision-maker, where individuals, businesses, and governments work together to promote economic progress and the well-being of societies. The prologue sets the stage for a journey that will empower you to make informed choices, navigate the complexities of our economic landscape, and be a catalyst for positive change in the world of economics.

Thank you for embarking on this journey with us. The world of "Economic Production" is waiting for you, filled with insights, discoveries, and the potential to shape a brighter economic future. Together, we will unlock the secrets of economic production and empower you to become a force for positive change.

Brief Overview

In "Economic Production," we embark on a captivating journey through the multifaceted world of economic production and its fundamental role in shaping our economies and livelihoods. This book is designed to provide you with a comprehensive understanding of key concepts, theories, and practical applications related to production in economics, making it an essential read for students, professionals, and enthusiasts eager to master this critical subject.

Chapter 1: Production in economics

Our exploration begins with a foundational chapter on "Production (economics)," offering a thorough examination of the production process, its factors, and its impact on economic growth. By delving into the core principles of production, you will lay a solid foundation for understanding the subsequent chapters that build upon this fundamental concept.

Chapter 2: Growth accounting

"Chapter 2: Growth accounting" takes you on a journey to uncover the tools and methods economists use to measure and assess economic growth. This vital knowledge is essential for policymakers, business leaders, and anyone interested in the factors that drive economic progress.

Chapter 3: Microeconomics

"Chapter 3: Microeconomics" invites you to discover the fundamentals of microeconomics. We delve into the core concepts, principles, and models that underpin the study of individual economic agents and their decision-making. Gain a solid grasp of the microeconomic landscape and how it shapes our everyday lives.

Chapter 4: Capital intensity

Discover the intricacies of "Capital intensity" in Chapter 4, where we explore how capital investments and productivity are intertwined. This chapter sheds light on the pivotal role of capital in economic production and its impact on various industries.

Chapter 5: Production function

"Production function" is the focus of Chapter 5, where you will uncover how economists model and analyze production processes. This key concept is essential for understanding how inputs, such as labor and capital, translate into outputs.

Chapter 6: Productivity

Chapter 6 delves into "Productivity," a topic of paramount importance for both individual success and national economic growth. Learn how to enhance productivity and its role in economic prosperity.

Chapter 7: Output in economics

In "Chapter 7: Output (economics)," we explore the critical concept of output and its connection to economic performance. Understanding the nuances of output is crucial for evaluating the health and vitality of economies.

Chapter 8: Capital accumulation

Chapter 8 examines "Capital accumulation," an essential factor for long-term economic growth. Learn how the accumulation of capital drives economic development and leads to higher living standards.

Chapter 9: Total factor productivity

"Total factor productivity" is the subject of Chapter 9, offering insights into the efficiency and innovation that underpin economic advancement. By grasping the principles of total factor productivity, you will gain a profound understanding of how economies evolve and thrive.

Chapter 10: Surplus product

Chapter 10 explores the concept of "Surplus product" and its relevance in the context of production. This concept is integral to understanding economic distribution and the creation of wealth.

Chapter 11: Prices of production

Unearth the intricacies of "Prices of production" in Chapter 11, as we delve into the fundamental theories and principles that guide price determination in various economic systems.

Chapter 12: Net output

"Chapter 12: Net output" takes you on a journey to understand the concept of net output, shedding light on the distinctions between gross and net measures of production.

Chapter 13: Productivity model

Chapter 13 introduces you to the "Productivity model," a powerful tool used by economists to analyze and enhance production processes. This model provides invaluable insights into optimizing efficiency and output.

Chapter 14: Measurement in economics

"Chapter 14: Measurement in economics" is your guide to understanding how economists collect, analyze, and interpret data to gain insights into production, consumption, and economic performance.

Chapter 15: Factor market

Explore the "Factor market" in Chapter 15, uncovering the pivotal role of labor, land, and capital markets in the production process and how they shape economic outcomes.

Chapter 16: Technological theory of social production

Chapter 16 takes you on a journey through the "Technological theory of social production," which examines how technology revolutionizes and shapes modern economies.

Chapter 17: Fei-Ranis model of economic growth

Dive into the "Fei-Ranis model of economic growth" in Chapter 17, and explore this influential model that highlights the intricate relationship between population, employment, and economic growth.

Chapter 18: Cambridge capital controversy

Chapter 18 uncovers the "Cambridge capital controversy," which delves into the debates and discussions surrounding the role of capital in economic theory, offering critical insights into economic thought.

Chapter 19: Socially necessary labor time

"Chapter 19: Socially necessary labor time" explores the concept's significance in understanding the value of labor and its connection to economic production.

Chapter 20: Surplus value

Chapter 20 delves into the concept of "Surplus value" and its implications for understanding economic distribution and class struggle.

Chapter 21: Macroeconomics

Our journey concludes with "Chapter 21: Macroeconomics" we set the stage by defining the very essence of macroeconomics. You'll explore key concepts, such as Gross Domestic Product (GDP), inflation, and unemployment, which serve as the building blocks for understanding economic performance. We examine the historical development of macroeconomics and lay the groundwork for the chapters to come..

Join us in this engaging exploration of economic production, where you will gain the knowledge and insights necessary to navigate the complex world of economics and contribute to its ongoing evolution. Each chapter is a stepping stone on this educational voyage, and together they form a comprehensive resource that will empower you to make informed decisions and contribute to the broader discourse on economic production.

From the Inside Flap

Welcome to an enlightening journey through the intricate world of "Economic Production." This book invites you to explore the heartbeat of modern civilization, where resources are transformed into the goods and services that drive our economies, shape our societies, and impact our lives. It delves into the hidden forces that influence our daily choices, from the products we buy to the careers we pursue. Whether you're a student, a professional, or simply someone with an innate curiosity about the world, this book serves as your gateway to understanding the pivotal role of production in our interconnected global landscape.

- The Seeds of Understanding: Begin your voyage with a comprehensive look at the foundations of economic production. Unearth the factors that drive the creation of wealth and prosperity, explore the processes that underlie economic growth, and gain insight into the critical role that production plays in shaping the world.

- The Power of Knowledge: Economic theory can be complex, but it need not be intimidating. "Economic Production" takes a step-by-step approach, breaking down intricate concepts into digestible, real-world narratives. Our aim is to empower you with the knowledge needed to navigate the complexities of production confidently, regardless of your familiarity with economics.

- The Global Connection: Production knows no borders. This book takes a global perspective, showing how economies are interwoven and how production is central to international trade and cooperation. You'll gain an appreciation for the shared challenges and opportunities that define our interconnected world.

- Unlocking Decision-Making: Whether you're a student, a business leader, a policymaker, or an informed citizen, the knowledge you gain here will empower you to make meaningful decisions. It will equip you to participate in shaping economic outcomes and to contribute to the prosperity and well-being of individuals, communities, and nations.

- Beyond Academics: "Economic Production" offers not just academic insight but practical wisdom. The book bridges the gap between theory and real-world application, enabling you to engage with the implications of production in your personal and professional life. It's more than a textbook; it's a guide to understanding the forces that shape our world.

The world of economics is not just for experts and scholars; it's for everyone who wants to be a more informed, engaged citizen. It's for anyone who wants to unravel the complexities of production, understand the global economy, and contribute to the betterment of our society. We invite you to dive into this book, embark on this intellectual journey, and embrace the knowledge that will empower you to make a difference in the world of economics.

Unlock the Secrets of Economic Production and Empower Your Future. Grab Your Copy Today!

From the Back Cover

Discover the Essence of Economic Prosperity: "Economic Production"

In a world of ever-evolving economies, "Economic Production" serves as your compass, guiding you through the intricate dynamics of the economic engine that fuels our daily lives. From the food we eat to the technologies we embrace, production is the cornerstone of modern existence, and this book unveils its profound influence on our world. Whether you are a student seeking to grasp the essentials, a professional navigating the complexities of production, or a curious mind eager to delve into the heart of economics, this book is your key to unlocking the mysteries of economic production.

- Uncover the Foundations: Begin your journey with an exploration of the fundamentals of production, dissecting the elements that underpin economic growth and prosperity. This book provides a comprehensive introduction to the factors that drive production and the pivotal role it plays in shaping our economies.

- Delve into Real-World Application: "Economic Production" goes beyond theory, offering a bridge between academic knowledge and practical understanding. Engage with the real-world implications of production, discovering how it impacts industries, businesses, and the day-to-day choices we make as consumers and citizens.

- Demystify Complex Concepts: Economics need not be a daunting subject. This book distills intricate theories into clear and accessible narratives, ensuring that readers of all backgrounds can embark on a journey of enlightenment. Unlock the wisdom of economic thinkers and gain the tools needed to navigate economic landscapes with confidence.

- Global Perspective: Production is not confined by borders. This book takes a global approach, shedding light on the interconnectivity of economies and the shared challenges and opportunities that shape our world. Gain a deeper appreciation for the forces that drive international trade and economic cooperation.

- Become an Informed Decision-Maker: Empower yourself with the knowledge to make informed decisions in your personal and professional life. Whether you are a student, business leader, policymaker, or simply a curious individual, this book equips you to contribute to the prosperity and growth of economies and societies.

"Economic Production" is your invitation to embark on a captivating exploration of a subject that impacts us all. Whether you are driven by a thirst for knowledge, a desire to excel in your career, or a passion for contributing to the world's economic progress, this book has been crafted with your aspirations in mind. Join us in unraveling the intricate world of economic production, and let the knowledge you gain here be your compass for navigating the complexities of the economic realm. This book promises not just to inform, but to inspire you to be an active participant in the world of economics.

Unlock the Secrets of Economic Production and Empower Your Future. Grab Your Copy Today!

From the Author

Dear Reader,

I am delighted to share with you our book, "Economic Production." As the author of this work, I have poured my passion for economics and my commitment to fostering a deeper understanding of economic production into every page. My aim is to take you on a journey that transcends the realms of theory and engages with the practical and real-world significance of production in our lives.

Economic production is the cornerstone of modern civilization, an intricate dance of resources and innovation that shapes the world we live in. It is a subject that underlies the daily choices we make, the businesses we engage with, and the policies that govern our economies. My aspiration is for this book to serve as your trusted guide in navigating this complex landscape, unraveling the intricacies of production, and empowering you to make informed decisions in your academic pursuits, professional endeavors, or personal life.

Throughout "Economic Production," I have endeavored to distill complex economic concepts into accessible and engaging narratives. Whether you are well-versed in economics or are approaching the subject for the first time, I have striven to provide clarity and relevance, bridging the gap between theory and practice. My intent is to awaken your curiosity, ignite your passion for economics, and invite you to become a critical thinker in the realm of economic production.

As you turn the pages of this book, you will find not only a comprehensive exploration of economic production but also a deep commitment to fostering economic literacy. I believe that understanding the principles that govern production is the first step toward contributing to the prosperity of societies and the well-being of individuals. This book aims to equip you with the tools and knowledge needed to make meaningful contributions to the field of economics and to enrich your own life through a deeper understanding of the forces that drive our world.

I invite you to immerse yourself in the world of "Economic Production." Explore the intricate theories, discover the fascinating history, and engage with the real-world applications. Let the knowledge you gain here be a catalyst for your personal and professional growth. I look forward to being your guide as we traverse the intricate landscapes of economics, and I hope that this book sparks your enthusiasm and empowers you to contribute to the ongoing discourse on economic production.

Thank you for choosing "Economic Production." Together, we embark on a journey of discovery, insight, and empowerment in the ever-evolving world of economic thought. Your quest for knowledge is the key to unlocking new horizons and forging a brighter economic future, and I am honored to be a part of your intellectual journey.

Warm regards,

Fouad Sabry

Chapter 1: Production in economics

Production is the process of combining material and immaterial inputs (such as metal, wood, glass, and plastics) to create output. This output should ideally be a valuable good or service that contributes to the utility of individuals. Generally, the degree to which needs are met is regarded as an indicator of economic welfare. There are two aspects of production that explain rising economic welfare. The first is improving the quality-to-price ratio of goods and services and increasing incomes as a result of growing and more efficient market production, while the second is total production, which contributes to the growth of GDP. The most essential methods of production are:

market production

public production

household production

To comprehend the origin of economic prosperity, it is necessary to comprehend these three production processes. All of them produce valuable goods that contribute to the well-being of individuals.

Utilization of produced commodities results in the fulfillment of needs. When the quality-to-price ratio of the commodities improves and more satisfaction is obtained at a lower cost, the level of need satisfaction rises. Improving the quality-to-price ratio of commodities is essential for a producer to increase the competitiveness of their products, but these gains cannot be measured using production data. Increasing the competitiveness of a product frequently necessitates lower product prices and, consequently, income losses that must be offset by an increase in sales volume.

Additionally, economic well-being improves as a result of the increase in incomes generated by a growing and more efficient market production.

Only market production generates and distributes profits to stakeholders.

Public production and household production are financed by market production earnings.

Thus, market production plays a dual role in the creation of happiness, i.e.

the responsibilities of producing goods and services and generating income.

Because of this dual function, market production is the "primus motor" of economic well-being and therefore here under review.

The underlying assumption of production is that the producer's primary objective is to maximize profit. Calculated profit is the difference between the value of production values (output value) and costs (associated with production factors). Efficiency, technological, pricing, behavioral, consumption, and productivity changes are among the crucial factors that have a substantial impact on production economics.

In production, efficiency plays a crucial role in reaching and maintaining full capacity, as opposed to producing at an inefficient (less-than-optimal) level. Changes in efficiency correspond to the positive shift in current inputs, such as technological advancements, relative to the position of the producer. Effectiveness is determined by dividing the maximum potential output by the actual input. The efficiency of the output is 0.6, or 60 percent, if the inputs have the potential to produce 100 units but are only producing 60 units. In addition, economies of scale determine the point at which production efficiency (returns) can be increased, decreased, or held constant.

This factor places the continuous adaptation of technology at the forefront of the production function. As noted throughout economic histories, such as the industrial revolution, technological change is a significant factor in advancing economic production outcomes. Consequently, it is essential to continue monitoring its effects on production and to encourage the development of new technologies.

There is a strong correlation between the producer's behavior and the production's underlying assumption; both assume profit-maximizing conduct. As a result of consumption and other variables, production can either increase, decrease, or remain constant. In accordance with the economic theory of supply and demand, the relationship between production and consumption mirrors that of supply and demand. Consequently, when production decreases more than factor consumption, productivity decreases. In contrast, an increase in production over consumption is viewed as increased productivity.

As the producer is the price taker in an economic market, input and output prices are assumed to be determined by external factors. Pricing is therefore an essential aspect of the practical application of production economics. If the price is too high, the product cannot be manufactured profitably. In addition, there is a strong relationship between pricing and consumption, which influences the overall production scale.

Production and consumption are the two primary activities in an economy, in general. There are also two types of actors: producers and consumers. Through efficient production and interaction between producers and consumers, well-being is made possible. In the interaction, consumers play two roles, both of which contribute to well-being. Consumers can function as both customers and suppliers for producers. Customers' well-being derives from the commodities they purchase, while suppliers' well-being derives from the compensation they receive for the production inputs they have supplied to producers.

Stakeholders of production are individuals, groups, or entities with an interest in a producing company. Economic prosperity stems from efficient production and is distributed through the interaction of a business's stakeholders. Companies' stakeholders are economic actors with an economic interest in the company. In order to differentiate their interests and mutual relationships, stakeholders can be categorized into three groups based on their shared interests. The three groups are as described below::

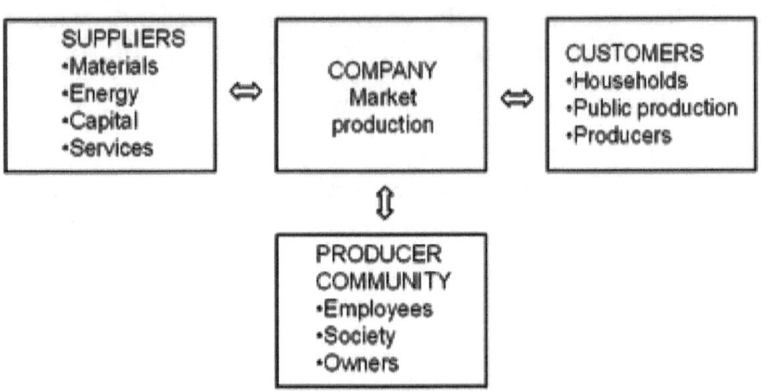

Interactive contributions of a company's stakeholders (Saari, 2011,4)

Customers

Customers of a business are typically consumers, other market producers, or public sector producers. Each has their own distinct production functions. As a result of competition, the price-to-quality ratios of commodities tend to improve, resulting in increased customer productivity. Customers pay less for more. This means that in households and the public sector, more needs are met at a lower cost. Therefore, customers' productivity can increase over time even if their incomes remain constant.

Suppliers

Typically, companies' suppliers are manufacturers of materials, energy, capital, and services. They each have distinct production functions. Changes in the prices or qualities of supplied commodities have an effect on the production functions of both actors (company and suppliers). We conclude that the production functions of the company and its suppliers are in a constant state of flux.

Producers

Collectively, those involved in production, including the labor force, society, and owners, are known as the producer community or producers. The producer community generates revenue through the development and expansion of production.

The price-quality relationships of the commodities determine the level of happiness attained through their consumption. As a result of market competition and growth, the price-quality relationships of commodities tend to improve over time. Typically, a commodity's quality improves and its price declines over time. This innovation benefits the production functions of customers. Customers pay less for more. Customers receive greater satisfaction at a lower cost. The production data can only partially calculate this type of well-being generation. In this study, the situation is described. The producer community (labor force, society, and owners) is compensated for the inputs they've contributed to the production. When production increases and becomes more efficient, income typically rises. This increases the production's ability to pay salaries, taxes, and profits. Increased production and productivity generate additional revenue for the producing community. Similarly, the high income level in the community is a result of the high production volume and its high quality. As mentioned previously, this type of well-being generation can be reliably calculated from production data.

A producing company can be divided into sub-processes in a variety of ways; however, the following five processes have been identified as the most important, each with its own logic, objectives, theory, and key figures. To be able to measure and comprehend them, it is necessary to examine each of them separately and as a component of the whole. The primary business processes are as follows::

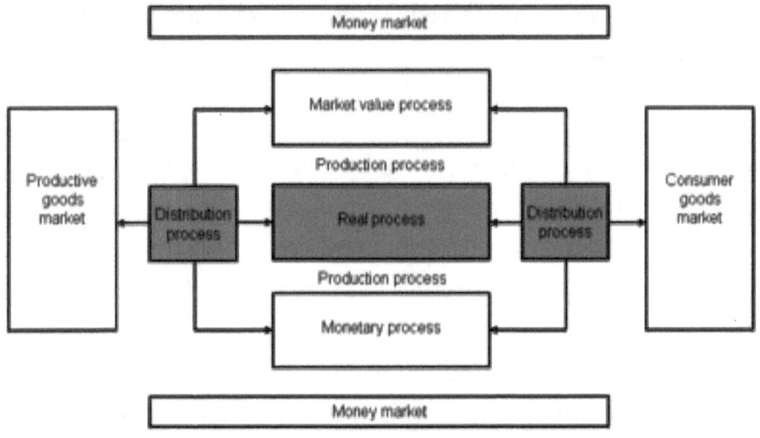

Main processes of a producing company (Saari 2006,3)

real process.

income distribution process

production process.

monetary process.

market value method.

The real process creates production output, the income distribution process distributes production gains, and these two processes comprise the production process. The production process and its sub-processes, the real process, and the income distribution process all occur simultaneously, but only the production process is identifiable and quantifiable according to conventional accounting practices. Real process and income distribution process can be identified and measured through additional calculation; therefore, they must be analyzed separately to comprehend the logic of production and its effectiveness.

Real processes generate production output from input, and they can be characterized by the production function. It refers to a series of production events in which inputs of varying quality and quantity are combined to create outputs of varying quality and quantity. Products can be tangible goods, intangible services, and, most frequently, combinations of both. The characteristics that the producer incorporates into the product confer surplus value to the consumer, and based on the market price, this value is split between the consumer and the producer in the marketplace. This is the mechanism by which both the consumer and the producer acquire surplus value. Customers' surplus values cannot be calculated from production data. Instead, the producer's surplus value can be measured. It can be expressed in nominal and real value terms. The real surplus value to the producer is the result of the real process, real income, and productivity as measured proportionally.

The concept "real process" in the meaning quantitative structure of production process was introduced in Finnish management accounting in the 1960s.

Since then, it has served as a pillar of Finnish management accounting theory.

(Riistama and Co. 1971)

The income distribution process of the production refers to a series of events in which the unit prices of constant-quality outputs and inputs change, resulting in a shift in the income distribution among exchange participants. The magnitude of the change in income distribution is proportional to the change in the prices and quantities of output and inputs. Productivity gains are distributed, for instance, to customers in the form of lower product sales prices or to employees in the form of higher income pay.

Real process and income distribution process comprise the production process. Profitability is both an outcome and a success metric for the owner. Profitability of production is the portion of the real process result that the owner was able to retain in the process of income distribution. Returns and costs are the components of profitability that describe the production process. The components of profitability are assigned nominal prices, whereas the factors of the actual process are assigned periodically fixed prices.

Monetary process refers to events associated with financing an organization. The market value process is the sequence of events by which investors determine the market value of a company on the investment markets.

Economic expansion can be defined as a rise in the output of a production process. It is typically expressed as a percentage representing the growth of the actual output of production. The real output is the real value of the products produced in a production process, and the real income is calculated by subtracting the real input from the real output. The real process of production from the real inputs generates the real output and real income.

The actual process is characterized by the production function. The production function is a graphical or mathematical expression illustrating the relationship between production inputs and output. Both mathematical and graphical expressions are presented and illustrated. The production function is a straightforward description of the income-generating mechanism in the production process. It is comprised of two parts. These elements are a shift in production input and a shift in output.

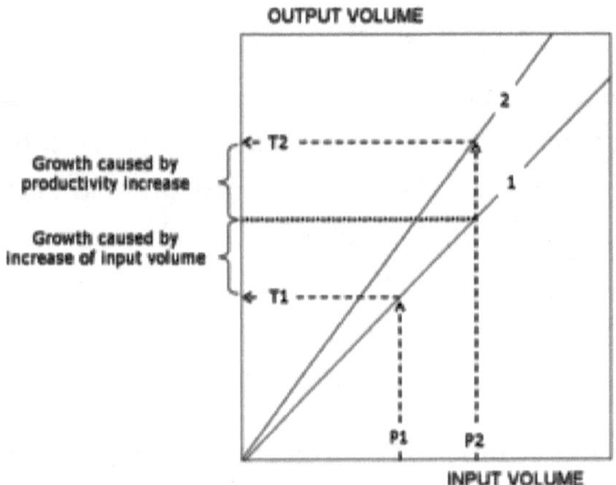

Components of economic growth (Saari 2006,2)

The diagram depicts a revenue generation process (exaggerated for clarity). The Value T2 (value at time 2) represents the increase in output from Value T1 over Time Period (value at time 1). Each measurement period has its own graph depicting the production function for that period (the straight lines). The output measured at time 2 is greater than the output measured at time 1 due to an increase in both inputs and productivity. Line 1 displays the portion of growth attributable to the increase in inputs, which does not alter the relationship between inputs and outputs. The portion of growth attributable to an increase in productivity is represented by the steeper slope of line 2. Therefore, increased productivity signifies increased output per unit of input.

The increase in production output reveals nothing about the effectiveness of the production process.

The production's performance is measured by its ability to generate revenue.

Because production revenue is generated in the actual process, referred to as the real income.

Similarly, As the production function reflects the actual process,, we could also call it "income generated by the production function".

The generation of real income adheres to the logic of the production function. Two components can also be distinguished in the change in income: the income growth attributable to an increase in production input (production volume) and the income growth attributable to an increase in productivity. Moving along the production function graph determines the increase in income due to an increase in production volume. Increased productivity generates the income growth associated with a shift in the production function. Thus, the change in real income represents a shift from point 1 to point 2 on the production function (above). To maximize production performance, we must maximize the revenue generated by the production function.

Following are explanations of the causes of increased productivity and production volume. Innovation is viewed as the leading economic indicator of productivity growth. The successful introduction of new products and new or modified processes, organizational structures, systems, and business models results in output growth that exceeds inputs growth. This leads to an increase in output per unit of input or productivity. Without innovation, income growth is also possible through the replication of established technologies. Without innovation and with only replication, output will grow proportionally to inputs. (2014) Jorgenson et al. This is an example of income growth via production volume expansion.

Jorgenson et al. (2014,2) provide an illustrative instance. They demonstrate that the vast majority of economic growth in the United States since 1947 has been attributable to the replication of existing technologies through investments in equipment, structures, and software as well as labor force expansion. In addition, they demonstrate that innovation accounts for less than 20% of US economic growth.

In the case of a single production process (described above), the output is defined as the economic value of the products and services produced. When analyzing an entity comprised of multiple production processes, we must add the value added by each individual process. This is done to prevent double-counting of intermediate inputs. Subtracting the intermediate inputs from the outputs yields value-added. GDP is the most well-known and widely-used measure of value-added (Gross Domestic Product). It is widely employed as a measurement of the economic expansion of nations and industries.

The performance of the production can be measured as a mean or absolute income. Understanding the welfare effects of production is enhanced by expressing performance in both average (avg) and absolute quantities (abs). For measuring average production performance, we employ the established productivity ratio.

True output / True input.

Subtracting the actual input from the actual output yields the absolute income of performance:

Real income (abstract) equals real output minus real input.

Real income growth is the increase in distributable economic value among production stakeholders. We can perform both average and absolute accounting with the help of the production model. To maximize production performance, the real income and its derivatives must be used as the performance metric.

Increasing productivity results in a phenomenon known as "jobless growth." This refers to economic growth as a result of productivity growth, but without the creation of new jobs and the resulting new incomes.

A concrete illustration illustrates the point.

When an unemployed person obtains a job in market production, we may assume the position is low-productivity.

As a consequence, average productivity declines while real per capita income increases.

Furthermore, The prosperity of the society also increases.

This example illustrates the difficulty in correctly interpreting the total productivity change.

The combination of volume increase and total productivity decrease leads in this case to the improved performance because we are on the "diminishing returns" area of the production function.

If we are on the part of "increasing returns" on the production function, The combination of increased production volume and total productivity results in enhanced production performance.

Unfortunately, We do not know which part of the production function we are performing in practice.

Therefore, Only by measuring the real income change can the correct interpretation of a performance change be obtained.

In the short term, the production function assumes the presence of at least one fixed input factor. The production function establishes a relationship between the amount of factor inputs utilized by a business and the output that results. There are three production and productivity measures. The first is output total (total product). In manufacturing industries such as the automobile industry, it is straightforward to quantify output. In tertiary industries, such as the service and knowledge industries, it is more difficult to quantify outputs because they are less tangible.

The average output is the second method of measuring production and efficiency. It measures output per employed worker or output per capital unit. The marginal product is the third production and efficiency metric. In the short run, it is the change in output caused by increasing the number of workers used by one individual or by adding one more machine to the production process.

According to the law of diminishing marginal returns, as more units of a variable input are added to fixed amounts of land and capital, the change in total output will initially increase and then decrease.

The amount of time required for all production factors to become flexible varies by industry. In the nuclear power industry, for instance, it takes many years to commission a new nuclear power plant and increase capacity.

Real-world examples of the company's short-term production equations may differ from the department's smooth production theory. In order to improve efficiency and promote the structural transformation of economic growth, it is essential to establish the corresponding industrial development model. Simultaneously, a shift should be made to models that incorporate industry-specific characteristics, such as specific technological changes and substantial differences in the likelihood of substitution before and after investment.

A production model is a numerical description of the production process based on input and output prices and quantities.

There are two primary operationalization strategies for the concept of production function.

We may employ mathematical formulas, which are frequently employed in macroeconomics (in growth accounting) or mathematical models, typical in microeconomics and management accounting.

We do not present the former approach here but refer to the survey "Growth accounting" by Hulten 2009.

Additionally, see Sickles and Zelenenuk's (2019) extensive discussion of various production models and their estimations, (Chapters 1 and 2).

We use arithmetic models because, like management accounting models, they are illustrative and easily understood and applied in practice. In addition, they are integrated with management accounting, a practical advantage. The ability of the arithmetic model to depict production function as part of the production process is a significant advantage. Therefore, production function can be comprehended, measured, and evaluated as part of the production process.

There are various production models to accommodate various interests. Here, we employ a production income model and a production analysis model to illustrate production function as a phenomenon and a quantifiable quantity.

	Period 1			Period 2		
	Quantity	Price	Value	Quantity	Price	Value
Product 1	210.00	7.20	1512	247.25	7.10	1755
Product 2	200.00	7.00	1400	195.03	7.15	1394
Output			2912			3150
Labour	100.00	7.50	750	115.00	7.70	886
Materials	80.00	8.60	688	79.20	8.50	673
Energy	400.00	1.50	600	428.00	1.55	663
Capital	160.00	3.80	608	164.80	3.90	643
Input			2646			2865
Surplus value (abs.)		266.00			285.12	
Surplus value (rel.)		*1.101*			*1.100*	

Profitability of production measured by surplus value (Saari 2006,3)

The scope of a going concern's success is vast, Moreover, there are no universally applicable success criteria.

Nevertheless, There is a single criterion by which we can generalize the production success rate.

This criterion is the capacity to generate excess value.

As a profitability criterion, Excess value is the difference between returns and expenses, taking into account the costs of equity in addition to the costs typically included in the profit and loss statement.

Surplus value denotes that the output is more valuable than the costs incurred to produce it, that is to say, The output value is greater than the input value (production costs).

When the surplus is positive, the owner's profit expectation has been surpassed.

The table presents a calculation of surplus value.

This set of production data is referred to as a basic example, and it is used throughout the article to illustrate production models.

The fundamental example is a simplified calculation of profitability used for illustration and modeling.

Even as diminished, It includes all phenomena of a real-world measuring situation, most notably the change in output-input ratio between two periods.

Hence, the basic example works as an illustrative "scale model" of production without any features of a real measuring situation being lost.

In practice, There may be hundreds of products and inputs, but the logic of measuring does not differ from the example given.

In this context, we define the quality requirements for productivity accounting production data. The most important criterion for accurate measurement is the homogeneity of the object being measured. If the object is not homogeneous, the measurement result may include both changes in quantity and quality, but the proportions of each will remain unclear. This criterion in productivity accounting stipulates that all output and input items must be accounted for as identical. In other words, inputs and outputs cannot be aggregated for measuring and accounting purposes. If they are aggregated, they are no longer homogeneous, and measurement results may be biased as a result.

In the example, both the absolute and relative surplus value have been calculated. Absolute value is the difference between the output and input values, while relative value represents their respective relationship. The calculation of surplus value in the example is based on a nominal price determined by each period's market price.

		Period 1			$Q_1 \times P_2$	Period 2		
		1	2	3	4	5	6	7
		Quantity	Price	Value		Quantity	Price	Value
a	Product 1	210.00	7.20	1512.00	1491.00	247.25	7.10	1755.48
b	Product 2	200.00	7.00	1400.00	1430.00	195.03	7.15	1394.46
c	Output			2912.00	2921.00			3149.94
d	Labour	100.00	7.50	750.00	770.00	115.00	7.70	885.50
e	Materials	80.00	8.60	688.00	680.00	79.20	8.50	673.20
f	Energy	400.00	1.50	600.00	620.00	428.00	1.55	663.40
g	Capital	160.00	3.80	608.00	624.00	164.80	3.90	642.72
h	Input			2646.00	2694.00			2864.82
i	Surplus value (abs.)			266.00	227.00			285.12
j	Surplus value (rel.)			1.101				1.100
k	Change of distribution (abs.); i4-i3				-39.00			
l	Distribution index of output; c4/c3				1.003			
m	Distribution index of input; h4/h3				1.018			
n	Distribution index; l4/m4				0.985			

─── Distribution process ───

		$Q_1 \times P_2$	Period 2
p	Productivity; c4/h4, c7/h7	1.084	1.100
q	Productivity index; p7/p4		1.014
r	Change of productivity (abs.); (q7-1)×c4		41.12
s	Volume index of output; c7/c4		1.078
t	Volume index of input; h7/h4		1.063
u	Change of input volume (abs); (t7-1)×(4+r7)		17.00

─── Real process ───

		Period 2
v	Change of profitability; j7/j3	0.999
x	Change of returns; c7/c3	1.082
z	Change of costs; h7/h3	1.083

─── Production process ───

Production Model Saari 2004 (Saari 2006,4)

It is possible to calculate the outcome of the actual process, income distribution process, and production process with the aid of a typical production analysis model, which is used here. The starting point is a calculation of profitability using surplus value as the profitability metric. The calculation of surplus value is the only valid metric for understanding the relationship between profitability and productivity or the relationship between real process and production process. A valid measurement of total productivity must account for all production inputs, and the only calculation that satisfies this requirement is the surplus value calculation. If we omit an input in productivity or income accounting, the omitted input can be used indefinitely in production without affecting accounting results' cost.

The term ceteris paribus, which translates to "all other things being the same" and states that only one variable should be changed at a time when examining a phenomenon, provides the best framework for understanding the calculation process. Consequently, the calculation can be presented as a sequential process. First, the effects of the income distribution process are determined, followed by the effects of the actual process on the production's profitability.

First, the impacts of the actual process and the income distribution process are separated from the change in profitability (285.12 - 266.0 = 19.12). This is accomplished by simply creating one auxiliary column (4) in which the quantities of Period 1 and the prices of Period 2 are used to calculate the surplus value. In the resulting profitability calculation, Columns 3 and 4 depict the effect of a change in the income distribution process on profitability, while Columns 4 and 7 depict the effect of a change in the actual process on profitability.

The accounting results are straightforward to interpret and comprehend. The real income has increased by 58.12 units, with 41.12 units attributable to productivity growth and the remaining 17.00 units attributable to production volume growth. The total increase in real income (58.12) is distributed to production stakeholders, in this case 39.00 units to customers and input suppliers and the remaining 19.12 units to owners.

Here, an important conclusion can be drawn. There is always a balance between income generation and income distribution in the process of producing income. The change in income generated by a real process (i.e., the production function) is always distributed as economic values to the stakeholders during the review period. Consequently, changes in real income and income distribution are always of equal economic value.

On the basis of the changes in productivity and production volume values that have been accounted for, we can conclusively determine which portion of the production function the production belongs to. The interpretation rules are as follows::

The production is on the part of "increasing returns" on the production function, when

productivity and output volume growth or

productivity and output volume are declining.

The production is on the part of "diminishing returns" on the production function, when

productivity declines while volume rises or

Productivity rises while volume falls.

In the basic illustration, the combination of volume growth (+17.00) and productivity growth (+41.12) reports explicitly that the production is on the part of "increasing returns" on the production function (Saari 2006 a, 138–144).

Another production model (Production Model Saari, 1989) also provides income distribution information (Saari 2011,14). Due to the fact that the accounting techniques of the two models are distinct, the analytical information they provide is distinct but complementary. However, the accounting outcomes are identical. The model is not described in detail here, but its detailed data on income distribution are used when the objective functions are formulated in the following section.

Formulating distinct objective functions in accordance with the objectives of the various interest groups is an effective method for enhancing understanding of production performance. To formulate the objective function, the variable to be maximized must be specified (or minimized). Then, subsequent variables are evaluated as constraints or free variables. Profit maximization, the most common objective function, is also included in this case. Profit maximization is an objective function derived from the owner's interest, and all other variables are constraints with respect to profit maximization in the organization.

INCOME FORMATION - changes between two periods			
Income generation		**Income distribution**	
		= Real income	+58.12
		+/- Customers	+9.00
		+/- Suppliers	-28.00
+/- Productivity	+41.12	= Producer income	39.12
+/- Volume	+17.00	- Labour compensation	-20.00
		- Taxes	N/a
= Real income	+58.12	= Owner income	+19.12
TOTAL GENERATION	58.12	TOTAL DISTRIBUTION	58.12

Summary of objective function formulations (Saari 2011,17)

Next, the procedure for formulating distinct objective functions within the context of the production model is presented. Following objective functions can be identified in the formation of income from production:

maximizing the actual revenue

maximizing producer earnings

maximizing owner earnings.

These instances are depicted using the numbers from the fundamental example. These icons are utilized in the presentation: The equal sign (=) represents the starting point of the computation or the result of the computation, whereas the plus or minus sign (+ / -) represents a variable to be added or subtracted from the function. Here, a producer refers to the producer community, which includes the labor force, society, and owners.

Formulations of objective functions can be expressed in a single calculation that concisely illustrates the logic of income generation, income distribution, and variables to be maximized.

The calculation resembles an income statement beginning with the generation of income and concluding with the distribution of income. The income generation and distribution are always in equilibrium, with equal amounts of each. In this instance, there are 58.12 units. During the same period, the income generated by the actual process is distributed to the stakeholders. There are three variables whose optimization is possible. They are the real income, the income of the producer, and the income of the owner. Producer income and owner income are practical quantities because they can be added and calculated with relative ease. Real income is typically not a number that can be added, and it is frequently difficult to calculate.

Additionally, the change in real income can be calculated from the changes in income distribution. We must determine the unit price changes of outputs and inputs and the resulting profit impacts (i.e. unit price change x quantity). Change in real income equals the sum of these impacts on profits and the change in owner income. This method is known as the dual method because the framework is viewed in terms of prices rather than quantities (ONS 3, 23).

Long acknowledged in growth accounting, the dual approach's interpretation has remained opaque.

The following question has remained unanswered: "Quantity based estimates of the residual are interpreted as a shift in the production function, but what is the interpretation of the price-based growth estimates?" (Hulten 2009, 18).

Above, we demonstrated that the real income change is the result of quantitative changes in production, while the change in income distribution to stakeholders is its dual.

In this instance, Accounting for the change in total income generation (real income) and the change in total income distribution yields the same accounting result.

{End Chapter 1}

Chapter 2: Growth accounting

In economics, growth accounting is a method for measuring the contribution of varied factors to economic growth and indirectly calculating the residual rate of technological progress in an economy. Growth accounting decomposes the growth rate of an economy's total output into that which is attributable to increases in the contributing amount of the factors used — typically the increase in the amount of capital and labor — and that which cannot be explained by observable changes in factor utilization. The unexplained portion of GDP growth is attributed to increases in productivity (producing more with the same inputs) or a measure of technological advancement as broadly defined.

The technique has been applied to virtually every economy in the world, and a common finding is that observed levels of economic growth cannot be simply explained by changes in the stock of capital or population and labor force growth rates. Therefore, technological progress is crucial to the economic growth of nations, or lack thereof.

This methodology was introduced by Robert Solow and Trevor Swan in 1957.

Typically, the growth accounting model is expressed as an exponential growth function.

Consider, as an abstract example, an economy whose total output (GDP) grows by 3 percent annually.

Over the same time period, its capital stock increases by 6% per year, while its labor force increases by 1% per year.

The contribution of the growth rate of capital to output is equal to this growth rate multiplied by the proportion of capital in total output, while the contribution of labor is given by the growth rate of labor multiplied by labor's proportion of income.

If capital's share in output is (1/3), then labor's share is (2/3) (assuming these are the only two factors of production).

This means that the portion of growth in output which is due to changes in factors is $0.06 \times (2/4) + .01 \times (2/3) = .027$ or 2.7%.

This indicates that 0.3% of the growth in output remains unexplained.

This remainder represents the increase in productivity caused by factors that occurred during the period, or the measure of technological advancement throughout this period.

Accounting for growth can also be expressed using the arithmetic model, which is used because it is more descriptive and easier to comprehend.

Simple is the accounting model's underlying principle.

Inputs (factors of production) growth rates are subtracted from output growth rates.

Because the accounting result is obtained through subtraction, it is commonly referred to as a "residual.".

The residual is often defined as the growth rate of output not explained by the share-weighted growth rates of the inputs.

Using the production model's actual process data, we can demonstrate the logic of the growth accounting model and identify potential differences with the productivity model. When production data is identical between models, differences in accounting results are solely attributable to accounting models. The following growth accounting is derived from production data.

The accounting for growth procedure is as follows. First, the output and input growth rates are determined by dividing the Period 2 numbers by the Period 1 numbers. Then, the input weights are computed as input percentages of the total input (Period 1). Weighted growth rates (WG) are obtained by applying weights to growth rates. Subtracting the weighed growth rates of the inputs from the growth rate of the output yields the accounting result. In this instance, the accounting result is 0.015, which indicates a 1.5 percent increase in productivity.

Using the same production data, the productivity model predicts a 1,4% growth in productivity. The difference (1.4% versus 1.5%) is due to the different production volumes utilized by the two models. In the productivity model, input volume is used as a measure of output volume, yielding a growth rate of 1.063. In this instance, productivity is defined as output volume divided by input volume. In the growth accounting model, output volume is used as a measure of production volume, yielding a growth rate of 1.078. In this instance, productivity is defined as input consumption per output volume unit. The case is easily verifiable using a productivity model with output as the production volume.

In this instance, the accounting result of the growth accounting model is expressed as an index number, 1.015, which represents the average productivity change. As previously demonstrated, we cannot draw accurate conclusions from average productivity figures. This is because productivity is treated as a separate variable from the entity to which it belongs, namely real income formation. If we compare two growth accounting results of the same production process in a practical setting, we cannot determine which one is superior in terms of production performance. In order to determine which outcome is superior and by how much, we need to know the income effects of productivity change and production volume change separately or their combined income effect.

This kind of scientific mistake of wrong analysis level has been recognized and described long ago.

In economic models, the total output of an economy is modeled as being produced by numerous factors of production, with capital and labor in modern economies being the most important ones (although land and natural resources can also be included). Typically, this is represented by an aggregate production function:

$$Y = F(A, K, L)$$

where Y is total output, K is the stock of capital in the economy, L is the labor force (or population), and A is a "catch-all" factor for technology, the role of institutions, and other relevant forces that measures how efficiently capital and labor are used in production.

Standard assumptions on the form of the function F(.) are that it is increasing in K, L, and A (if you increase productivity or the number of factors used, output increases) and homogeneous of degree one, or that there are constant returns to scale (which means that if you double both K and L you get double the output). The assumption of constant returns to scale enables the assumption of perfect competition, which entails that factors receive their marginal products:

$$dY/dK = MPK = r$$

$$dY/dL = MPL = w$$

where MPK represents the additional units of output produced with an additional unit of capital and MPL represents the same. w represents wages paid to labor, while r represents the rate of profit or the real interest rate. Noting that the assumption of perfect competition enables us to accept prices as given, we can accept prices as given. Assuming unit price (P = 1) for simplicity, quantities also represent values in all equations.

If we completely distinguish the preceding production function, we obtain;

$$dY = F_A dA + F_K dK + F_L dL$$

where F_i

denotes the partial derivative with respect to factor i, or with regard to capital and labor, the marginal items.

With ideal competition, the following equation becomes:

$$dY = F_A dA + MPK dK + MPL dL = F_A dA + r dK + w dL$$

When we divide by Y and convert each change to growth rates, we obtain:

$$dY/Y = (F_A A/Y)(dA/A) + (rK/Y) * (dK/K) + (wL/Y) * (dL/L)$$

or denoting a growth rate (percentage change over time) of a factor as

$$g_i = di/i$$

we get:

$$g_Y = (F_A A/Y) * g_A + (rK/Y) * g_K + (wL/Y) * g_L$$

Then rK/Y

is the share of total income that goes to capital, which can be denoted as α

and wL/Y

is the share of total income that goes to labor, denoted by $1 - \alpha$

.

This enables us to write the preceding equation as:

$$g_Y = F_A A/Y * g_A + \alpha * g_K + (1 - \alpha) * g_L$$

In principle the terms α

, g_Y

, g_K

and g_L

are all observable and can be measured using standard national income accounting methods (with capital stock being measured using investment rates via the perpetual inventory method).

The term
$$\frac{F_A A}{Y} * g_A$$

however is not directly observable as it captures technological growth and improvement in productivity that are unrelated to changes in use of factors.

This term is commonly known as the Solow residual or Total factor productivity growth.

This is the portion of the increase in total output that is not attributable to the (weighted) growth of factor inputs, as measured by a slight modification of the previous equation:

$$SolowResidual = g_Y - \alpha * g_K - (1 - \alpha) * g_L$$

The same concept can also be expressed in per capita (or per worker) terms by subtracting the growth rate of labor force from both sides:

$$SolowResidual = g_{(Y/L)} - \alpha * g_{(K/L)}$$

which states that the rate of technological growth is the portion of the per capita income growth rate that is not attributable to the (weighted) growth rate of capital per person.

{End Chapter 2}

Chapter 3: Microeconomics

Microeconomics is a subfield of mainstream economics that investigates how people and businesses allocate limited resources and how their actions affect one another. Instead of looking at the economy as a whole, as macroeconomics does, microeconomics examines smaller economic units such as markets, sectors, and industries.

Microeconomics analyzes the market mechanisms that enable buyers and sellers to establish relative prices among goods and services.

A picture of a market in Delhi.

The study of microeconomics seeks, among other things, to shed light on how markets determine the relative prices of different goods and services and how scarce resources are divided among competing demands. The study of microeconomics reveals the circumstances under which market forces produce optimal distributions. Market failure, in which markets fail to produce optimal outcomes, is also examined.

Macroeconomics examines the economy as a whole, addressing national policies regarding growth, inflation, and unemployment, whereas microeconomics studies individual businesses and consumers. Many recent macroeconomic theories, especially those developed in response to the Lucas critique, have relied heavily on micro foundations, or fundamental assumptions about individual behavior.

Traditionally, general equilibrium theory has been applied to the study of microeconomics, developed by Léon Walras in Elements of Pure Economics (1874) and partial equilibrium theory, created by Alfred Marshall and published in his book "Principles of Economics" (1890).

The study of a single, hypothetical, economically rational, and utility-maximizing individual is often where microeconomic theory gets its start. According to economic theory, a rational person has fixed, exhaustive preferences that change over time.

Utility functions can only exist under the technical assumption that preference relations are continuous. However, without this assumption, comparative statics would be rendered useless because there would be no assurance that the resulting utility function would be differentiable.

A subset of the consumption set the competitive budget set is a key concept in modern microeconomic theory. Economists assume, for technical reasons, that people's preferences are not fully satisfied even in their immediate surroundings. There is no absolute guarantee, but individual utility should rise rationally in the absence of LNS (local non-satiation). The utility maximization problem (UMP) is created after collecting the data and making the necessary assumptions.

The core concept of consumer theory is the utility maximization problem. Through the imposition of rationality axioms on consumer preferences and subsequent mathematical modeling and analysis, the utility maximization problem seeks to provide an explanation for the action axiom. In addition to providing a solid mathematical basis for consumer theory, the utility maximization problem also provides a philosophical justification for it. That is, economists use the utility maximization problem to explain not just what or how people make decisions, but also their motivations for doing so.

The utility maximization problem is a form of constrained optimization in which an individual attempts to maximize utility while being limited by available resources. The extreme value theorem is relied on by economists as proof that the utility-maximizing problem can be solved. In other words, the utility maximization problem has a solution because the budget constraint is both bounded and closed. A Walrasian demand function or correspondence is what economists use to describe the optimal solution to the utility maximization problem.

To this point, the utility maximization problem has been built with consumers' preferences (i.e., utility) as the fundamental unit of analysis. However, consumer choice can also serve as a starting point for developing microeconomic theory. The term "revealed preference theory" is used to refer to this particular type of microeconomic theory.

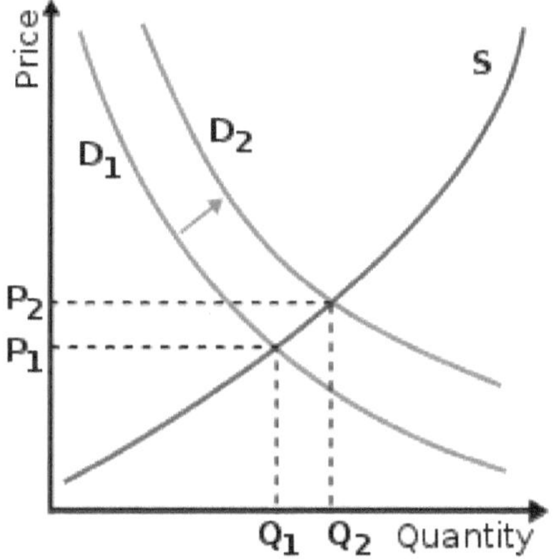

The supply and demand model describes how prices vary as a result of a balance between product availability at each price (supply) and the desires of those with purchasing power at each price (demand).

The graph depicts a right-shift in demand from D1 to D2 along with the consequent increase in price and quantity required to reach a new market-clearing equilibrium point on the supply curve (S).

In most applications of supply and demand theory, perfectly competitive markets are taken for granted. Because of the high number of buyers and sellers in the market, prices for goods and services are unlikely to be significantly influenced by any single participant. Because some buyers or sellers can affect prices in many real-world transactions, the assumption often fails. The demand-supply equation of a solid model is not always easy to grasp without resorting to complex analysis. However, when these conditions hold, the theory excels.

In contrast to widespread belief, mainstream economics does not take it as a given that market economies are optimal. In fact, a lot of thought is put into situations where deadweight loss is produced by inefficient resource allocation due to market failures. The provision of public goods is often criticized as an illustration of inefficient use of resources. Economists may try to find waste-avoidance policies in these cases through direct government control, indirect regulation that induces market participants to act in a manner consistent with optimal welfare, or through the creation of "missing markets" to enable efficient trading where none previously existed.

Collective action theory and public choice theory investigate this phenomenon. Most discussions of "optimal welfare" employ the Paretian norm, a mathematical extension of the Kaldor-Hicks approach. Since this does not take into account how goods are distributed among people, it may deviate from the Utilitarian goal of maximizing utility. When the economist's faith and theory are kept separate, the implications of market failure in positive economics (microeconomics) are constrained.

One common explanation for consumer demand is that people are trying to maximize their own utility within the constraints of their available resources and their established pattern of consumption when making purchasing decisions.

Companies and people have to make choices about how to spend scarce resources so that everyone in the economy benefits. When deciding what to produce, businesses weigh the costs of labor, materials, and capital against the expected profits. Consumers make their purchases based on what they believe will bring them the greatest amount of satisfaction relative to the amount of money available to them.

Microeconomists and macroeconomists are two common classifications among economists. The Norwegian economist Ragnar Frisch, who shared the first Nobel Memorial Prize in Economic Sciences in 1969, is widely credited with introducing the distinction between microeconomics and macroeconomics in 1933.

According to consumer demand theory, individuals have a connection between their preferences for goods and services and their willingness to spend money on those goods and services. Individual preferences, discretionary income, and the demand curve are some of the most investigated connections in economics. In order to maximize utility within the constraints of a consumer's budget, this method analyzes the ways in which consumers can strike a balance between their wants and their ability to spend.

The field of study known as production theory examines the economic activity of turning raw materials and labor into finished goods. Production makes use of resources to make something that can be used, given as a gift, or traded for other goods and services. Production, stocking, transport, and packaging are all possible examples. Production, in the broad sense, is what happens in the economy other than consumption, according to some economists. They consider anything that happens in a store other than the actual purchase to be production.

Production expenses According to the theory of value, a product's or service's value is equal to its total cost of production. All production inputs (labor, capital, and land) and taxes count as cost. Both fixed capital (such as an industrial plant) and circulating capital (such as a computer) can be considered forms of technology (e.g., intermediate goods).

Short-term total cost in the production cost model equals fixed cost plus total variable cost. The term "fixed cost" is used to describe expenses that remain constant regardless of the volume of output. The variable cost varies with the output of a given good. The economic duality theory, pioneered by Ronald Shephard (1953, 1970) and others, employs the cost function to characterize production (Sickles & Zelenyuk, 2019, ch.2).

Costs that do not vary with output are called fixed costs (FC). Rent, salaries, and utilities are all part of the cost of doing business.

In contrast to fixed costs, variable costs (VC) shift in proportion to output. Materials, transportation fees, and other manufacturing expenses fall under this category.

Over a relatively brief time limit (a few months), the majority of a company's expenses will be fixed, such as payroll, contracted shipping, and the cost of raw materials. Over a longer time, frame (say, two to three years), expenses may fluctuate. Producing less, buying less, and possibly even selling some machineries are all options for companies. Most expenses become malleable after the first decade, when workers can be let go and old equipment can be replaced.

The concept of opportunity cost is intrinsically linked to the concept of limited time. Since it is impossible to multitask, we must constantly choose between various alternatives. The opportunity cost of any activity is the value of the next-best alternative thing one may have done instead. The value of the best available alternative is all that matters when calculating opportunity cost. It makes no difference if one has five options or five thousand.

If you know the opportunity cost of doing something, you will know when not to do it. One might enjoy both waffles and chocolate, for instance. One would accept waffles alone if that were all that was offered. A chocolate bar would be chosen over waffles any day. Eating waffles means passing up chocolate, which is an opportunity cost. Choosing the waffles over the chocolate would be irrational because of the opportunity cost of missing the chocolate. Of course, there is still the opportunity cost of forgoing waffles if one opts for chocolate. However, one is prepared to make this sacrifice because the advantages of the chocolate outweigh the opportunity cost of forgoing the waffle. Because choosing one option over another requires foregoing the next-best option, opportunity costs inevitably limit behavior.

To emphasize the importance of prices in relation to buyers and sellers, microeconomics is sometimes referred to as price theory. Supply and demand are the theoretical foundation of the economics subfield known as "price theory," which seeks to explain and predict consumer behavior. It has ties to the Department of Economics at the University of Chicago. The goal of studying competitive equilibrium in markets from the perspective of price theory is to generate falsifiable hypotheses.

The study of prices is distinct from microeconomics. Although price theory is central to the study of microeconomics, it pays little attention to strategic behavior, such as the interactions between sellers in a market with a small number of sellers. Competitive markets, according to price theorists, provide a reasonable description of most markets and can be extended to include the study of consumer preferences and technological developments. Consequently, microeconomics is more likely to make use of game theory than price theory.

Although its primary focus is on price responses by agents, the framework of price theory can be applied to many other socioeconomic issues. The advancement of public choice theory and the study of law and economics can both be attributed to the work of price theorists. Criminology, marriage, and substance abuse are just a few of the fields where price theory has been successfully applied.

In a perfectly competitive market, prices are determined by the economic model of supply and demand. To sum up, it states that a good's unit price is the price at which the quantity demanded by consumers equals the quantity supplied by producers in a perfectly competitive market free of externalities, per-unit taxes, and price controls. Because of this price, the economy is in a state of equilibrium.

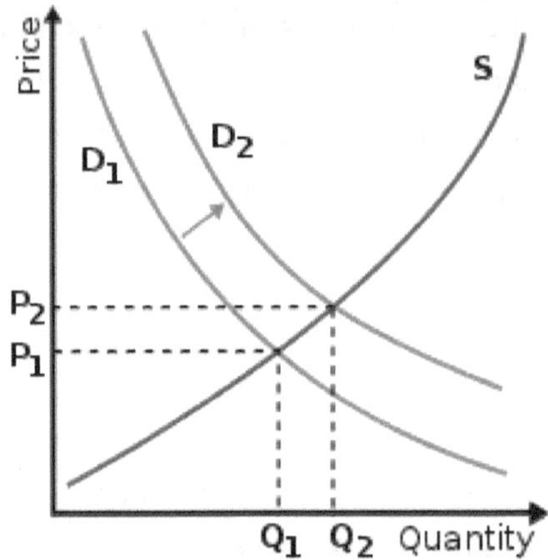

The supply and demand model describes how prices vary as a result of a balance between product availability and demand.

An ascending line in the graph indicates progress, right-shift) in demand from D1 to D2 along with the consequent increase in price and quantity required to reach a new equilibrium point on the supply curve (S).

It has been said that in a market economy, the most easily observable characteristics of goods are their prices and quantities traded. How production and consumption are kept in equilibrium is explained by the theory of supply and demand. It is a condition of perfect competition in microeconomics that neither buyers nor sellers can exert monopoly power over prices in the market.

Demand in a commodity market is defined as the ratio of the quantity that would be purchased by all buyers at each unit price of the good. Tables and graphs that display price and quantity demanded are common representations of demand (as in the figure). Given their income, price range, preferences, etc., consumers, according to demand theory, will choose the optimal quantity of each good. The term "constrained utility maximization" describes this situation (with income and wealth as the constraints on demand). Utility is the assumed connection between how much a consumer values various sets of goods and services.

According to the law of demand, in a competitive market, demand falls as price rises. In other words, people's willingness to purchase a product decrease as its price rises (other things unchanged). Consumers shift their purchasing habits toward less expensive commodities as their prices drop (the substitution effect). In addition, the rise in purchasing power was due to the drop in prices (the income effect). The demand curve for a typical good, as shown in the figure, would move further away from the origin if income were to increase. Everything is assumed to be constant, including the factors that affect supply and demand.

The price at which a product is offered for sale is related to its supply. It can be shown as a table or a graph connecting selling price and available stock. Businesses and other manufacturers are assumed to be profit maximizers that aim to produce and sell as much of their wares as possible. If all other factors remain constant, the supply curve is a function of price and quantity.

To rephrase, the figure shows that production increases as the selling price rises. Because of the increased price, it is worthwhile increasing output. The supply side can move, too, for several reasons, such as when the price of a productive input decreases or increases or when there is a breakthrough in technology. In accordance with the "Law of Supply," supply increases as prices go up and decreases as prices go down. The price of substitutes, the cost of production, the technology used, and the numerous factors of inputs to production are also assumed to remain constant over the evaluation period of supply in this case.

If we look at the point where the supply and demand curves intersect, we can see that this is where market equilibrium takes place. When the price falls below the point of equilibrium, supply falls short of demand. A higher price is expected as a result of this. When the price is higher than the point of equilibrium, supply exceeds demand. The result is a lower price. Price and quantity are forecast to level off at the point where the supply curve meets the demand curve, according to the supply and demand model. Like the figure, a change in demand (or supply) is expected to result in a different price-quantity dynamic, according to demand-and-supply theory.

Consumers' willingness to pay per unit of a product's quantity purchased is represented by the point on the demand curve. Consumers' willingness to pay for that specific unit is quantified by this indicator.

On the supply side of the market, the cost of adjusting output levels is affected by factors of production that are described as (relatively) variable in the short run. Electricity, raw materials, overtime, and contract labor all have flexible utilization rates. Other inputs, such as plant and equipment and key personnel, are more permanent. Over time, management may change any and all inputs. These variations are reflected in the price-quantity response to a change in supply or demand, as well as the elasticity (responsiveness) of the supply curve in the short and long runs.

Producers try to maximize profits within their own constraints, which include the demand for goods produced, technological limitations, and the cost of inputs, while consumers try to achieve most-preferred positions within their income and wealth levels. There is no longer any benefit to the consumer from increasing consumption beyond a certain point, as measured by the good's marginal utility less its price. Similarly, marginal profit is the difference between marginal revenue (which is the same as price for a perfect competitor) and marginal costs. When a product's marginal profit is zero, no additional units are produced. Price and quantity change "at the margin" for both the movement to market equilibrium and the changes in equilibrium: more or less of something, rather than all or nothing.

Factor markets use demand and supply to allocate resources like labor and capital among the various participants in the production process. For instance, in a competitive labor market, the quantity of workers employed, and the wage rate are both influenced by the demand and supply of workers (from potential workers). Labor economics looks at how workers and businesses interact through markets to shed light on things like wage and income fluctuations, worker mobility and (un)employment rates, human capital productivity gains, and related public policy concerns.

The term "market structure" is used to describe the characteristics of a market, such as its size, the number of participating firms, the composition of market share among those firms, the degree to which firms offer similar products, the ease with which new firms can enter the market, and the nature of competition among those firms. Multiple market systems of varying types can interact within a given market structure. Capitalism and market socialism both feature markets, but market socialists and state socialists have different views on markets and aim to substitute or replace them with government-directed economic planning.

Market systems rely on competition as a form of regulation, with government stepping in to regulate areas where market forces alone would fail. When the private equilibrium of the market does not correspond to the social equilibrium, regulations help to mitigate the negative externalities of goods and services. The absence of building codes, for instance, in a purely competition-regulated market system could lead to several horrific injuries or deaths before companies would begin improving structural safety. This is because, at the outset, consumers may not be as concerned or aware of safety issues to begin putting pressure on companies to provide them, and because, at the outset, providing proper safety features would cut into companies' profits.

There is a distinction to be made between "market type" and "market structure." However, here it is important to note that there is a wide range of markets to choose from.

Depending on the market structure, prices follow different curves. Marginal cost, average total cost, average variable cost, average fixed cost, and marginal revenue all appear on the production cost curve, which is sometimes equal to demand, average revenue, and price in a firm that sets its own prices.

In a perfectly competitive market, numerous small firms all making the same goods would face off against one another. When there are no barriers to entry, firms will produce the socially optimal level of output at the lowest possible cost per unit thanks to perfect competition. Companies operating in a genuinely competitive market have no choice but to "price take" (they do not have enough market power to profitably increase the price of their goods or services). Online auction houses like eBay are a great illustration of this phenomenon because they facilitate the sale of identical goods by multiple vendors to numerous buyers. In an ideal competitive market, consumers know everything there is to know about the goods on the market.

Some characteristics of competitive markets are present in imperfectly competitive markets. Since there are so many suppliers in an environment of perfect competition, it is impossible to gain monopoly status. As a result, costs are covered, and prices are adjusted accordingly. When a single company controls the market, monopoly pricing causes profits to exceed expenses. Businesses that operate in markets that are neither perfectly competitive nor monopolistic fall somewhere in the middle. The soft drink and video game markets are dominated by the likes of Pepsi and Coke and Sony, Nintendo, and Microsoft, respectively. Companies in this sector face only limited competition.

When many companies offer nearly identical goods, the market is said to be monopolistic. Society reaps benefits from product differentiation despite production costs that exceed what could be achieved by perfectly competitive firms. Restaurants, breakfast cereal, clothing, footwear, and urban service industries all have market structures that are similar to monopolistic competition.

A monopoly is a type of market structure in which a single firm controls the majority of customers and the price of a product or service. Monopolies, with no rivals to worry about, charge more for their wares and turn out less than what society needs. In industries where the costs of competing would outweigh the benefits, monopolies may actually be beneficial (i.e., natural monopolies).

A natural monopoly occurs when a single firm can produce goods or services at a lower price than a large number of smaller firms.

In an oligopoly, a small group of companies controls the majority of the market (oligopolists). Competition is reduced, prices are raised, and overall market output decreases when firms in an oligopoly have an incentive to collude and form cartels.

Two-firm oligopoly is a subset of the broader category duopoly. Duopolies and oligopolies can benefit from the insights provided by game theory.

In a monopsony, one buyer dominates a market with multiple sellers.

A market with a monopoly (one seller) and a monopsony (two sellers) is called a bilateral monopoly (a single buyer).

In an oligopsony, a small number of sellers dominate a large pool of potential buyers.

Mathematical economics and business frequently employ game theory to model the competitive actions of interacting agents. In this context, the study of games can refer to the analysis of any form of strategic human interaction. Auctions, bargaining, M&A pricing, fair division, duopolies, oligopolies, social network formation, agent-based computational economics, general equilibrium, mechanism design, voting systems, and a host of other phenomena and approaches from the fields of experimental economics, behavioral economics, information economics, industrial organization, and political economy are just some of the many areas in which these applications can be found.

The field of microeconomics known as "information economics" investigates the impact of data and technological infrastructure on economic activity and policymaking. The characteristics of information are unique. Easy to make, but difficult to rely on. It is simple to disperse but difficult to contain. It is a major factor in a lot of choices. In comparison to other products, these unique features present challenges for many established economic theories.

United States Capitol Building: meeting place of the United States Congress, where a lot of tax legislation is enacted, whose effects are felt immediately in the economy.

This is the focus of research in public economics.

Numerous subfields within applied microeconomics make use of approaches from other academic disciplines.

Economists, geographers, sociologists, psychologists, and political scientists all contribute to economic historians' quest to understand how economies and economic institutions have developed over time.

The field of study known as "education economics" delves into the positive and negative effects of schooling on economic output.

The field of financial economics investigates issues like the most effective portfolio layout, the rate of return on investment, statistical analysis of stock returns, and the fiscal practices of businesses.

Health economists investigate how medical facilities and government agencies run, from staffing to insurance.

The field of industrial organization investigates issues like new company formation, product development, and the function of trademarks.

The field of law and economics analyzes the effectiveness of various legal systems by applying the tools of microeconomics to the decision-making process.

The field of study known as "political economy" investigates how government structures affect economic outcomes.

The field of public economics analyzes the way governments set tax rates and spend money (e.g., social insurance programs).

When analyzing urban problems like sprawl, pollution (air and water), gridlock (transportation), and poverty (economics), urban geographers and sociologists often consult one another.

Despite its name, the field of labor economics encompasses far more than just the study of the labor market.

{End Chapter 3}

Chapter 4: Capital intensity

Capital intensity refers to the ratio of fixed or real capital to other factors of production, particularly labor. On the level of a production process or the economy as a whole, it can be estimated by the capital to labor ratio, such as from the points along a capital/labor isoquant.

The use of tools and machinery increases the efficiency of labor, so rising capital intensity (or "capital deepening") increases labor productivity. Long-term, capital-intensive societies tend to have a higher standard of living.

Robert Solow's calculations suggested that technological progress (productivity growth) rather than capital and labor inputs drove economic growth. Recent economic research has refuted Solow's theory because he failed to properly account for changes in both investment and labor inputs.

Dale Jorgenson, Cornell University, The American Economic Association's president in 2000, concludes: "Griliches and I demonstrated that changes in the quality of capital and labor inputs as well as the quality of investment goods accounted for the majority of the Solow residual.".

We estimated that capital and labor inputs were responsible for 85 percent of growth between 1945 and 1965, while only 15 percent could be attributed to productivity growth... This has precipitated the sudden obsolescence of earlier productivity research employing the conventions of Kuznets and Solow.'

Considering the G7 and other major economies, Jorgenson and Vu conclude: 'the growth of world output between input growth and productivity... input growth greatly predominated... Productivity growth accounted for only one-fifth of the total during 1989-1995, whereas input growth accounted for nearly 80% of output growth.

Similarly, after 1995, input growth accounted for more than 70 percent of growth, whereas productivity contributed less than thirty percent.

relating to variations in output per capita Jorgenson and Vu conclude that differences in per capita output levels are primarily explained by differences in per capita input, as opposed to variations in productivity.

According to some economists, the Soviet Union failed to learn the lessons of the Solow growth model because, beginning in the 1930s, the Stalin government attempted to force capital accumulation through state control of the economy. However, Solow's calculations have been shown to be invalid, so this explanation is inadequate. Modern research indicates that the primary factor for economic growth is the expansion of labor and capital inputs, not productivity gains. Therefore, factors other than capital accumulation must have contributed significantly to the Soviet economic crisis.

Free market economists tend to believe that capital accumulation should be determined by market forces rather than by the government. Then, capital accumulation would be promoted by monetary stability (which increases confidence), low taxation, and greater freedom for entrepreneurs.

The Austrian School contends that the capital intensity of any industry is a result of the industry's cyclical nature and consumer demand.

Compared to their labor costs, capital-intensive industries devote a substantial portion of their capital to the purchase of expensive machinery. The term was coined in the mid- to late-nineteenth century, when factories such as steel or iron mills began to appear throughout the newly industrialized world. The added expense of equipment increased the financial risk. This results in a small market share for new capital-intensive factories with high-tech machinery, despite their increased productivity and output. Railways, aircraft manufacturing, airlines, oil production and refining, telecommunications, semiconductor fabrication, mining, chemical plants, electric power plants, etc. are considered to be capital-intensive industries.

Capital intensity is straightforward to quantify in nominal terms. It is the ratio between the total monetary value of capital equipment and the total output potential. However, this metric need not be related to real economic activity because it is susceptible to inflationary increases. The question then becomes, how do we measure the "real" quantity of capital goods? Utilize book value (historical cost)? or cost of replacement? or the price justified by the present value of discounted future profits? Or do we simply "deflate" the total present value of capital equipment by the average cost of capital goods?

This capital controversy illustrates that the measure of capital intensity is not independent of the income distribution, so that changes in the ratio of profits to wages lead to changes in measured capital intensity.

{End Chapter 4}

Chapter 5: Production function

A production function in economics describes the technological relationship between physical inputs and outputs of goods. The production function is one of the central concepts of mainstream neoclassical theories, used to define marginal product and differentiate allocative efficiency, a central concept in economics. One of the primary purposes of the production function is to address allocative efficiency in the use of factor inputs in production and the resulting distribution of income to those factors, while abstracting away the technological issues of achieving technical efficiency, as an engineer or professional manager might understand them.

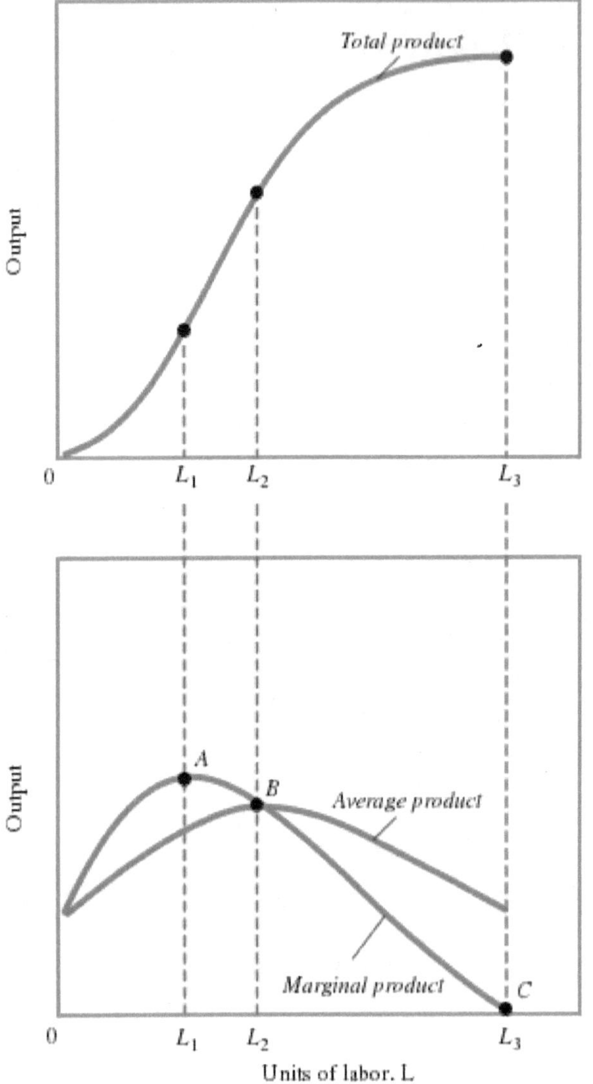

Graph of total, average, and marginal product

For modeling the case of many outputs and many inputs, researchers frequently employ so-called Shephard's distance functions or, alternatively, directional distance functions, which are economic generalizations of the simple production function.

Any given set of inputs can produce a variety of outputs, so economic output is not a (mathematical) function of input in general. To satisfy the mathematical definition of a function, it is commonly assumed that a production function specifies the maximum output achievable from a given set of inputs. Therefore, the production function describes a boundary or frontier that represents the maximum output that can be obtained from each feasible combination of inputs. Alternately, a production function may be defined as the specification of the minimal input requirements necessary to produce specified output quantities. Assuming maximum output from given inputs allows economists to abstract away from technological and managerial problems associated with achieving such a technical maximum and to focus solely on the problem of allocative efficiency, which is associated with the economic choice of how much of a factor input to use, or the degree to which one factor may be substituted for another. In the production function itself, the relationship between output and inputs is non-monetary; that is, prices and costs are not reflected in the function.

In the decision framework of a firm making economic decisions regarding production—how much of each factor input to use to produce how much output—and facing market prices for output and inputs, the production function represents the opportunities made available by an exogenous technology. Under specific conditions, the production function can be used to calculate the marginal product of each factor. The profit-maximizing firm in perfect competition (assuming output and input prices are constant) will choose to add input until the marginal cost of additional input equals the marginal product of additional output. This implies a perfect division of the income generated from output into the income due to each input factor of production, which is equal to the marginal product of each input.

Inputs to the production function are often referred to as factors of production and may represent stocks of primary factors. Historically, the primary production factors were land, labor, and capital. In the production process, neither the primary factors nor the primary factors themselves are incorporated into the final product. As a theoretical construct, the production function may ignore the secondary factors and intermediate products utilized in a production process. The production function is not a comprehensive model of the production process; it abstracts on purpose from inherent aspects of physical production processes that some would argue are essential, such as error, entropy, and waste, as well as energy consumption and co-production of pollution. In addition, production functions typically do not model business processes, ignoring the role of strategic and operational business management. (For an introduction to the basic elements of microeconomic production theory, see production theory fundamentals).

The production function is fundamental to the marginalist orientation of neoclassical economics, its definition of efficiency as allocative efficiency, its analysis of how market prices can govern the achievement of allocative efficiency in a decentralized economy, and its analysis of the distribution of income, which attributes factor income to the marginal product of factor input.

The right side of a production function expressed in functional form is.

$$Q = f(X_1, X_2, X_3, \ldots, X_n)$$

where Q

is the quantity of output and $X_1, X_2, X_3, \ldots, X_n$

are the quantities of factor inputs (such as capital, labor, (land or resources).

For $X_1 = X_2 = \ldots = X_n = 0$

it must be $Q = 0$

since we cannot produce anything without inputs.

If Q

is a scalar, Therefore, this form does not include co-production, which production method yields multiple co-products?

On the contrary, if f

maps from $\mathbb{R}^n$

to $\mathbb{R}^k$

then it is a joint production function expressing the determination of k

diverse types of output based on the joint usage of the specified quantities of the n

inputs.

As a linear function is one formulation:

$$Q = a_1 X_1 + a_2 X_2 + a_3 X_3 + \cdots + a_n X_n$$

where $a_1, \ldots, a_n$

are parameters that are determined empirically.

Linear functions imply that production inputs are perfect substitutes.

Additionally, as a Cobb–Douglas production function:

$$Q = a_0 X_1^{a_1} X_2^{a_2} \cdots X_n^{a_n}$$

where a_0

is the so-called total factor productivity.

The Leontief production function is applicable when inputs must be utilized in fixed proportions; beginning with these proportions, if one input is increased without another input also being increased, the output will decrease, the result will not alter.

This function of production is provided by.

$$Q = \min(a_1 X_1, a_2 X_2, \ldots, a_n X_n).$$

Other types consist of the constant elasticity of substitution production function (CES), which is the generalized Cobb–Douglas function, together with the quadratic production function.

The best form of the equation to use and the values of the parameters (

$$a_0, \ldots, a_n$$

) vary from company to company and industry to industry.

In the near term, production function at least one of the X

's (inputs) is fixed.

Over the long term, all factor inputs are variable at management's discretion.

Moysan and Senouci (2016) provide an analytical formula for all neoclassical two-input production functions.

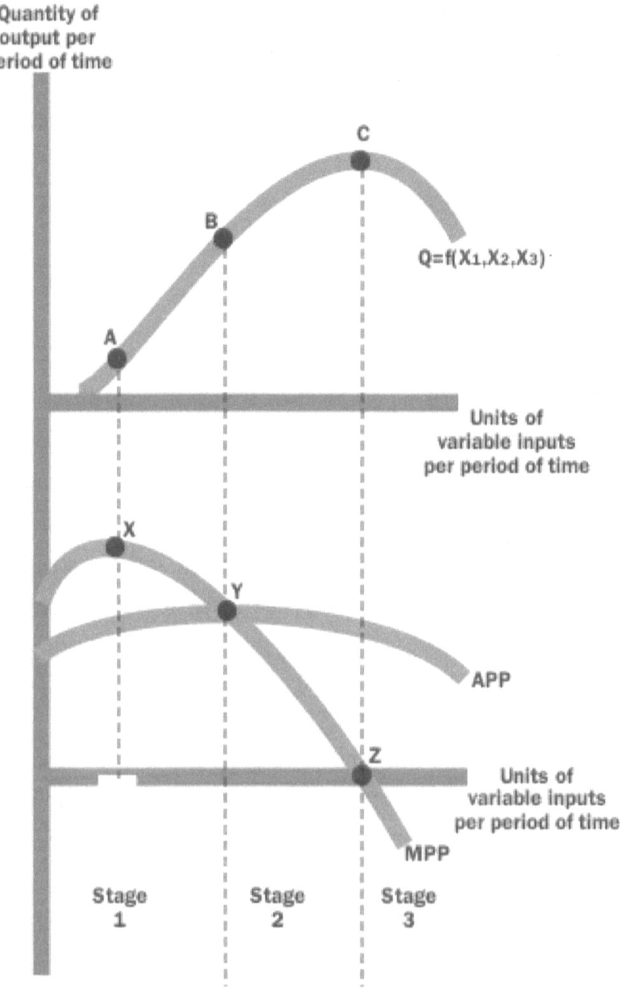

Quadratic production function

Any one of these equations can be graphed. The diagram below depicts a typical (quadratic) production function under the assumption of a single variable input (or fixed ratios of inputs so they can be treated as a single variable). All points above the production function are infeasible with current technology, all points below are technically feasible, and all points on the function represent the maximum amount of output achievable at the specified level of input consumption. From point A to point C, the firm's variable input generates positive but decreasing marginal returns. As more units of input are utilized, the output rises at a decreasing rate. The diminishing slope of the average physical product curve (APP) beyond point Y indicates that point B is the point beyond which there are diminishing average returns. Point B is tangent to the origin's steepest ray, so the average physical product is at its maximum. Beyond point B, mathematical necessity dictates that the marginal curve must be below the average curve. (See production theory basics and Sickles and Zelenyuk (2019) for more in-depth discussions of various production functions, their generalizations, and estimates.).

It is common to divide the range of a production function into three stages in order to simplify its interpretation. In Stage 1 (from the origin to point B), variable input is utilized with rising output per unit, which reaches a maximum at point B. (since the average physical product is at its maximum at that point). Because the output per unit of the variable input increases as stage 1 progresses, a price-taking firm will always operate beyond this stage.

In Stage 2, the rate of output growth slows, and both the average and marginal physical product decrease. However, the average product of fixed inputs (not shown) continues to increase, as output increases while fixed input usage remains constant. In this stage, the addition of variable inputs increases output per unit of fixed input while decreasing output per unit of variable input. The optimal input/output combination for a firm with a price-taking strategy will be in Stage 2, while a firm with a demand curve that slopes downwards may find it most profitable to operate in Stage 2. In Stage 3, variable inputs are overutilized relative to fixed inputs: variable inputs are overutilized in the sense that their presence at the margin hinders the production process rather than facilitating it. Throughout this stage, the output per unit of both the fixed and variable inputs decrease. At the transition between stages 2 and 3, the fixed input produces the maximum possible output.

Long-term, the firm can change the scale of its operations by adjusting the level of fixed inputs in the short term, thereby shifting the production function plotted against the variable input upward. Adjustments to the scale of operations may be more significant than what is required to simply balance production capacity with demand if fixed inputs are lumpy. For instance, you may only need to increase production by 1 million units per year to meet demand, but the available production equipment upgrades may involve a 2 million unit increase in productive capacity.

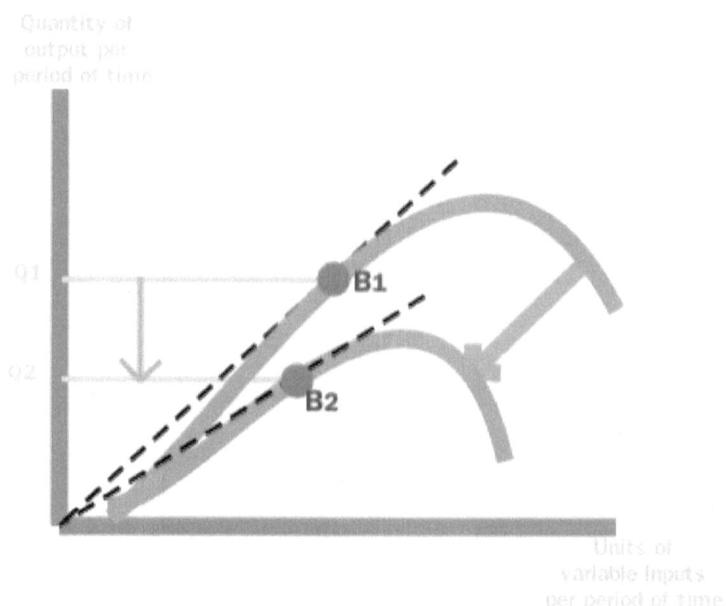

Shifting a production function

Eventually, if a company is operating at a profit-maximizing level in stage one, it may decide to scale back its operations (by selling capital equipment). By decreasing inputs of fixed capital, the production function will shift downwards. B1 gives way to B2 at the beginning of stage 2. The profit-maximizing output level will now be in stage 2 (unaltered).

Two distinct categories of production functions are frequently analyzed.

The production function $Q = f(X_1, X_2, \ldots, X_n)$

is said to be homogeneous of degree m

, if given any positive constant k

,

$$f(kX_1, kX_2, \ldots, kX_n) = k^m f(X_1, X_2, \ldots, X_n)$$

.

If $m > 1$

, The function exhibits rising returns with increasing scale, and it exhibits decreasing returns to scale if $m < 1$

.

If it is homogeneous of degree 1

, It demonstrates consistent returns to scale.

In the presence of increasing returns, a one percent increase in the usage levels of all inputs would result in an output increase that is greater than one percent; The presence of diminishing returns indicates that the output would increase by less than one percent.

Constant returns to scale are the intermediate situation.

In the above-mentioned Cobb–Douglas production function, returns to scale are increasing if $a_1 + a_2 + \cdots + a_n > 1$

, decreasing if $a_1 + a_2 + \cdots + a_n < 1$

, and constant if $a_1 + a_2 + \cdots + a_n = 1$

.

If a production function is homogeneous to the first degree, it is said to be, it is often referred to as "linearly homogeneous.".

A linearly homogeneous production function with capital and labor as inputs possesses the property that the marginal and average physical products of both capital and labor can be expressed as functions of the capital-labor ratio alone.

Moreover, in this instance, if each input is paid at a rate equal to its marginal product, then the total cost of production is zero, the firm's revenues will be exactly exhausted and there will be no excess economic profit.

Homothetic functions are functioning whose marginal technical rate of substitution (slope of the isoquant graph) is equal to zero, A curve drawn through the set of points in, say, labor-capital space where the same quantity of output is produced for different combinations of inputs is homogeneous of degree zero.

As a result of this, along with rays emanating from the beginning, the isoquants will have the same slopes.

Homothetic functions are of the form $F(h(X_1, X_2))$

where $F(y)$

is a monotonically increasing function (the derivative of $F(y)$

is positive ($\mathrm{d}F/\mathrm{d}y > 0$

)), and the function $h(X_1, X_2)$

is a homogeneous function of any degree.

Sometimes, aggregate production functions for entire nations are constructed in macroeconomics. Theoretically, they are the sum of all the production functions of individual producers; however, there are methodological issues with aggregate production functions, and economists have vigorously debated the concept's validity.

There are two major criticisms of the conventional production function form.

Throughout the 1950s, 1960s, and 1970s, there was a lively discussion regarding the theoretical validity of production functions (see the Capital controversy). Even though the majority of the criticism was directed at aggregate production functions, microeconomic production functions were also scrutinized. In 1953, Joan Robinson criticized the method of measuring factor input capital and how the concept of factor proportions had distracted economists. She penned:

"The production function has been a potent tool for miseducation.".

The student of economic theory is taught to write $Q = f(L, K)$

where L

is a quantity of labor, K

a quantity of capital and Q

a rate of output of commodities.

They are instructed to assume that all employees are equal, and to measure L

in man-hours of labor; They are informed of the index-number dilemma when selecting a unit of output; subsequently, they are rushed to the next question, in the hopes that they will forget to ask how K is measured in units.

Before they ever inquire, he or she is now a professor, Thus, sloppy mental habits are transmitted from one generation to the next.

According to the argument, it is impossible to conceive of capital whose quantity is independent of interest and wage rates. This independence is a prerequisite for constructing an isoquant, which presents a problem. In addition, the slope of the isoquant aids in determining relative factor prices, but the curve cannot be constructed (or its slope measured) without prior knowledge of the prices.

It has been asserted that empirical evidence strongly supports the use of neoclassical aggregate production functions with well-behaved behavior, despite criticisms of their theoretical basis. Anwar Shaikh has shown, however, that they lack empirical relevance so long as the alleged good fit is based on an accounting identity and not on any underlying production/distribution laws.

Typically, natural resources are absent from production functions. When Robert Solow and Joseph Stiglitz attempted to develop a more realistic production function by incorporating natural resources, they did so in a manner that economist Nicholas Georgescu-Roegen criticized as a "magic trick": Solow and Stiglitz failed to account for the laws of thermodynamics, as their variant allowed man-made capital to serve as a complete substitute for natural resources. Despite an invitation in the September 1997 issue of the journal Ecological Economics to respond to Georgescu-criticism, Roegen's neither Solow nor Stiglitz did so.

It is possible to interpret Georgescu-Roegen as criticizing Solow and Stiglitz's approach to mathematically modeling production factors. We will use the example of energy to illustrate the advantages and disadvantages of the two in question approaches.

Robert Solow and Joseph Stiglitz outline a method for modeling energy as a factor of production based on the following assumptions:

Only labor, capital, energy input, and technical change (omitted for brevity) are relevant production factors, The factors of production are independent of one another such that the production function takes the general form

$$Q = f(L, K, E)$$

, Labor, capital, and energy input only depend on time such that

$$K = K(t), L = L(t), E = E(t)$$

.

This approach yields an energy-dependent production function given as

$$Q = AL^\beta K^\alpha E^\chi$$

.

Consider the following instances which support the revision of this model's underlying assumptions:

If workers at any stage of the production process rely on electricity to perform their duties, then electricity must be provided, A power failure would substantially reduce their maximum output, a prolonged power outage would render their maximum output null.

Therefore L

should be modeled as depending directly on time-dependent energy input

$$E(t)$$

.

In the event of a power outage, no machines would be able to function, Consequently, their maximum output would decrease to zero.

Therefore K

should be modeled as depending directly on time-dependent energy input

$$E(t)$$

.

It has also been demonstrated that this model predicts a 28% decrease in output for a 98% reduction in energy, which further supports the revision of this model's assumptions. Note that while an "independent" modeling approach is inappropriate for energy, it may be appropriate for modeling other natural resources such as land.

The "independent" energy-dependent production function can be revised by considering energy-dependent labor and capital input functions

$$L = L(E(t))$$

$$K = K(E(t))$$

,

.

This approach yields an energy-dependent production function given generally as $Q = f(L(E), K(E))$

.

Details regarding the derivation of a particular functional form of this production function and empirical support for this form of the production function are discussed in more recent publications.

Noting that similar arguments could be used to develop more realistic production functions that take other depleting natural resources besides energy into account:

If a geographical region runs out of the natural resources required to produce a given machine or maintain existing machines and is unable to import more or recycle, it will be unable to produce or maintain the machine, Eventually, the machines in that region will fall into disrepair, and their maximum output will be reduced to near zero.

This should be modeled as having a significant impact on total output.

Therefore, therefore K

should be modeled as depending directly on time-dependent natural resource input $N(t)$

The theory of the production function illustrates the relationship between the physical outputs of a production process and the physical inputs, or production factors. The practical application of production functions is obtained by assigning monetary values to physical outputs and inputs. The income generated by the production process is equal to the economic value of physical outputs minus the economic value of physical inputs. By holding prices constant between two periods under consideration, we can determine the change in income caused by a change in the production function. This is the principle that makes the production function a practical concept, i.e., one that is measurable and understandable in real-world situations.

{End Chapter 5}

Chapter 6: Productivity

Productivity is the efficiency with which goods or services are produced, as measured by some metric. Measurements of productivity are frequently expressed as a ratio of an aggregate output to a single input, or an aggregate input used in a production process, i.e., output per unit of input, typically over a predetermined time period.

Partial productivity are productivity measures that utilize a single class of inputs or factors, but not multiple factors.

Prior to the widespread use of computer networks, partial productivity was monitored using hand-drawn tables and graphs. In the 1920s and 1930s, tabulating machines for data processing became popular and remained so until the late 1960s and early 1970s, when mainframe computers became prevalent. By the late 1970s, affordable computers enabled industrial operations to perform process control and productivity tracking. Today, data collection is largely computerized, and virtually every variable can be viewed graphically in real time or retrieved for specific time intervals.

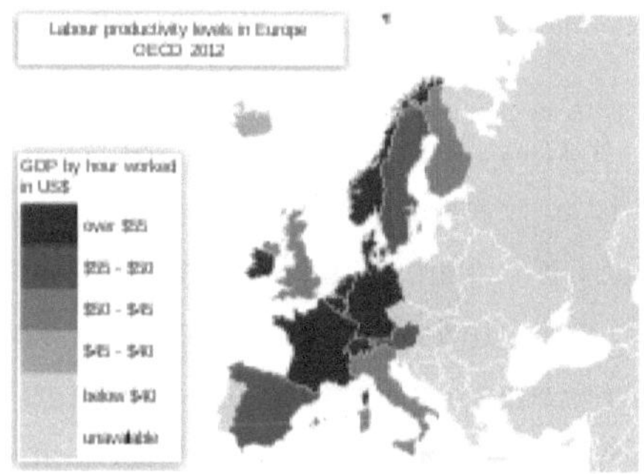

Labor productivity levels in 2012 in Europe.

OECD

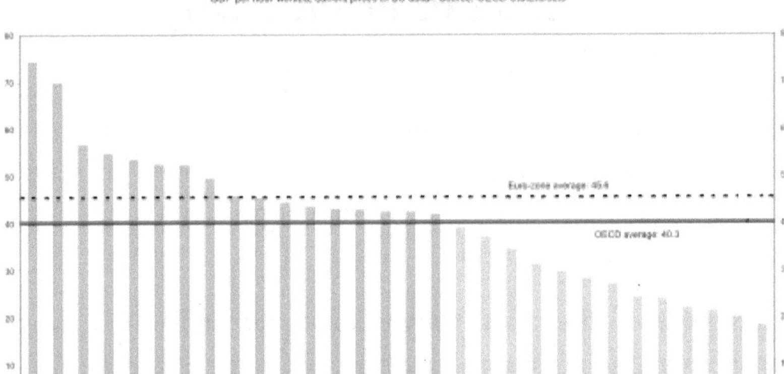

Comparison of average labor productivity levels between the OECD member states.

Productivity is measured by gross domestic product per hour worked.

Blue bars indicate above-average OECD productivity.

Yellow bars are below average.

Labor productivity is a common partial productivity measure in macroeconomics. Labor productivity is a revealing indicator of several economic indicators because it provides a dynamic measurement of an economy's economic growth, competitiveness, and living standards. It is the labor productivity measure (and everything this measure takes into account) that helps explain the primary economic foundations required for both economic growth and social development. In general, labor productivity equals the ratio between an output volume measure (gross domestic product or gross value added) and an input use measure (the total number of hours worked or total employment).

$$\text{labour productivity} = \frac{\text{output volume}}{\text{labor input use}}$$

Typically, the output measure is net output, or the value added by the process under consideration, which is the difference between the value of outputs and the value of intermediate inputs. This is done to prevent double counting when one firm's output is used as an input by another in the same measurement. There are both benefits and drawbacks associated with the various input measures utilized in the calculation of labor productivity. It is generally accepted that the total number of hours worked is the most appropriate measure of labor input because a simple headcount of employed individuals can conceal changes in average hours worked and has difficulty accounting for variations in work, such as part-time contracts, paid leave, overtime, or shifts in normal hours. However, estimates of hours worked are not always accurate. Particularly difficult to use are statistical establishment and household surveys due to the varying quality of hours-worked estimates and the varying degree of international comparability.

GDP per capita is an approximation of average living standards or economic prosperity and is one of the primary indicators of economic performance. This measure (output per worker) is however more problematic than the GDP or even invalid because it allows for the maximization of all inputs, i.e., materials, services, energy, and capital, at the expense of producer income.

Chart 2. Percentage point contributions to growth in output per hour in the private nonfarm business sector, 1987-2014

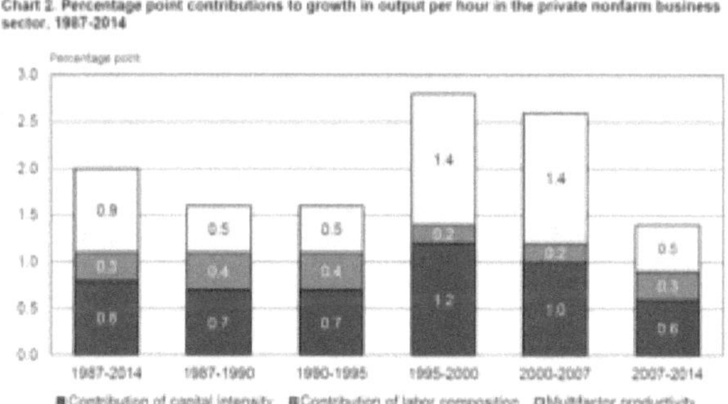

Trends in U.S. the output of labor, Capital, and multiple-factor sources from 1987 to 2014

When multiple inputs are considered, the productivity measure is referred to as MFP or multi-factor productivity.

It is called total productivity when all outputs and inputs are included in the productivity measurement. A valid measurement of total productivity must account for all inputs into production. If we omit an input in productivity (or income accounting), the omitted input can be used in production without affecting accounting results indefinitely. Because total productivity encompasses all production inputs, it is utilized as an integrated variable when attempting to explain how the production process generates income.

Davis has considered suggesting that the measurement of productivity shall be developed so that it" will indicate increases or decreases in the productivity of the company and also the distribution of the 'fruits of production' among all parties at interest."

Consequently, to Davis, the price system is a mechanism for the distribution of productivity gains, in addition to the business enterprise, receiving parties could include its customers, Personnel and providers of production inputs.

In the main article, the function of total productivity as a variable in describing how income formation in production is always a balance between income generation and income distribution is discussed. During the review period, the income change generated by the production function is always distributed to the stakeholders as economic values.

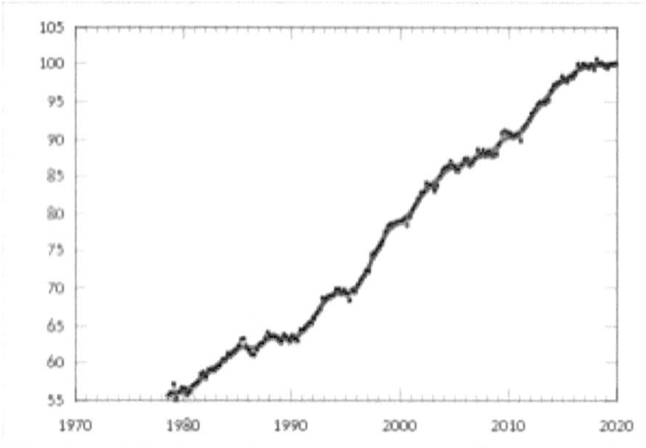

Labor productivity growth in Australia since 1978, calculated using GDP per hour worked (indexed)

Productivity growth is a key contributor to rising living standards. Productivity growth implies that more value is added to production, and consequently, there is more income available for distribution.

The benefits of productivity growth can be distributed in a variety of ways at the firm or industry level:

to the workforce by means of improved wages and conditions; to shareholders and retirement funds via increased profits and dividend payments; to customers through price reductions; to the environment by means of stricter environmental protection; to governments through tax payment increases (which can be used to fund social and environmental programs).

Productivity growth is important to the company because it enables it to meet its (possibly expanding) obligations to workers, shareholders, and governments (taxes and regulations) while maintaining or even enhancing its market competitiveness. Adding more inputs will not increase the per-unit-of-input earnings (unless there are increasing returns to scale). In fact, it is likely to result in lower average wages and profit margins. However, when productivity increases, even the current allocation of resources generates more output and income. The yield generated per unit of input rises. Additionally, additional resources are attracted to production and can be utilized profitably.

In the most direct sense, productivity is determined by the available technology or expertise for converting inputs into outputs, as well as the way inputs are organized to produce goods and services. Historically, productivity has increased through evolution, as inefficient processes are abandoned, and newer forms are utilized. Process enhancements may involve organizational structures (such as core functions and supplier relationships), management systems, work arrangements, manufacturing techniques, and a shifting market structure. The assembly line and the process of mass production, which appeared in the decade following the commercial introduction of the automobile, are well-known examples.

Physical capital, including machinery, equipment, and buildings, is the object of investment. In general, the more capital workers have at their disposal, the better they are able to perform their jobs, resulting in greater and higher-quality output.

Innovation is the effective application of novel concepts. Innovative ideas can manifest as innovative technologies, new products, or new organizational structures and methods of operation. Accelerating the spread of innovations can increase productivity.

A skill is the quantity and quality of diverse types of labor available in an economy. Complementing physical capital, competencies are necessary to capitalize on investments in innovative technologies and organizational structures.

Enterprise is defined as the pursuit of new business opportunities by both new and established companies. New enterprises compete with existing businesses by introducing innovative concepts and technologies that increase competition. Entrepreneurs are able to combine production factors and innovative technologies, compelling incumbents to adapt or leave the market.

Competition increases productivity by encouraging innovation and ensuring that resources are allocated to the most productive firms. It also compels existing businesses to organize their work more efficiently by copying organizational structures and technology.

Computers, spreadsheets, email, and other technological advancements have made it possible for knowledge workers to appear to produce more in a day than in a year. Improved or intensified exchange with peers or coworkers is a driver of productivity growth for creative and knowledge workers, as more productive peers have a stimulating effect on one's own productivity.

Bullying in the workplace reduces productivity, as measured by self-reported job performance. After World War II, Japanese manufacturers adopted the Kaizen system of bottom-up, continuous improvement, most notably as part of The Toyota Way.

One of the primary concerns of business management and engineering is productivity. Numerous businesses have formal programs for enhancing productivity on an ongoing basis, such as a production assurance program. Whether or not they have a formal program, businesses are always looking for ways to increase quality, decrease downtime, and reduce inputs of labor, materials, energy, and purchased services. Typically, the greatest productivity gains result from adopting innovative technologies, which may necessitate the purchase of new capital equipment, computers, or software. Modern productivity science owes a significant amount to formal studies associated with scientific management.

From the 1970s to the early 1990s, overall productivity growth was comparatively moderate, To measure the productivity of a nation or an industry, it is necessary to operationalize the same concept of productivity as in a production unit or a company, despite the fact that the object of modeling is significantly broader and the data is more aggregate. Calculations of national or industry productivity are based on the time series of the System of National Accounts (SNA). National accounting is a system based on UN recommendations (SNA 93) for measuring a nation's total production and total income and how they are utilized.

Productivity growth at the international or national level results from a complex interaction of factors. In addition to economies of scale and scope, the most significant immediate factors include technological change, organizational change, industry restructuring, and resource reallocation. The transfer of resources from low-productivity to high-productivity industries and activities can also have an effect on a nation's average productivity level. Over time, other factors such as research and development and innovative effort, the development of human capital through education, and incentives from stronger competition encourage the pursuit of productivity gains and the ability to attain them. Many policy, institutional, and cultural factors ultimately determine a country's success in enhancing productivity.

Nationally, productivity growth raises living standards because an increase in real income enables individuals to purchase more goods and services (whether necessities or luxuries), enjoy leisure, improve housing and education, and contribute to social and environmental programs. Some have suggested that the "productivity puzzle" in the United Kingdom must be addressed immediately by policymakers and businesses in order to sustain economic growth. that includes both labor and multifactor productivity measures.

{End Chapter 6}

Chapter 7: Output in economics

Output is the "quantity (or quality) of goods or services produced in a given time period by a firm, industry, or country," according to economics. The concept of national output is fundamental to macroeconomics. It is national output, not large sums of money, which makes a nation wealthy.

Output is the result of an economic process in which inputs are used to produce a product or service that is for sale or used elsewhere.

Net output, also known as netput, is a quantity that is positive if it is the output of the production process and negative if it is an input to the production process.

The profit-maximizing output condition for producers equates the relative marginal cost of any two goods with their respective relative selling prices, i.e.

$$\frac{MC_1}{MC_2} = \frac{P_1}{P_2}$$

One can also derive the ratio of marginal costs from the slope of the production–possibility frontier, which indicates the rate at which a society can transform one good into another.

When a certain amount of output is generated, the same amount of income is generated because the output belongs to somebody. Thus, we have established that output equals income (where an identity is an equation that is always true regardless of the values of any variables).

Output can be subdivided into components according to whose demand generated it – total public consumption C (including on imported goods) minus imports M. (the difference being consumption of domestic output), The government is spending G, foreign buyers of domestically manufactured X, planned inventory accumulation I(planned inven), unplanned inventory accumulation I(unplanned inven) resulting from incorrect predictions of consumer and government demand, and fixed investment I(f) on machinery and the like.

Similarly, income can be subdivided according to its uses: consumption spending, taxes T paid, and the portion of income that is neither taxed nor spent (saving S).

Since output and income are identical, the preceding leads to the following identity:

$$C + I_{\text{planned inven}} + I_{\text{unplanned inven}} + I_f + G + X - M \equiv C + S + T,$$

where the triple-bar symbol represents an identifier. This is distinct from the condition of goods market equilibrium, which is met when unplanned inventory investment equals zero:

$$C + I_{\text{planned inven}} + I_f + G + X - M = C + S + T.$$

Output is the result of an economic process in which inputs are used to produce a product or service that is for sale or used elsewhere.

Net output, also known as netput, is a quantity that is positive if it is an output of the production process and negative if it is an input to the production process.

The question of why national output fluctuates is a crucial one in macroeconomics. Although no consensus has been reached, there are a number of factors that economists agree cause fluctuations in output. Most economists agree that there are three fundamental sources of economic growth: an increase in labor utilization, an increase in capital utilization, and an increase in the effectiveness of the factors of production. Just as increases in the utilization or efficiency of factors of production can cause output to rise, anything that causes labor, capital, or their efficiency to decline will result in a decline in output or at least a slowing of its growth rate.

Exchange of output between two nations is a common occurrence, as trade is constantly taking place between nations around the globe. For instance,

Japan may exchange its electronics for German-made automobiles. If the value of the trade being conducted by both countries is equal at that time, then their trade accounts are balanced: exports and imports in both countries would be equal.

{End Chapter 7}

Chapter 8: Capital accumulation

Capital accumulation is the driving force behind the pursuit of profit, involving the investment of money or any financial asset with the objective of increasing the initial monetary value of said asset in exchange for a financial return in the form of profit, rent, interest, royalties, or capital gains. The purpose of capital accumulation is to create new fixed and working capitals, to expand and modernize existing ones, to expand the material basis of social-cultural activities, and to provide the necessary resources for reserve and insurance.

The definition of capital accumulation is contested and ambiguous, as it may refer to:

a net increase in existing wealth

redistributing the wealth.

Typically, capital accumulation entails both a net addition and a redistribution of wealth, which raises the question of who gains the most. If more wealth is produced than was previously present, a society becomes wealthier; the total stock of wealth rises. However, if some acquire capital at the expense of others, wealth is simply transferred from A to B. It is also possible that some individuals accumulate wealth much more rapidly than others. When a person is enriched at the expense of another under circumstances deemed unjust by the law, this is referred to as unjust enrichment. It is theoretically possible for a few individuals or organizations to accumulate capital and become wealthier while the total wealth of society declines.

Capital accumulation is frequently equated in economics and accounting with the investment of profit income or savings, particularly in real capital goods. Capital concentration and centralization are two outcomes of such accumulation (see below).

Typically, capital accumulation refers to:

Real investment in tangible means of production, such as acquisitions, R&D, etc., can increase the flow of capital.

Investment in paper-based financial assets that yield profit, interest, rent, royalties, fees, or capital gains.

Investment in non-productive physical assets that appreciate in value, such as residential real estate or works of art.

therefore also:

Human capital, i.e., new education and training that increases the skills of the (potential) labor force, can boost earnings from employment.

Social capital is the wealth and productive capacity that a society's members hold collectively, as opposed to individuals or corporations.

etc.

Typically, both non-financial and financial capital accumulation are required for economic growth, as additional production requires additional funds to expand the production scale. A more intelligent and productive production organization can also increase output without increasing capital. Inventions or improved organization that increase productivity, discoveries of new assets (oil, gold, minerals, etc.), the sale of property, etc. can generate capital without increased investment.

In contemporary macroeconomics and econometrics, "capital formation" is frequently preferred to "accumulation," although the United Nations Conference on Trade and Development (UNCTAD) uses "accumulation" today. Occasionally, the term is used in national accounts.

Accumulation can be measured by the monetary value of investments, the amount of reinvested income, or the change in the value of assets owned (the increase in the value of the capital stock). Government statisticians estimate total investments and assets for the purposes of national accounts, national balance of payments, and flow of funds statistics using company balance sheets, tax data, and direct surveys as a basis. Typically, reserve banks and the Treasury interpret and analyze this information. Capital formation, gross fixed capital formation, fixed capital, household asset wealth, and foreign direct investment are standard indicators.

The International Monetary Fund, UNCTAD, the World Bank Group, the Organization for Economic Cooperation and Development (OECD), and the Bank for International Settlements used national investment data to estimate global trends. The Bureau of Economic Analysis, Eurostat, and Japan Statistical Office provide respective data on the United States, Europe, and Japan.

Business magazines such as Fortune, Forbes, The Economist, Business Week, etc., and various corporate "watchdog" organizations and non-governmental organization publications are additional useful sources of investment information. Review of Income and Wealth is a reputable scientific publication. In the case of the United States, the "Analytical Perspectives" document (an appendix to the annual budget) provides useful estimates of national wealth and capital.

In macroeconomics, modelled after the Harrod–Domar, the savings ratio (s) and the capital coefficient (k) are regarded as critical factors for accumulation and growth, assuming that all savings are invested in fixed assets.

The rate of growth of the real stock of fixed capital (K) is:

$$\frac{\Delta K}{K} = \frac{\frac{\Delta K}{Y}}{\frac{K}{Y}} = \frac{s}{k}$$

where Y

is the real national income.

$$k = \frac{K}{Y}$$

If the capital-output ratio or capital coefficient (

) is constant, the rate of growth of Y

is equal to the rate of growth of K

.

This is determined by s

(the ratio of net fixed investment or saving to Y

) and k

.

A nation could, for instance, save and invest 12 percent of its national income, and if the capital coefficient is 4:1 (i.e., \$4 billion must be invested to increase the national income by \$1 billion), the annual growth rate of the national income could be 3 percent. Keynesian economics demonstrates, however, that savings do not necessarily imply investment (as liquid funds may be hoarded for example). Investment may also not constitute fixed-asset investment (see above).

Assuming that the turnover of total production capital invested remains constant, the proportion of total investment that merely maintains the stock of total capital, as opposed to increasing it, will typically increase as the stock of total capital grows. In order to accelerate the growth of the capital stock, the growth rates of incomes and net new investments must also accelerate. Simply put, the larger capital grows, the greater the amount of capital required to maintain its growth, and the greater the need for market expansion.

The Harrodian model has a problem with unstable static equilibrium, as production tends to extreme points if the growth rate is not equal to the Harrodian warranted rate (infinite or zero production). The Sraffian Supermultiplier model differs from the Harrodian model in that it considers investment to be induced rather than autonomous. In this model, the autonomous components are Autonomous Non-Capacity-Creating Expenditures, such as exports, credit-led consumption, and public spending. The growth rate of these expenditures determines the rate of long-term capital accumulation and output expansion.

Marx borrowed the concepts of capital accumulation and capital concentration from early socialist authors like Charles Fourier, Louis Blanc, Victor Considerant, and Constantin Pecqueur. According to Karl Marx's critique of political economy, capital accumulation is the process by which profits are reinvested in the economy, thereby increasing the total amount of capital. Marx viewed capital as expanding value, or, in other words, as a sum of capital, typically expressed in monetary terms, which is transformed by human labor into a greater value and extracted as profits. Capital is defined as the value of economic or commercial assets that capitalists use to create additional value (surplus-value). This necessitates the establishment of property relations that allow objects of value to be appropriated and owned, as well as trading rights.

With the expansion of productive forces, the Marxist analysis of capital accumulation and the evolution of capitalism identifies systemic issues with the process. A crisis of overaccumulation of capital occurs when the rate of profit exceeds the rate of new profitable investment outlets in the economy, as a result of rising organic composition of capital and rising productivity (higher capital input to labor input ratio). This depresses the wage bill, resulting in stagnant wages and high unemployment rates for the working class, as excess profits seek new profitable investment opportunities. Marx believed that this cyclical process would be the primary reason for the demise of capitalism and its replacement by socialism, which would operate under a different economic dynamic.

According to Marxist theory, socialism would replace capitalism as the dominant mode of production when the accumulation of capital could no longer be sustained due to declining profit rates in real production relative to rising productivity. A socialist economy would not be based on the accumulation of capital, but rather on the satisfaction of human needs and the direct production of use-values. This concept is encapsulated by the production for use principle.

Marx asserts that capital tends to concentrate and centralize in the hands of the wealthiest capitalists. Marx describes:

"It is the concentration of already-formed capitals, the destruction of their individual independence, the expropriation of capitalists by capitalists, and the transformation of numerous small capitals into a small number of large ones. ... Capital accumulates in a single hand in one location because it has been lost by many in another. ... The battle of competition is fought through the devaluation of goods. The affordability of goods is contingent, all else being equal, on the productivity of labor and, in turn, on the scale of production. Therefore, larger capitals are superior to smaller ones. In addition, it should be recalled that as the capitalist mode of production develops, the minimum amount of individual capital required to operate a business under normal conditions rises. Therefore, smaller capitals crowd into production spheres that Modern Industry has only sporadically or incompletely captured. Here, competition is fierce. It always results in the ruin of numerous small capitalists, whose capitals pass in part to their conquerors and in part vanish."

Marxian economic theory, (1) The value of the real net increase in the stock of capital during an accounting period is the definition of the rate of accumulation, (2) the proportion of realized profit or surplus value that is reinvested, instead of being consumed.

This rate can be expressed using a variety of ratios involving the initial investment, the realized revenue, (see surplus-value or profit and reinvestment), e.g., the writings of the economist Michał Kalecki).

If all else is equal, the greater the proportion of profit-income that is distributed as personal earnings and used for consumption, the lower the savings rate and accumulation rate are likely to be. However, income spent on consumption can also increase market demand and investment levels. This is the source of endless debates in economic theory regarding "how much to spend and save.".

In a period of booming capitalism, the growth of investments is cumulative, meaning that one investment leads to another, resulting in an ever-expanding market, a growing labor force, and an increase in the standard of living for the majority of the population.

In a decadent, stagnant capitalism, the accumulation process is increasingly focused on investments in the military and security forces, real estate, financial speculation, and luxury consumption. In that case, income from value-adding production will decline in favor of interest, rent, and tax income, and permanent unemployment will rise as a result.

In general, the greater the total amount of capital invested, the greater the return on investment. The greater one's capital holdings, the greater one's ability to borrow and reinvest capital at a higher rate of profit or interest. This is a factor in the widening gap between the wealthy and the poor.

Ernest Mandel emphasized that (1) the division of a society's social product into necessary product and surplus product, and (2) the division of the surplus product into investment and consumption were crucial to the rhythm of capital accumulation and growth. This allocation pattern was a result of competition among capitalists, competition between capitalists and workers, and competition among workers. Therefore, the pattern of capital accumulation cannot be explained solely by economic factors; it also involves social factors and power relationships.

Strictly speaking, capital is only accumulated when profit income is reinvested in capital assets. According to the first volume of Marx's Das Kapital, the process of capital accumulation in production has at least seven distinct but interconnected phases:

Initial investment of capital (which may be borrowed capital) in production means and labor force.

The authority over surplus labor and its allocation.

The process of increasing the value of capital through the creation of new outputs.

The acquisition of the value-added new output created by employees.

The achievement of surplus value via output sales.

Appropriation of realized surplus value as (profit) income after costs have been deducted.

Investment of profit earnings in production.

All of these instances are not limited to economic or commercial processes. Rather, they presuppose the existence of legal, social, cultural, and economic power conditions, without which the creation, distribution, and circulation of new wealth would be impossible. This becomes especially apparent when an attempt is made to create a market where none exists or where individuals refuse to engage in commerce.

Marx contends that the original or primitive accumulation of capital is frequently the result of violence, plunder, slavery, robbery, extortion, or theft. He argues that the capitalist mode of production necessitates that people be forced to work in value-adding production for someone else, and that they must be cut off from all other sources of income for this purpose.

Marx continues the story in volume 2 of Das Kapital, demonstrating that, with the assistance of bank credit, capital in search of growth can more or less smoothly mutate from one form to another, alternately taking the form of money capital (liquid deposits, securities, etc.), commodity capital (tradeable goods, real estate, etc.), and production capital (means of production and labor power).

His discussion of the simple and expanded reproduction of production conditions provides a more sophisticated model of the accumulation process's overall parameters. At simple reproduction, enough is produced to sustain a given standard of living; the stock of capital remains constant. At expanded reproduction, more product-value is produced than is required to sustain society at a given standard of living (a surplus product); the surplus product-value is available for investments that increase the scale and variety of production.

According to the bourgeois, there is no economic law mandating the reinvestment of capital in the expansion of production; rather, it depends on anticipated profitability, market expectations, and investment risk perceptions. Such statements explain only the subjective experiences of investors while ignoring the objective realities that would influence their opinions. According to Marx in Volume 2, simple reproduction is only possible if the variable and surplus capital realized by Department 1 (producers of means of production) precisely equals that of Department 2 (producers of articles of consumption) (pg. 524). This equilibrium relies on a number of assumptions, including a constant labor supply (no population growth). Accumulation does not necessarily imply a change in the total magnitude of value produced but can simply refer to a change in an industry's composition (pg. 514).

Ernest Mandel introduced the additional concept of contracted economic reproduction, i.e., reduced accumulation where businesses operating at a loss outnumber growing businesses, or economic reproduction on a decreasing scale, for instance as a result of wars, natural disasters, or devaluation.

Balanced economic growth requires that various accumulation process factors expand in proportional amounts. But markets cannot create this equilibrium on their own; in fact, the imbalances between supply and demand are what drives economic activity: inequality is the engine of growth. This partially explains why the global pattern of economic growth is so uneven and unequal, despite the fact that markets have existed virtually everywhere for centuries. Some argue that it explains government regulation of market trade and protectionism as well.

According to Marx, capital accumulation has two sources: trade and expropriation, which can be legal or illegal. The reason for this is that a capital stock can be increased not only through exchange or "trading up," but also by taking an asset or resource from another person without compensation. David Harvey refers to this as accumulation by expropriation. Marx neither discusses gifts and grants as sources of capital accumulation nor analyzes taxation in depth (he could not, as he died even before completing his major book, Das Kapital). Today, the tax take is frequently so high (25-40% of GDP) that some authors refer to it as state capitalism. This results in the proliferation of tax havens to avoid tax obligations.

The continuation and growth of capital accumulation is contingent on the elimination of barriers to the expansion of trade, which has historically been a violent process. As markets grow, opportunities for capital accumulation increase because increased types of goods and services can be exchanged. But capital accumulation may also encounter resistance when individuals refuse to sell or purchase (for example a strike by investors or workers, or consumer resistance).

In Marxist writings, "accumulation of capital" can also refer to the reproduction of capitalist social relations (institutions) on a larger scale over time, i.e., the growth of the proletariat and the bourgeoisie's wealth.

This interpretation emphasizes that capital ownership, based on control over labor, is a social relationship: the expansion of capital implies the expansion of the working class (a "law of accumulation"). Marx illustrated this concept in the first volume of Das Kapital by referencing Edward Gibbon Wakefield's theory of colonization:

"Wakefield discovered in the Colonies that...", property in cash, a source of subsistence, machines, and additional methods of production, does not yet label a man as a capitalist if he is seeking the corresponding term — wageworker, The other man is forced to sell himself against his will.

He realized that capital is not a physical entity, but a social relationship between individuals, based on the instrumentality of objects.

Mr. Peel, he moans, carried along from England to Swan River, West Australia, means of subsistence and of production to the amount of £50,000.

Mr. Peel was foresighted enough to bring with him, besides, 3,000 individuals from the working class, men, women, and children.

Once he reached his destination, "Mr. Peel was left without a servant to make his bed or fetch him water from the river." Unhappy Mr. Peel, who provided everything but the export of English production methods to Swan River!"

— Das Kapital, vol. 1, Ch. 33

Marx states in the third volume of Das Kapital that the "fetishism of capital" reaches its zenith with interest-bearing capital, because capital now appears to grow on its own without anyone's intervention. In this instance, "Interest-bearing capital represents the most externalized and fetishized form of capital relations."

We have here $M - M'$

, Money generating more cash, self-growing worth, Without the mechanism that produces these two extremes,

In business capital, $M - C - M'$

, At least the general form of the capitalist movement exists, Despite the fact that it is limited to the realm of circulation, Thus, profit appears to be derived solely from alienation; However, it is viewed as the result of a social relationship, not the result of a simple entity.

(...) This is obliterated in $M - M'$

, The form of capital that earns interest.

[...] The item (money), commodity, even as a mere object, value is now capital, and capital appears to be an object.

The result of the entire reproduction process appears as an inherent property of the thing.

It depends on the money's owner, i.e., the form in which the commodity is continuously exchanged, whether he desires to spend it as cash or lend it as capital.

Investments in interest-bearing capital, therefore, this innate fetish, self-growing worth, Money producing money, are released in their purest form, and in this state, it no longer bears traces of its origin.

In the relation of a thing is consummated the social relationship, of money, to itself — Rather than the transformation of money into capital, we see only form and no content here."

— "Das Kapital", vol.3, Ch. 24

It has been demonstrated that product recommendations and information about previous purchases significantly influence consumers' choices for music, movies, books, and other products. Frequently, social influence causes the rich-get-richer phenomenon (Matthew effect), in which popular products tend to become even more popular.

{End Chapter 8}

Chapter 9: Total factor productivity

Total-factor productivity (TFP), also known as multi-factor productivity, is typically measured in economics as the ratio of aggregate output (such as GDP) to aggregate inputs.

Technology growth and efficiency are considered to be two of the largest sub-sections of total factor productivity, with the former possessing "special" inherent characteristics such as positive externalities and non-rivals that bolster its role as a driver of economic growth.

Total factor productivity (TFP) is frequently regarded as the primary factor in determining the GDP growth rate. In addition to labor inputs, human capital, and physical capital, other contributing factors include human capital, physical capital, and human capital. Total factor productivity measures output growth that cannot be explained by the accumulation of traditional inputs such as labor and capital. Since this cannot be directly measured, the process of calculating TFP yields the residual, which accounts for effects on total output that are not caused by inputs.

It has been demonstrated that there is a correlation between TFP and energy conversion efficiency in the past.

Frequently, the following equation (in Cobb–Douglas form) is used to represent total output (Y) as a function of total-factor productivity (A), monetary input (K), labor effort (L), and the two inputs' respective shares of output (α and β are the share of contribution for K and L respectively).

As is customary for equations of this type, a rise in either A or B, Either K or L will increase output.

$$Y = A \times K^{\alpha} \times L^{\beta}$$

TFP is dependent on estimates of the other components as a residual.

Total implies that all inputs have been measured.

Official statisticians typically use the term "multifactor productivity" (MFP) rather than "total factor productivity" (TFP) because inputs such as energy are typically not included.

External expenses including workforce attributes, public infrastructure such as highways and environmental sustainability costs such as mineral depletion and pollution are not traditionally included. The units of the quantities in the Cobb–Douglas equation is:

Y: widgets/year (wid/yr)

L: man-hours/year (manhr/yr)

K: capital-hours/year (caphr/yr; this raises issues of heterogeneous capital)

α, β: pure numbers (non-dimensional), owing to being examples

A: (widgets $\times$ year$^{\alpha + \beta - 1}$) / (caphr$^{\alpha}$ $\times$ manhr$^{\beta}$), a balancing amount, that is TFP.

In this context, the units of A would not have a straightforward economic interpretation, and TFP appears to be a modeling artifact. Instead of measuring levels, official statistics construct unitless growth rates for output and inputs, as well as for the residual.

{End Chapter 9}

Chapter 10: Surplus product

Karl Marx theorized surplus product (German: Mehrprodukt) in his critique of political economy. Roughly speaking, it refers to the surplus of goods produced over the amount necessary for a community of workers to maintain their current standard of living. Marx began developing the concept of surplus product in his 1844 notes on James Mill's Elements of political economy.

Marx explains in Theories of Surplus Value that in classical economics, "surplus" referred to an excess of gross income over cost, implying that the value of goods sold exceeded the value of the costs associated with producing or supplying them. That was the way to "make money" The surplus represented a net increase in the wealth stock. Even if they might agree that the value of production must equal the sum of the new revenue that it generates for the producers, a central theoretical question was to explain the types of influences on the size of the surplus, or how the surplus originated, because this had important implications for the funds available for reinvestment, tax levies, national wealth, and (especially) economic growth.

Originally, political economy was considered a "moral science" that arose from the moral and legal ambiguities of trading processes.

Marx divides the new "social product" of the working population (the flow of society's total output of new products in a specified time interval) into the necessary product and the surplus product in Das Kapital and other works. The "necessary" product refers, from an economic standpoint to the output of goods and services required to maintain a population of workers and their dependents at the prevailing standard of living (effectively, their total reproduction cost). The "surplus" product consists of whatever is produced in excess of the essentials. Socially speaking, this distribution of the social product reflects the claims of the working class and the ruling class on the newly created wealth.

Such an abstract and general distinction is, however, a simplification for at least three reasons.

A society must typically reserve a portion of its new social product at all times. These reserves (sometimes referred to as "strategic stocks"), by definition, are not typically available for immediate distribution but are stored in some manner; however, they are essential for long-term survival. Such reserves must be maintained even if no other surplus to immediate needs is produced; therefore, they can be viewed over a longer period of time as a permanent reproduction cost rather than a true surplus.

A further complicated factor is population growth, as a growing population necessitates the production of "more products" for the population's survival. In primitive societies, insufficient output simply results in death, whereas in complex societies, "producing more" is physically required to sustain a growing population (this is admitted by Marx in Capital, Volume III, chapter 48 where he writes: "A definite quantity of surplus labor is required as insurance against accidents, and by the necessary and progressive expansion of the process of reproduction in keeping with the development of the needs and the growth of population, which is called accumulation from the viewpoint of the capitalist").

At any given time, a portion of the adult population of working age does not work, yet these individuals must also be supported. As far as they are not directly dependent on the producers of the necessary product for their sustenance, they must rely on communal or state resources, or other means, for support.

The concept of a social surplus product appears simple and straightforward at first glance, but it is actually quite complex for social scientists. When attempting to quantify the surplus product of a given economic community, a number of complexities become apparent.

In producing, people must continually maintain their assets, replace their assets, and consume goods, but, assuming sufficient labor productivity, they can also produce more.

This social surplus product is capable of being:

destroyed or squandered

kept in reserve or stockpiled.

consumed

exchanged or otherwise transferred with others.

reinvested Nevertheless, if, for instance, 90 people own 5 sacks of grain and 10 people own 100 sacks of grain, it would be physically impossible for those 10 people to use all that grain themselves; they would likely trade it or hire others to farm it. Since 5 sacks of grain are insufficient for 90 individuals, it is likely that the 90 individuals would be willing to work for the 10 individuals who possess more grain than they can consume in order to obtain additional grain.

If the surplus is simply held in reserve, wasted, or consumed, there is no economic growth (or enhanced economic reproduction). Only when the surplus is traded and/or reinvested is it possible to increase production scale. Throughout the majority of the history of urban civilization, surplus foodstuffs were the primary source of surplus products, whether appropriated through trade, tribute, taxation, or other means.

In Marxism, the existence of a "surplus product" typically presupposes the ability to perform surplus labor, i.e., extra labor beyond what is required to maintain the direct producers and their family dependents at their current standard of living. In Capital, Volume 1, Chapter 9, Section 4, Marx defines the capitalist surplus product exclusively in terms of the relationship between the value of necessary labor and surplus labor; at any given time, this surplus product is lodged simultaneously in money, commodities (goods), and claims to labor-services, and thus is not merely a "physical" surplus product (a stockpile of additional goods).

Marx's view, as expressed in the Grundrisse, is that all frugality is reducible to the economy of human labor-time. The greater human productivity, the more time there is to potentially produce more than is required for population reproduction. Alternately, this additional time can be devoted to leisure, but who gets the leisure and who gets the extra work is typically heavily influenced by the prevailing power and moral relations, not just economics.

The corollary of rising societal wealth and productivity is the expansion of human needs and desires. Consequently, as the surplus product increases, so does the necessary product per person, which typically results in an increase in the standard of living. Marx distinguishes in this context between the physical minimum requirements for human life and a moral-historical component of earnings from work.

However, this distinction is somewhat deceptive for a number of reasons.

At least in more complex societies, minimum living costs include social and infrastructure services, which incur costs and are essential from a survival standpoint.

It is difficult to define which products constitute "luxury." For instance, owning a car may be considered a luxury, but if it is required for commuting to work and shopping, it is a necessity.

Michael Hudson notes that in the contemporary United States, households spent only about a quarter of their income directly on consumer goods and services. The remaining expenditures are for interest, rent, taxes, loans, retirement provisions, and insurance. Some of these financing payments could be considered "moral-historical," but others are physical necessities, as people could die without them (for example, because they cannot get health care, or have no shelter).

Marxian authors such as Ernest Mandel and V. Gordon Childe argued that for the majority of human prehistory, there was no economic surplus product of any kind, except for exceedingly small or incidental surpluses.

The primary causes were:

the lack of techniques to store, preserve, and package surpluses securely in large quantities or to transport them reliably over significant distances; The productivity of labor was insufficient to produce much more than a small tribe could consume; Early tribal societies were not typically oriented toward producing more than they could actually use, let alone maximizing their output. Thus, anthropologist Marshall Sahlins estimated that the utilization by ethnic groups of the "carrying capacity" of their habitat ranged from 7% among the Kuikuro of the Amazon basin to approximately 75% among the Lala of Zambia.

In general, diverse groups of people did not rely on trade for survival, and the total amount of trading activity remained proportionally low.

The formation of the first permanent surpluses is linked to the settlement of tribal groups in a single territory and the storage of food. Once there are sufficient reserves and surpluses, tribes can diversify their production, and members can specialize in the manufacture of tools, weapons, containers, and ornaments. Archaeological discoveries of the modern era indicate that this development originated in the more complex hunter-gatherer (foraging) societies. Initial technical or economic division of labor involving the exchange of products is made possible by the formation of a reliable surplus product. In addition, a secure surplus product enables population growth by reducing starvation, infanticide, and the abandonment of the elderly and infirm. Lastly, it establishes the material basis for a social hierarchy in which those at the top of the hierarchy possess prestige goods to which commoners have no access.

The first real "takeoff" in terms of surpluses, economic growth, and population growth likely occurred during what V. Gordon Childe termed the neolithic revolution, or the beginning of the widespread use of agriculture, from about 12,000 to 10,000 years ago onwards, when the world population was estimated to have been between 1 and 10 million.

Archaeologist Geoffrey Dimbleby offers his observations:

"It has been estimated that if man had never advanced beyond the hunting and gathering stage, the world's surface could support a maximum of 20–30 million people at any given time."

Modern anthropologists and archaeologists differentiate between "staple finance" and "wealth finance" in terms of the extraction of a surplus from the working population (whether as a tax, tribute, rent, or other method). They dislike the term "surplus product" due to its Marxist connotations and definitional controversies, but it refers to the same concept.

In the case of staple finance, common households provide staples (often foodstuffs and occasionally standard items of handicraft) as payment to the political center or property owner. This is a straightforward "payment in kind" The ruling elite owns the land and in exchange for use rights receives a portion of the food produced by the commoners. It is a simple system, but it creates logistical issues with physical storage and transport, as well as the need to safeguard stores from theft and environmental hazards.

In the case of wealth finance, commoners do not provide necessities, but rather valuables (wealth objects or prestige goods) or currencies that are more or less freely convertible in the exchange of goods. Typically, monetary systems are found in state-organized societies; large states employ monetary systems for taxation and payment purposes. Valuables and currencies are significantly more transportable, centralizable, and do not depreciate through spoilage. The disadvantage is that they cannot be consumed directly; they must be traded on markets for consumables. Therefore, if markets are disrupted for some reason, wealthy objects and currencies suddenly lose value.

The surplus-extraction system could also be a combination of staple finance and wealth finance. The use of "finance" to describe the allocation of a surplus is just as problematic as "surplus product." Commoners required to pay a levy, tax, or tribute to landowners on pain of imprisonment or death are not making an "investment" that yields a return; rather, they are compelled to pay for the use of land they do not own.

The increasing economic and social divisions of labor are closely related to the expansion of international trade and occur simultaneously. According to Ashley Montagu, "barter, trade, and commerce is largely dependent on the exchangeable surpluses of a society."

The surplus product is then produced within a class relationship in which the exploitation of surplus labor combines with active or passive resistance to that exploitation.

To maintain social order and enforce basic morality among a growing population, a centralized state apparatus with soldiers and officials emerges as a distinct group of society that is subsidized from the surplus product through taxes, tributes, rents, and confiscations (including war booty). Because the ruling elite controls the surplus product's production and distribution, it also controls the state. This, in turn, gives rise to a moral or religious ideology that justifies superior and inferior positions in the division of labor and explains why some individuals have a natural right to appropriate more resources than others. Archaeologist Chris Scarre offers his observations:

"There has been some debate over whether states should be considered beneficent institutions, operating for the benefit of all, or whether they are fundamentally exploitative, with elites gaining wealth and power at the expense of the majority. In the majority of documented instances, the latter appears more accurate. In terms of scale, however, large populations can only be integrated and supported with the assistance of centralized state control; the collapse of states... is inevitably followed by population decline."

Archaeologist Bruce G. Trigger makes remark:

"Regardless of the agricultural system employed, it appears that between 70 and 90 percent of the labor input in early civilizations was required to be devoted to food production. This implies that the predominant economic activity of all early civilizations was agriculture. It also implies that the surplus resources available to the upper classes were never disproportionately large to total production and had to be utilized with caution. Due to this, strategies for increasing revenue had to be primarily political: increasing the number of controlled farmers, creating situations in which ruling groups shared available resources more disproportionately based on rank, or convincing farmers to surrender marginally greater amounts of surplus production without increasing the cost of the mechanisms required to maintain social control."

Given the relatively low labor productivity of agrarian societies, the ancient world required a disproportionately large amount of (surplus-)labor to produce a relatively small amount of physical surplus.

Archaeologist Brian M. Fagan offers his observations:

The combination of economic productivity, control over sources and distribution of food and wealth, the development and maintenance of a stratified social system and its ideology, and the capacity to maintain control through the use of force was the essential ingredient in the formation of early states.

According to Gil Stein, Mesopotamia (3700 B.C.), Egypt (3300 B.C.), the Indus Valley (2500 B.C.), and China were the earliest known states (1400 BC). In various regions of the world, such as Africa and Australasia, tribal societies and chiefdoms persisted for a significantly longer period of time than state formation. Many modern states have their origins in colonialism. At its height, the British empire contained a quarter of the world's population. Many of the colonized nations did not have a state apparatus at first, but rather chiefdoms.

Based on a certain level of productivity, the size of the surplus product has implications for how it may be distributed. Simply put, if there is insufficient to go around, it cannot be distributed equally. If 10 products are produced and there are 100 people, it is obvious that not all of them can be consumed or utilized; it is likely that some people will receive the products while others must go without. According to Marx and Engels, this is the ultimate cause of socioeconomic inequality and the reason, for millennia, all attempts to establish an egalitarian society failed. Thus, they composed:

"Until now, all conquests of liberty have been based on restricted productive forces. The production that these productive forces could provide was insufficient for the whole of society and made development possible only if some persons satisfied their needs at the expense of others; thus, some—the minority—obtained the monopoly of development, while others—the majority—due to the constant struggle to satisfy their most basic needs—were for the time being (i.e. until the birth of new revolutionary productive forces) excluded from any development. Thus, society has always developed within the context of a contradiction: in antiquity, between free men and slaves, in the Middle Ages, between nobility and serfs, and today, between the bourgeoisie and the proletariat."

However, it would be incorrect to infer the pattern of socioeconomic inequality from the surplus product alone. This is equivalent to saying, "People are poor because they are poor." At each stage of human society's evolution, there have always been numerous opportunities for a more equitable distribution of wealth. It is not only a matter of technique or productivity as to which of these possibilities have been realized, but also of the assertion of power, ideology, and morals within the prevailing system of social relations governing legitimate cooperation and competition. The prosperity of some may depend on the destitution of others.

Other scarcity is purely socially constructed, meaning that people are excluded from wealth not because of physical scarcity but because of how the social system functions (the system of property rights and distributing wealth that it has). In modern times, it has been determined that a levy of 5,2 percent on the fortunes of the world's 500 or so billionaires would be sufficient to provide for the basic needs of the entire human population.

In this case, there is no longer a physical scarcity of goods that satisfy fundamental human needs. To improve the lot of the poor requires political will and social organization, or, alternatively, for the poor to organize themselves to improve their lot.

The category of surplus product is a transhistorical economic category, which means that it applies to any society with a stable division of labor and a significant labor productivity, regardless of how the surplus product is produced, what it consists of, and how it is distributed. Within the context of a society's unique social and production relations, surplus labor is carried out. Thus, the precise forms surplus products take depend on the type of society that generates them.

If economic growth or population growth rates were plotted on a graph beginning in zero, we would obtain a tangent curve with a sharp bend in the nineteenth century. New forms of technology and labor-cooperation have contributed to a tremendous increase in productivity over the past century. According to Marx, this was the "revolutionary" aspect of the capitalist mode of production, and it resulted in a substantial increase in the surplus product created by human labor. Marx believed it could serve as the material foundation for a future transition to communism, a form of human society in which everyone could live up to their full potential, because there was enough to satisfy all human needs for everyone.

Commentary from economic historian Paul Bairoch:

"...the average agricultural worker in traditional societies produced only 20 to 30 percent more food than his family consumed. These percentages—this 20 to 30 percent surplus—take on new significance when we consider a factor frequently omitted from theories of economic development: the yearly fluctuations of agricultural yields, which can amount to an average of over 25 percent on a national scale. As a result, periodic subsistence crises became inevitable, crises of varying severity that, at their worst, could lead to a decline in economic life and, by extension, in the civilization they supported. As a result, as long as agricultural productivity remained at that level, it was practically impossible to conceive of a continuous progression in the development of civilizations, let alone the accelerated scientific and technological progress that is a defining feature of the modern era. The profound changes to the agricultural production system that preceded the industrial revolution ended this particular impasse. In the course of 40 to 60 years, the resultant increase in productivity led to a transition from an average surplus of 25 percent to a surplus of 50 percent or more, thus surpassing—for the first time in human history—what might be called the risk-of-famine limit; in other words, a truly poor harvest no longer meant severe shortage or actual famine. The agricultural revolution laid the groundwork for the industrial revolution."

Roberto Sabatino Lopez, an economic historian, adds:

"Despite the fact that the majority of farmers and peasants produced very little surplus on an individual basis, the surplus of millions of agricultural workers was easily sufficient to support a large number of towns and foster the growth of industry, commerce, and banking. Despite their admiration for and dependence on agriculture, the Romans equated "civilization" with cities (civitates)."

As Marx discusses in Das Kapital, the surplus product in capitalist society is characterized by the following key characteristics (among others):

The surplus product no longer consists solely of "physical" surpluses or tangible use-values, but increasingly of tradable goods or assets that can be converted into cash. Claims to the social product are primarily realized through monetary transactions, and the social product itself can be valued in monetary terms. The division of necessary and surplus products among various uses and social classes is increasingly expressed in terms of monetary quantities. The focus is on maximizing wealth as such, based on calculations of abstract price relationships.

As the capitalist mode of production expands and supplants other modes of production, the surplus-product and surplus-value become essentially identical. In a strictly capitalist society, they would be identical (but such a society is unlikely ever to exist, other than in economic models and analogies).

The ability to claim the surplus value created in production through the production of new output as profit income depends heavily on market sales and purchasing power. If goods and services cannot be sold due to a lack of funds, the business owner is left with surpluses that are useless to him and will likely lose value. This results in an ongoing need to maintain and expand market demand, as well as a growing global market for goods and services.

A substantial portion of surplus products must be accumulated (invested) to maintain and improve market position, as opposed to being consumed, due to the intense pressure exerted by competition among numerous private enterprises. Failure to do so would result in the closure of businesses. This, according to Marx, was the primary reason for the nineteenth century's enormous economic expansion.

Corollary to the tremendous increase in physical productivity (output of goods) is the fact that an ever-increasing proportion of the monetary value of the social product consists of the production and consumption of services. This leads to a redefinition of wealth: not only a stockpile of assets, but also the capacity to consume life-improving services (note: many activities called "services" supply tangible products).

The dialectic of scarcity and surplus begins to gradually invert: the problem of optimal allocation of scarce resources gives way to the problem of optimal allocation of abundant resources. High productivity results in excess capacity: more resources can be produced than can be consumed, in large part because the masses lack purchasing power. This can result in practices of dumping. At the same time, wealth ownership becomes highly concentrated, preventing vast numbers of people from possessing significant assets.

As a ruling class, the bourgeoisie is historically unusual because it emerges and exists independently from the state, rather than being the state (like many earlier ruling classes). As a "political class" or polity, the various competing fractions of the bourgeoisie appoint others (typically middle-class professionals, such as lawyers and economists) to govern on their behalf; the bourgeoisie itself is primarily concerned with conducting business. Typically, the business class becomes wealthy through business, not by imposing taxes and tributes on themselves (that would often be regarded as a criminal protection racket, not valid trade). The bourgeois state typically lacks an independent economic base sufficient to finance its own activities; it is perpetually reliant on taxation with the consent of the populace and bourgeois loans. In a bourgeois state, taxpayers have the option of electing their own representatives to state office, which enables them to influence the taxation system and the justice system in general. Rarely has this possibility existed in non-capitalist states; there, any criticism of the state results in a fine, imprisonment, or death for the critic.

Marx believed that by separating purely economic-commercial considerations from legal-moral, political, and religious considerations, capitalist society enabled, for the first time in history, the economic functions applicable to all types of society to be expressed in their purest forms. In pre-capitalist society, neither "the economy" nor long-term mass unemployment existed as separate abstractions or realities (other than in exceptional cases, such as wars or natural disasters). Only when the "cash nexus" mediates the majority of resource allocation is "the economy" viewed as a distinct domain (the domain of commercial activity), quantifiable via money-prices.

Marxian economists contend that a socialist society also has an economic surplus product because more goods are produced than are consumed. However, the creation and distribution of the surplus product would begin to be governed by different principles. Particularly, the distribution of the new wealth would be determined much more in accordance with populist-democratic and egalitarian principles, utilizing a variety of property forms and allocative methods that have been empirically demonstrated to best meet the human needs of all. The experience of the 20th century with economic management demonstrates that there is a wide range of options; if some options are chosen and others are not, this has more to do with who holds political power than with anything else.

The magnitude of the surplus product can be measured in physical use-value stocks, monetary values, or labor hours.

If it is known, then:

What and how much was made in a given year? what the population demographics are, what earnings or income were received, how many hours were worked in various professions? the average actual consumption pattern, what producers contribute to taxes or tribute

Then, it is theoretically possible to estimate the necessary product and surplus product quantities.

However, it is never possible to obtain mathematically precise or completely objective distinctions between necessary and surplus product, as social needs and investment requirements are always the subject of moral debate and political competition among social classes. Some statistical indicators can at best be developed. Marx himself was less concerned with measurement issues in Das Kapital than with the social relations involved in the surplus product's production and distribution.

In a capitalist economy, the techniques for estimating the size of the surplus product are essentially identical to those for measuring surplus-value. However, some surplus product components may not be marketable products or services. The existence of markets always requires a substantial amount of non-market labor. The quantities of surplus product, surplus labor, and surplus value can vary.

Although it is possible to measure the number of hours worked in a country with reasonable precision, social statisticians have made few attempts to calculate the surplus product in terms of labor hours.

Nonetheless, time use surveys have yielded a wealth of remarkably interesting data regarding the average time utilization of the population. It is evident from these data just how dependent modern market economies are on the performance of unpaid (i.e., volunteer) labor. That is, the forms of labor that are subject to commercial exploitation represent a quantitatively insignificant portion of the total labor performed in a society and are contingent on non-market labor being performed.

In turn, this creates a distinct and distinguishable way in which various labor activities are valued and prioritized. Some types of labor can command a high wage, whereas others have no value or are priceless. Nevertheless, in a capitalist society, all labor is influenced by value relations, regardless of whether a price is assigned to it or not. However, the commercial value of labor may not necessarily reflect the social or human value of labor.

Marxist theory suggests that decadence involves a waste of a large portion of the surplus product from any balanced or nuanced human perspective, and it is typically accompanied by a growing indifference to the well-being and fate of other humans; to survive, people are forced to shut out of their consciousness the horrors that appear to be beyond their control. Marx and Engels suggest in The German Ideology that the productive forces are converted into destructive forces in this scenario. Declining or decadent societies are primarily characterized by the fact that:

The difference between what is produced and what could theoretically (or technically) be produced (sometimes referred to as the "GDP gap" or "output gap") widens dramatically.

A substantial portion of the surplus product is wasted or allocated to luxury consumption, speculation, or military expenditures.

To the detriment of activities that are healthier for human life as a whole, a variety of activities and products that are utterly useless or even harmful from the perspective of improving human life have emerged.

The coexistence of enormous wealth and abject poverty and squalor suggests that society has lost its sense of moral and economic priorities. The ruling elite no longer cares about the well-being of the population it governs and may be internally divided.

A consensus morality and sense of trust has eroded, criminality is on the rise, and the ruling elite has lost legitimacy in the eyes of the people, to the point where it can only maintain power through the crudest means (violence, propaganda, and intimidation whereby people are cowed into submission).

A regression to the beliefs, values, and practices of an earlier period in human history, which may include the dehumanization of others.

In the sense of undermining the very conditions of its own reproduction, society "fouls its own nest.".

Marxist scholars such as Ernest Mandel argued that this condition typically involves a stalemate in the balance of power between social classes, with none of them able to assert their dominance and thus implement a constructive program of action that would ensure genuine social progress and benefit the entire population. Herbert Marcuse argues that a society is "sick" if its fundamental institutions and relationships prevent the optimal development of human life.

However, there is a great deal of disagreement among historians and politicians regarding the existence and nature of decadence because value judgments and biases regarding the significance of human progress are often involved. Throughout the course of history, people have defined decadence in a variety of ways. Hedonism, for instance, is not necessarily decadent; it is only decadent in a particular context. Thus, accusations of decadence may be made that reflect only a certain moral sentiment of social classes and not the objective truth.

On a basic level, it is argued that in trade, one person's gain is another's loss; therefore, if total losses were subtracted from total gains, the result would be zero. How else could there be a surplus, if not for goods that are not exchanged? It is not difficult to demonstrate that the gains and losses may not balance out, leading to economic crises, but numerous arguments have been presented to demonstrate that any surpluses are "accidental" or "temporary." Nonetheless, even based on a crude estimate of value added, the gross output value of production exceeds the cost of labor and raw materials. If there is no surplus, it is difficult to explain how economic growth (the increase in output) can occur and why there was more to distribute than before (see surplus value). Somehow, the output of production exceeds the input. The majority of surplus comes from human labor, which is a 'renewable resource'; the first form of surplus in many societies, excess food, is the result of agricultural innovations that enable farmers to produce more than they will consume.

Therefore, the denial that a surplus product exists tends to focus on its precise definition, i.e., "surplus" in relation to what?

Another type of criticism asserts that the very concept of surplus product is merely relative and circumstantial, or even subjective, because anyone can regard something as a "surplus" if he has command or effective control over it and is in a position to use it as he sees fit, even if others do not consider it a "surplus." In this sense, "surplus product" may appear to be primarily a moral concept referring to the tendency of humans to "reap what they did not show," whether criminally/immorally, with a legally sanctioned justification, or by asserting brute force.

The broad division of the annual new social product in net terms into consumer items and investment items does not directly correspond to the value of costs and revenues generated in its production. Accounting for what is a "cost" and what represents an "income" is always somewhat controversial from a social perspective, since the costs incurred by some correspond to the income received by others. The precise procedures adopted for "grossing and netting" flows of income, expenditures, and products always reflect a theory or interpretation of the economy's social nature. Thus, it is possible that the categories employed do not accurately reflect the real relationships involved.

The Cambridge economist Piero Sraffa returned to the classical economic meaning of "surplus." Marxists have frequently responded that this view of the matter merely remains at the level of double-entry bookkeeping (where the uses of funds balance against the sources of funds), in part because it equates the surplus to net value-added in double-entry accounting terms. The "accounting perspective" is never questioned because accounting methods are inevitably used to make concepts "more scientifically precise".

People who assert what is surplus and what is not engage in a never-ending struggle over how the social product of their labor should be divided and distributed when there is a surplus product. In this context, Marxist archaeologist Randall H. McGuire emphasizes that:

In V. Gordon Childe's system, the social surplus exists before the ruling class emerges to exploit it. This perspective assumes that there is a fixed number of resources required for social reproduction, and that when primary producers produce more than this amount, they have produced a social surplus. However, there is no fixed amount of material required for social or biological reproduction. The quantity and quality of calories, protein, clothing, shelter, and education required to reproduce the primary producers can vary greatly across time and space. The distinction between necessary and surplus labor reflects an underlying relationship, class, in which one group, an elite class, has the ability to take labor or the products of labor from another group, the primary producers. This relationship is the definition of social surplus".

Additionally, anthropologist Robert L. Carneiro comments:

The major flaw in [Gordon Childe's] theory is that agriculture does not automatically produce a food surplus. We know this because many agricultural communities around the world do not produce such a surplus. Almost all Amazonian Indians, for instance, were agriculturalists, but they did not produce a food surplus in prehistoric times. It was technically feasible for them to produce such a surplus because, in response to European settlers' hunger, a number of tribes grew manioc in quantities far in excess of their own needs for the purpose of trading. Thus, the technical means to generate a food surplus existed, but the social mechanisms required to actualize it did not.

Several authors have argued, therefore, that "it is not the surplus that generates stratification, but rather stratification that generates surplus by activating an unrealized surplus potential in the productive system." It depends entirely on the extent of exploitation. So, for instance, a law might require peasants to pay a fixed amount of their produce as tax, regardless of whether the harvest was good or bad. If the harvest was poor, the peasants might not have enough food for their own needs.

The "natural" human propensity to trade, barter, and exchange, according to Adam Smith, was the origin of the division of labor. He stated that "the certainty of being able to exchange the surplus portion of the product of one's own labor for such portions of the product of another man's labor as he may require, induces every man to apply himself to a particular occupation, and to cultivate and perfect whatever talent or genius he may possess for that particular type of business".

Marx believed that commercial trade strongly stimulated the growth of a surplus product, not because the surplus product is itself generated by trade, or because trade itself creates wealth (wealth must be produced before it can be distributed or transferred through trade), but rather because the ultimate goal of such trade is capital accumulation, i.e., because the purpose of commercial trade is to become richer through it, to accumulate wealth. If traders did not earn a profit from trading (i.e., if their sales revenue did not exceed their expenses), they would not engage in it. Ultimately, income growth can only occur if the total stock of assets available for distribution increases as a result of increased production. The greater the surplus, the greater the amount that can be appropriated and traded to make money. If people only consume what they produce, others cannot become wealthy from that.

As a result, because the accumulation of capital stimulates the growth of productive forces, the size of the surplus product that can be traded will typically increase as well. The greater the expansion of the trading network, the more complex and specialized the division of labor will become, and the more surplus goods people will produce. The gradual replacement of the old system of subsistence production with commercial production necessitates that people engage in commerce in order to meet their needs ("market civilization"). Their labor becomes social labor, i.e., cooperative labor that produces goods for others — goods that they do not consume.

Obviously, it is also possible to amass wealth by appropriating it from others, but once this has occurred, the source of additional wealth disappears, and the original owners are less motivated to produce surpluses because they know their products will be appropriated (they no longer reap the rewards of their own production, in which case the only way to extract more wealth from them is by forcing them to produce more). It is like killing the golden egg-laying goose.

Adam Smith acknowledged in The Wealth of Nations the crucial importance of the division of labor to economic growth on the grounds that it increased productivity ("industriousness" or "efficiency"). However, Marx argues that Smith failed to adequately explain why the division of labor stimulated economic growth.

The existence of an efficient division of labor among producers did not necessitate any particular method of product distribution among producers. In theory, given a division of labor, products could be distributed in a variety of ways — market trade being only one of them — depending on how property claims were organized and enforced using the available technologies. Economic growth was not a logically necessary consequence of the division of labor, as it depended entirely on what was done with the newly distributed wealth and how it was distributed. There are numerous types of distributive norms that could be applied, with varying effects on wealth creation.

Smith conflated the technical division of work tasks between co-operatively organized producers, in order to increase production efficiency, with the system of property rights defining the social division of labor between different social classes, in which one class could claim the surplus product from the surplus labor of another class because it owned or controlled the means of production.

As a result of Smith's theoretical omissions, the real relationship between wealth production and distribution became a mystery. According to Marx, this effect in economic theory was not coincidental; it served an ideologically justifiable purpose, namely reinforcing the notion that only market expansion is beneficial for economic growth. In actuality, the argument becomes somewhat tautological, in that market expansion is considered to be "what you mean" by economic growth. The logical corollary of this concept was that all production should ideally be organized as market-oriented production, so that everyone is motivated to produce more for the purpose of accumulating wealth. The real purpose of the justification, however, was the private accumulation of capital by property owners, which depended on the social production of a surplus product by those who lacked adequate resources to survive. In other words, the justification reflected that market expansion was typically the primary legally sanctioned means by which capitalists could appropriate more of the wealth produced by others, and that any other method of producing and distributing products should be rejected for this purpose. Economic development then became a matter of establishing private property rights everywhere so that markets could expand (see also primitive accumulation). According to Marx, this perspective explains precisely why the concept of the social surplus product disappeared from official economic theory in the middle of the 19th century; after all, this concept raised the difficult political and legal question of who has the right to appropriate the labor and products of others. Henceforth, markets were justified on the basis that even if some stood to gain more than others from market trade, all stood to gain something, and if they did not, they would not trade. Marx's response was essentially that the majority of people were forced to trade because if they did not, they would perish, but they had little control over the terms of trade. In this regard, capital owners were vastly more powerful than workers who owned only a few personal possessions (and perhaps some small savings).

{End Chapter 10}

Chapter 11: Prices of production

Prices of production (or "production prices"; in German Produktionspreise) is a concept in Karl Marx's critique of political economy that is defined as "cost price plus average profit." It refers to the price levels at which producers would have to sell newly produced goods and services in order to achieve a normal, average profit rate on the capital invested to produce the goods (different from the profit on the turnover).

The significance of these price levels stems from the fact that a large number of other prices are derived from or based on them: according to Marx's theory, they determine the cost structure of capitalist production. The market prices of goods typically fluctuate around their production costs, whereas production costs fluctuate around product values (the average current replacement cost in labor-time required to make each type of product).

This understanding existed in classical political economy (the concept of market prices that gravitate toward "natural prices" or "natural price levels"), but according to Marx, political economists were unable to adequately explain how production prices were formed or how they could regulate the trade of commodities. In addition, political economists were unable to reconcile their labor theory of value with value/price deviations, unequal profit-to-wages ratios, and unequal capital compositions. Therefore, the labor theory of value of political economists prior to Marx was more of a metaphysical belief than a scientific assertion.

The concept of production prices is introduced and elaborated systematically in chapter 9 et seq. of the third volume of Das Kapital, despite Marx's references to it in earlier works. The first significant discussion is found in the Grundrisse (1857-1858), followed by numerous references in Theories of Surplus Value (1862-1863). The products must be sold at a profit and bought at a competitive price through market trade and the circulation of capital.

Marx intended to publish additional volumes but was unable to do so. Volume III of Capital argues that the capitalist mode of production regulates the sales of newly produced commodities through their production prices. The selling price of a product is determined by the cost of production plus a markup that ensures a normal average return on capital for the producing enterprise. For efficient producers, there will typically be a larger margin between their costs and sales-revenue (more profit), whereas for less efficient producers, this margin will be smaller (less profit) (less profit). Marx's controversial claim is that the magnitude of production prices for goods is ultimately determined by their current replacement costs in average labor time, i.e., by their value.

Marx never finalized the text of the third volume of Capital for publication, although he drafted it before publishing the first volume. This is likely the cause of much of the academic debate surrounding Marx's concept of production prices. Nonetheless, Marx's concept is frequently confused with concepts from other economic theories. According to the majority of economists, production prices roughly correspond to Adam Smith's concept of "natural prices" and the modern neoclassical concept of long-term competitive equilibrium prices subject to constant returns on scale. Marx's theory differs from both classical political economy and neoclassical economics with regard to the function of prices of production.

Marx believed that a production price for outputs always consists of two primary components: the cost-price of producing the outputs (including the costs of materials, equipment, operating expenses, and wages), and a gross profit margin (the additional value realized in excess of the cost-price, when goods are sold, which Marx calls surplus value).

Marx argues that price levels for products are determined by input cost-prices, turnovers, and average profit rates on output, which in turn are primarily determined by aggregate labor-costs, the rate of surplus value, and the growth rate of final demand. These price levels determine how much of the new output value created in excess of its cost price can be realized as gross profit by businesses.

It is hypothesized that, as a result of business competition, differences among the majority of producers regarding their profit rates on capital invested will tend to "even out," and a general norm for the profitability of industries will emerge.

In capitalist production, a profit levy is the standard prerequisite for the provision of goods and services. When competition for product markets intensifies, the producers' true income, which is the difference between cost prices and selling prices, decreases. In this case, producers can only maintain their profits by reducing their costs and increasing their productivity, or by increasing their market share and selling more product in less time, or by doing both (the only other option they can try is product differentiation). In an established product market, however, supply and demand fluctuations are typically not extreme.

Long before the beginning of the modern era in the 15th century, medieval merchant capitalists well understood this basic market logic.

A product's regulating price is a sort of modal average price level, above or below which people are much less likely to trade the product. If the price is too high, buyers will either be unable to afford it or seek cheaper alternatives. If the price is too low, sellers are unable to cover their expenses and generate a profit. Therefore, there is typically a price range within which the product can be traded, with upper and lower limits.

The production price is essentially the "normal or dominant price level" for a product type that prevails over an extended period of time. It assumes that both the inputs and outputs of production are priced goods and services, i.e., that production is fully integrated in relatively sophisticated market relations, allowing a sum of capital invested in it to be converted into a greater sum of capital. This was not the case in pre-capitalist economies; many inputs and outputs of production were not priced.

Marx argues that the production prices of goods are fundamentally determined by the comparative labor requirements of those goods and are thus constrained by the law of value.

Marx argues that the prices of new products sold will, assuming free competition for an open market, tend to settle at an average level that enables at least a "normal" rate of profit on the capital invested to produce them, and that if such a socially average rate of profit cannot be reached, it is highly unlikely that the products will be produced at all (because of comparatively unfavorable profitability conditions). Marx defines the "general rate of profit" as the (weighted) average of all the average profit rates in various production branches; it is the "grand average" profit rate on production capital. The most straightforward indicator of this rate is the ratio of total surplus value to total production capital employed.

According to Marx's theory, investment capital is likely to move away from production activities with a low profit rate and toward those with a higher profit rate; According to Marx, the relative movements of different production prices have a significant impact on how the total "cake" of newly produced surplus value is distributed as profit among competing capitalist enterprises. They are the foundation of the producers' competitive position because they determine profit yields relative to costs.

Some authors contend that Marx's production price is comparable to, or serves the same theoretical function as, the "natural prices" of classical political economy, which can be found in the works of Adam Smith and David Ricardo, among others (though the concept of natural prices is much older). This is the orthodox Marxist viewpoint, based on quotations from Marx in which he compares his concept of production prices to the classical notion of natural prices. Marx rejects the notion of a "natural" interest rate in Volume III of Capital, arguing that this term refers to the interest rate that results from free competition. According to this argument, there is nothing "natural" about purportedly "natural" prices; rather, they are the socially determined results of capitalist production and trade. Moreover, the existence of production prices does not logically rely on or assume a state of equilibrium.

If classical economists discussed the "naturalness" of price levels, this was ultimately a theoretical apologism; they were unable to reconcile their labor theory of value with the theory of capital distribution. They assumed market equilibrium without demonstrating how it could exist.

The general theory underlying the concept of natural prices was that the free play of markets, through successive adjustments in the trading process, would "naturally" converge on price levels at which sellers could cover their costs and make a normal profit, while buyers could afford to purchase products; with the result that relative labor requirements would be proportional to relative prices. However, classical political economy did not provide a plausible explanation for how this process could actually occur. Since it confused and conflated the value of labor power with the price of labor, commodity values with their production prices, and surplus value with profit, i.e., it conflated values and prices, it could only explain the normal price levels of commodities as "natural" phenomena in the end.

Marx argues that in the realm of capitalist production, commodity values are only directly observable as prices of production for outputs, which are established jointly by average input costs and the prevailing profit margins for outputs sold. It is the result of the establishment of regular, well-developed market trade; the production price averages reflect the fact that production has become completely integrated into the commodity trade circuits, where capital accumulation has become the driving force.

What prices of production simultaneously conceal, he argues, is the social nature of the valorization process, or how exactly production has led to an increase in capital value. Only cost prices and sale prices remain, and it appears that any of the factors of production (which Marx refers to as the "Holy Trinity" of capitalism) can contribute new value to output, paving the way for the conception of the production function.

The first interpretive challenge relates to the existence of varying production prices. For more than a century, virtually all Marxists, Sraffians, and Post-Keynesians simply accepted Marx's concept of production prices as roughly equivalent to Smith's and Ricardo's "natural price" theory (as it was taught and presented in textbooks), and they did not investigate the concept in detail. They believed the concept of a production price to be straightforward, obvious, and uncontroversial. Thus, they completely missed the fact that in Volume III of Capital, Marx identified (though not always very clearly) at least six primary types of production prices:

The private or enterprise production price that serves as the basis for the first chapter's analysis. This price is equal to the cost-price and normal profit on production capital invested that applies to the new output of a particular enterprise when it is sold (the "individual production price"). The profit rate reflected in this production price can be compared to the average profit rate for a sector or the nation.

The sectoral price of production. This price equals the cost-price and average profit rate on production capital invested for the output of a commodity produced by a particular industry, sector, or branch of production (at "producer's prices"). This is the production price that applies to a specific type or category of product; it reflects the average return that producers can normally anticipate in a given industry. Marx highlights the distinctions between industrial and agricultural production costs in his discussion of ground rent. It is hypothesized that there is a structural distinction between the average profit rates applicable to various sectors of production.

The intersectoral price of production. This price level refers to the sale of output at producers' prices, which reflects an average profit rate on a quantity of capital invested that is applicable to multiple industry sectors. Marx frequently refers to this fully formed industrial production price in his theoretical discussions of the equalization of profit rates; it reflects the producer's product-price at which the average rate of profit on production capital applicable to an entire economic community is obtained (for example, a net return of 10 percent).

Marx himself defines the so-called original price of production as the price of production for the commodity produced and sold by an industry plus the commercial profit made on reselling the commodity (warehousing, distribution and retailing etc.).

The so-called market price of production "This production price is not determined by the individual cost of production of a single industrialist, but rather by the commodity's average cost under the average conditions for capital in the entire sphere of production. In actuality, it is the market price of production; the average market price, as opposed to its fluctuations." This is roughly equivalent to what we refer to as the "average unit cost" of a product today.

the economic price of production. This price, a total cost-price (i.e. a replacement cost), equals the average cost price and average profit rate of an output at the point of sale to the final consumer, including all costs incurred by all the different enterprises participating in its production (factory, storage, transport, packaging, etc.), plus tax imposts, insurance levies, etc. In modern times, "costing" production in order to determine the expected return on capital invested typically entails evaluating the entire value chain in relation to the price at which products can be sold to the end consumer. How can the entire production of a product - from the factory gate to the final consumer - be organized so that it can be sold to the final consumer at a price that the market will bear - and still make a profit? Marx sometimes refers to an "economic production price" when, for argument's sake, he abstracts from everything that occurs between the factory gate and the final consumer of a commodity.

When analyzing the composition of a product's cost structure at various stages of production and distribution, these disparate prices become apparent. Marx's frequent assumption in his shorthand drafts that these six kinds of prices all refer to the same thing is a source of interpretive difficulty. However, this is only the case when one business sells directly to the final consumer.

Marx's analytical concern was likely not with pricing processes in and of themselves, but with the primary factors influencing the realization and distribution of new surplus-value produced when sales occur. In the end, his argument was that competition in capitalism revolves around the pursuit of maximizing surplus-value in the form of generic profit income (profit, interest, rent). How does a sum of capital invested in production become an even greater sum of capital? What are the dynamics and outcomes of this procedure? What are the implications for the economic reproduction procedure?

Marx's initial discussion of the leveling of profit rates through price competition omits the existence of diverse types of production prices, which implies a much more complex picture than he initially presents. Marx argues, for instance, in his discussion of ground rent, that farm products can be consistently sold for more than their cost of production but less than their value, whereas many manufactured goods only obtain their cost of production because they are sold for more than their value. In Marx's more developed theory of the circulation of commodities, the values of products, their costs of production, and their market prices are all semi-autonomous variables that can diverge and converge as a result of constant market fluctuations, influencing the profitability of businesses. Marx, nevertheless, asserts that they will converge overall.

Marx's draft manuscript is a second source of interpretive difficulty because he frequently conflates (1) capital advanced (to acquire inputs necessary for production) with (2) capital in use and (3) capital consumed (that fraction of the value of inputs used up in the production of new output). In his simplified quantitative examples, he abstractly assumes, for argument's sake, that:

The output value equals the sum of capital invested plus surplus value.

The sum of input expenses incurred in the production of output (the cost price) equals the amount of production capital invested.

There is no depreciation of fixed capital, as fixed capital expenditures equal fixed capital expenditures.

There is no difficulty selling anything because all output is sold simultaneously.

There are no variations in capital turnover.

The surplus value rate is uniform across all industries.

The profit rate of production capital is the same across all industries.

There are no impediments to the free circulation of labor and capital.

His real interest was most likely in the overall dynamics of capital accumulation, competition, and the realization of surplus value produced, presuming that output would sell. He was considering grand averages and overall outcomes. Marx himself explains that capitalist competition hinges on buying commodities below their value and selling them above their value, so the simplified depiction does not reflect reality (or, in the ideal competitive situation, to sell them below their value at a good profit, with a high turnover).

Marx's theory is frequently confused with input-output economics and the marginalist theory of capital, in which total inputs and total outputs are always exactly equal in value, an equality achieved by treating factor income, which is gross profit, as an input, so that gross profit is both a cost and a revenue. Marx did not discuss inputs and outputs in the sense of double-entry bookkeeping, where the source of funds balances against the use of funds; rather, he was concerned with how a sum of capital was transformed into a greater sum of capital through the net addition of new value created by workers in production. He was actually discussing the quantities of capital required for commodity production and the quantities of capital generated by commodity production, not the quantities of input and output commodities.

If the value of commodities purchased precisely matched the value of commodities sold, capitalists would not invest in production because there would be no profit. Their income would exactly equal their expenses, resulting in a net loss. So, from Marx's perspective, input-output economics obscured the "capital-relationship," i.e., the ability of the bourgeoisie to profit from the surplus labor of the labor force due to its ownership of the means of production.

A third source of interpretive difficulty is the question of what types of prices production prices are in reality.

The theoretical equilibrium output prices that would apply if supply and demand were equal or balanced (this equilibrium could be thought of as a simple market balance, or as some kind of system equilibrium or dynamic equilibrium - where market prices gravitate towards or oscillate around some underlying value or natural price).

regulating price levels of market prices for products that serve as trade standards, establishing upper and lower bounds for market-price fluctuations around an axis or level based on current labor demands for their supply.

Obtaining empirical price averages for products sold over a longer time period by averaging actual output prices for multiple accounting periods.

Consequently, it is unclear how such prices actually exist in the real world. The conceptual challenge of modeling is to demonstrate the relationship between these three variables. In principle, it could also be argued that certain types of production prices are empirical price averages, whereas others express only theoretical price levels. If production prices are viewed as merely "theoretical" entities, it is impossible to assert that they actually regulate actual prices. A theoretical price level that does not exist in reality cannot be said to determine actual price levels (other than in the sense of publicly available price information influencing market expectations).

The problem with the popular Newtonian metaphor of production prices as "centers of gravity" or the stochastic metaphor of production prices as "attractors" of market prices (both used in tectonophysics) is that they do not provide any causal explanation of how the "gravitation" or "attraction" process actually occurs as a social process in the real world. The metaphors' meaning fluctuates between empirical price levels, theoretical price levels, and regulatory price levels. Gravitation may be interpreted as a physical process, an empirical stochastic outcome, or a purely theoretical description. In any case, it is necessary to explain how gravitation actually operates. In the end, "price numbers" cannot replace a realistic ontology of prices and an accurate explanation of price structures.

Marx had pointed the way toward resolving the issues raised by classical political economists, but he had not provided a comprehensive solution. In reality, he lacked the data to prove that a "general rate of industrial profit" would be established for the entire economy (at least in the sense of the minimally acceptable profit rate that is the bottom line for the average business operation). He did not elaborate on the distinction between distributed and undistributed profit, tax requirements, or how this may impact profit statements. His discussion was limited to physical capital and employed labor, excluding ancillary costs and incomes unrelated to production that enterprises typically have (including taxes and subsidies), asset transactions, and market price changes.

Marx's theory of "the tendency of differences between rates of profit on production capital to level out through competition" aimed to solve a theoretical problem left unsolved by David Ricardo. The concept of production prices is a "building block" in Marx's theory. This problem involved the explanation of how an average or "normal" return on production capital invested (e.g., 8 to 16 percent) could be established, so that capitals of equal size earned equal profits, even though the enterprises differed in capital compositions and amounts of labor performed (see labor theory of value) and therefore generated different amounts of new value.

Intuitively, if the labor theory of value is accurate, firms that use more labor to produce goods will also create more value and earn greater profits. In reality, the opposite is true: firms that are more efficient and use less labor to produce goods earn greater profits.

Marx argued that this was not merely a logical problem, a social accounting problem, or a theoretical problem, but rather a structural contradiction inherent to the capitalist mode of production that had to be continually resolved. In his view, the fact that investors could appropriate more or less value from the labor-efforts of employed workers, and thus that different labor efforts were unequally rewarded, was fundamental to the competitive process - in which the norms of labor effort continually clashed with the norms of profitability.

On the surface, it appeared to the individual observer that profit yields on capital determine expenditures on labor, but taken together, according to Marx, it is the other way around, as the volume of labor-time worked determined how much profit could be distributed among producing capitalists via product sales. The quantity of surplus labor performed in the sphere of production limited the quantity of surplus value that could be distributed as profit in the sphere of circulation.

According to certain interpretations of the Marxian transformation problem, total "(production) prices" for output must by definition equal total "values," and total profits must by definition equal total surplus value. Marx explicitly denied, in chapter 49 of the third volume of Das Kapital, that this exact mathematical identity applies. Once synchronic and diachronic variability in labor productivity is acknowledged, the two well-known identities can no longer be true, even in theory.

Logically, Marx's only option for expressing the identity of aggregated output prices and aggregated output values is to assert that both totals are equivalent to the same amount of abstract labor time or gold. Nonetheless, this equality is only asserted "by definition." There are no causal forces in the real world that could guarantee such an exact match. Moreover, the identity cannot be empirically demonstrated directly, as a relationship between labor-time and money must be assumed in order to determine the quantitative relationship between labor-time and value.

Economists' "accounting" interpretation of production prices (value/price identity at the macro level), according to which price distributions and value distributions can be inferred from each other, would imply that the production price is empirically derived from a simple statistical averaging of aggregated cost prices and profits. In such a case, the production price is a theoretical median that fluctuating actual prices would match exactly only in exceptional circumstances.

In another interpretation, the production price merely reflects the empirical output price level that dominates the market for that output (a "norm" applying to a branch of production or economic sector, which producers cannot escape from). In other words, the prevailing value proportions and labor requirements establish a range or band within which product prices will fluctuate. In practice, this means that there exists a minimum sale price at which a commodity can be produced profitably and sustainably; if a product cannot be sold at this price, it is unlikely to be produced.

Adapting a concept from Michio Morishima, Emmanuel Farjoun and Moshe Machover (1984) reject the notion that a "uniform rate of profit" could ever exist in reality, contrary to Marx's theory that competition would tend to establish at least a minimally "acceptable" average rate of profit on production capital invested in producing outputs and returns proportional to capital size.

According to proponents of the Temporal Single System Interpretation, such as Andrew Kliman, Machover's inequality does not exist because, if Marx is correctly interpreted, there is no requirement for the value of total inputs to equal the value of total outputs or for inputs and outputs to be valued simultaneously.

It is true that transactions can be "simultaneous": both the buyer and seller can receive their money or goods simultaneously. However, this is not the case for production. It takes time to produce an output, which becomes an input for the subsequent cycle of production once an input has been acquired. The new output cannot be reduced to its inputs because it is a new use-value to which living labor has added value. A production price (or a unit cost price) can be set "after the fact" once the output has been produced and sold, but that price is based on the fixed capital outlays incurred prior to the output's production, plus a profit markup, and typically cannot be changed later (at least not very significantly, in the ordinary situation).

In practice, it is not true, as Machover suggests, that every commodity has a uniquely formed production price. At best, one could say that a specific commodity (such as a high-quality vacuum cleaner) has a normal, average production price. On the basis of the capital value of the entire new output being sold and the production price, a profit rate is typically calculated.

Rarely is the profit or surplus value component of a single commodity proportional to the total profit on the total turnover of that commodity type. If, for instance, the total gross profit markup in the unit-cost structure of a stick of butter at the point of sale to the consumer is (say) 45 percent, this does not imply that the profit rate on the total production capital of the butter producer is also 45 percent. To obtain such a high profit rate on his output, the butter producer would have to produce and sell an enormous quantity of butter in a very brief period of time.

According to McKinsey analysts, for every $1.00 of operating profit on consumer goods sold in the United States in 2008, retailers earned approximately $0.31 (down from $0.60 in 1999), while suppliers, packagers, and others along the value chain received $0.69. To achieve the same level of profit as in the past, fewer retail outlets must sell significantly more products in a shorter period of time. This can lead to the phenomenon of food deserts, among other things.

Marx provides a hint at the beginning of Volume III of Capital as to how he believes the "transformation problem" is resolved in reality. He implies that the issue can only be resolved by examining capital and profit distributions as a dynamic, rather than a static, process. His argument is that industrial competition revolves primarily around the difference between the value of newly produced commodities and their cost-prices, i.e., the potential surplus-value (the trading gain) that can be realized from them. There are constant disparities in space and time between labor-expenditures and capital returns, as well as attempts to overcome or exploit these disparities. Thus, unrestricted economic competition results in the law of value regulating the trade in newly produced commodities: the ultimate limits of what products will trade for, i.e., their supply price, are determined by comparative costs in labor-time.

The actual world, A uniform profit rate and surplus value rate for all industries do not exist, except in the sense of a minimum acceptable profit rate or a base productivity level (below which an enterprise is likely to go out of business, since it cannot better its capital costs).

The agents of capital do not simply seek the average rate of profit, but rather a rate of profit above the average (the maximum profit, or a "surplus profit").

The rate of surplus value and turnover time can differ between producers and production periods.

Technical, legal, or political factors may limit the migration of labor and capital.

Competition is not a "level playing field," but rather a process in which unequally positioned capitalists attempt to obtain or maintain extra profits, which may involve blocking competitors in many ways to improve their own market position. This process can be relatively benign and legal, but it can also become vicious and illegal, leading to all-out war.

The relationship between product-values and product-prices is mathematically expressible only in probabilistic (stochastic) terms, and not as a simultaneous equation based on accounting identities.

Total capital consumed diverges from total capital advanced, and total capital advanced exceeds total physical production capital, just as gross business income after expenses is typically greater than the profit component of the new value added.

Since the production price refers only to the cost prices and profit yields for newly produced outputs, the current production price can be determined definitively only after the newly produced output has been sold and the total turnover is known.

Marx was not primarily attempting to demonstrate that the two famous identities (total profit=total surplus value and total product value=total production price) are compatible with price-value divergences and with profit distributions according to capital employed when he created a simplified, abstract model of profit distributions (to the contrary: for analytical purposes, Marx assumes that they are compatible). Instead, he was attempting to model the fundamental parameters of business competition for a share of the working class's new surplus value. Marx was able to explain both what really motivates business owners and why the surface appearance of the business process as perceived by an individual is almost the exact opposite of the real economic process in society as a whole by identifying the ultimate purpose of business competition.

Many criticisms of Marx's concept stem from the ambiguities mentioned previously. According to some Marxists, a more precise definition of the cost, product, and revenue aggregates used, as well as the timing of transactions, can refute many of the criticisms (see e.g., Temporal Single System Interpretation).

In doing so, however, it must be acknowledged that Marx's draft manuscript frequently demonstrates sloppy use of terminology and concepts, and that Marx's purpose was frequently not entirely clear. His discussion of "capital invested" is limited to intermediate goods, fixed capital, and labor power at an elevated level of abstraction.

Sometimes the transformation is depicted as a purely quantitative change, while other times it is also depicted as a qualitative change.

Occasionally, he asserts that the transformation is a shift from one form of value to another, Sometimes it is suggested that a price category completely replaces a value category, whereas other times the two categories always coexist and are mutually dependent, so that production prices can adjust to product-values, but product-values can also adjust to production prices.

Sometimes the transformation from value to production price is presented as a logical progression, while other times it is presented as an irrational expression.

Sometimes the production price is presented as an observable characteristic, and other times as a hidden market price regulator.

Sometimes the transformation is presented as a historical process, sometimes as a logical process, and sometimes as a conceptual (or epistemic) shift.

Sometimes the sum of production prices and the sum of product values are equated, Marx's theory is difficult for academics to comprehend because it is never entirely clear how these disparate concepts can be reconciled, obscuring his intent. Marx probably would have eliminated inconsistencies if he had prepared his own draft for publication, but he did not, leaving his readers with significant interpretation issues.

Marx believed that a capitalist production process was a process in which new values were created. The theoretical problem was that this value-forming process - the crucial process for capital accumulation - occurred primarily outside the market, bracketed by the transactions M-C (purchase of inputs, C, with money, M) and C'-M' (sales of new output, C', for more money, M'). However, between each exchange, economic value was preserved, transferred, and increased. Management then attempted, without absolute certainty, to estimate the cost and profit implications of various production tasks and activities for the growth of capital.

In this instance, however, the domains of product-values and product-prices, as well as the domains of value relations and price relations, were distinct but overlapping and coexisting domains (unless one is willing to argue that goods have an economic value only at the point where they are being sold for a price). As far as prices were determined by markets over which individual producers had no control, "price management" was not feasible, but value-based management was.

The ability of goods to sell below or above their real or socially average value posed a significant issue for capitalists, as it affected their gross income and profit margins. The Marxian product values may be of no interest to capitalists, but the prevalent cost structures and price levels in their markets are undoubtedly of interest. Marx himself described the wealth of a capitalist society as "a mass of commodities," but before and after the commodities were sold, they existed outside the market as use values. At that time, they possessed only value and utility, but no market price (though obviously one could estimate a hypothetical selling price - see also real prices and ideal prices).

Thus, at the point of production, the "factors of production" themselves had no actual market price, only a value, because they were used to create new products rather than sold (indeed, what a particular business enterprise was currently "worth" in total, as a going concern, might be very difficult to say; it would depend on how much profit income it was expected to yield in the future compared to the capital assets invested in it, but even if a total price could be estimated, its individual assets might change in value continuously).

Enterprises produced a quantity of value, but it could not be determined beforehand how much of that value would be realized by an enterprise as income from sales or how gross revenues would be distributed among producers. Yet, the value of the total masses of output-values actually produced by all enterprises affected the market prices that each could obtain in distribution; it affected how the market would reward each producer, and there was a real, systematic relationship between total value produced and total sales revenue (even although these might not be equal).

Moreover, producers were constantly adjusting their commercial behavior to the emerging economic reality (the "market state"), to the greatest extent possible. Marx argued that this adjustment created a specific trajectory for capitalist development, guided by the pursuit of realizing additional surplus value. According to him, there is a permanent imperative to increase productivity, and producers seek to exploit every opportunity to gain a competitive edge (which includes blocking competition from others in some way).

How could this business reality be modeled most effectively? Corporate "value-based management" in the twenty-first century involves a constant cross-reference between past, present, and future prices, as there is practically no other way to do it for business purposes. Group controller Gerard Ruizendaal of Royal Philips Electronics stated: "The primary objective is to increase our economic value-added (EVA) annually so that our return on capital exceeds our cost of capital."

A McKinsey & Company partner comments:

"The guiding principle of value creation is that firms create value by employing capital raised from investors to generate future cash flows at rates of return exceeding the cost of capital (the rate investors require as payment). The quicker a company can increase its revenues and deploy additional capital at attractive rates of return, the more value it generates. What drives value is the combination of growth and return on invested capital (ROIC) relative to its cost." The more the market expands and the more there is buying and selling, the greater the value, according to this perspective. In reality, according to Marx, it is precisely the opposite: the more value workers create for their company, the faster it can increase revenues and deploy capital at attractive rates of return. Marx viewed the prices of production as the "outward expression" of the results of a valorisation process in production, and he believed that in order to discuss price aggregates at all, it was absolutely necessary to refer to value relations.

Not only was a value-theoretic principle required to group prices, relate them, and aggregate them (principles of value equivalence, comparable value, value transfer, value conservation, value creation, and value used up or destroyed), but the vast majority of an economy's stock of labor-products at any given time had no actual price because they were not being traded. The extent to which their value could be realized through exchange in the future could only be determined definitively "after the fact," i.e., after they had been sold and paid for. In the interim, one could only speculate on their price based on historical data. Finally, however, the attribution of value to products implied a social relationship, without which it would be impossible to comprehend value relations. A community of independent private producers expressed their coexistence and mutual adaptation through the trading prices of their products; the forms of value expressed how they were socially related.

The concept of "average profit" (a general profit rate) suggested that a process of competition and market-balancing had already established a uniform (or ruling average, or normal) profit rate; however, paradoxically, profit volumes (and consequently profit rates) could only be determined after sales by deducting costs from gross revenues. An output was produced before it was definitively valued in markets, but the quantity of value produced influenced the total price for which it was sold, and there was a "working knowledge" of normal returns on capital. This was the dynamic business reality Marx sought to model in a straightforward manner.

Marx's critics who interpret his models frequently argue that he assumes what he needs to explain, because rather than "transforming values into prices" by some quantitative mapping procedure, such that prices are truly deduced from labor-values, he either (1) equates value quantities and price quantities, or (2) combines both value quantities and price quantities into a single equation. In a somewhat perplexing manner, the cost price refers both to the capital invested (input) and to a component of the value of the new product (output).

Either Marx infers a rate of profit from a given capital composition and a given amount of surplus-value, or he assumes a rate of profit in order to calculate the amount of surplus-value applicable to a given amount of capital invested. If the objective is merely to determine the average profit a business or industry would earn after producing a certain output value with a particular capital composition, this approach may suffice. But this maneuver cannot contain a formal proof of a necessary quantitative relationship between values and prices, nor a formal proof that capitals of the same size but different compositions (and, consequently, different labor-time expenditures) must obtain the same profit rate. It is still only a theory.

Marx maintains that output prices will necessarily deviate from values produced, and that the sum of prices would equal the sum of values in a pure case. However, critics assert that he fails to demonstrate quantitatively how a distribution process could then occur such that price magnitudes map onto value magnitudes, and such that a uniform profit rate returns equal profits to capitals of equal sizes (a mapping relation is used here in the mathematical sense of a bijective morphism, involving one-to-one correspondence between value quantities and price quantities via mathematical equations). Then again, there is no formal proof of any necessary relationship between values and prices, and Marx's manuscript appears to be an endless, fruitless theoretical digression leading nowhere. In modeling, simple logical contradictions of the type:

In a static model, it is impossible to simultaneously uphold the postulates of a uniform profit rate and total values equal total prices; To find production prices, a uniform profit rate must be assumed, while to find a uniform profit rate, production prices must already be assumed; It is necessary to assume a price level rather than deduce it from labor-values.

Marx's examples do not make sense unless additional assumptions are introduced, raising the question of which assumptions are valid and whether they can solve anything without introducing further inconsistencies.

When attempting to model value and price aggregates mathematically in order to study capitalist competition, all the above-mentioned conceptual and logical concerns become crucial. Diverse types of theoretical hypotheses or interpretations will inevitably produce vastly different outcomes.

Many contemporary Marxists believe that Marx's concept of "transformation" was misinterpreted.

If market trade consisted solely of simple exchange (the exchange of items of equal value by the direct producers themselves), balancing production effort, output, and demand would be a relatively simple and straightforward task. However, this is not the case because capitalist market exchange is not a straightforward exchange. In a capitalist economy, production effort, output, and demand can only be in equilibrium if sufficient profits are earned, and capital accumulates. In actuality, products are continually sold above or below their value, based on what generates the greatest possible profit on the turnover, given market fluctuations.

No one can avoid the (simultaneous or sequential) reciprocal effects of individual business behavior and aggregate economic outcomes, regardless of their theoretical perspective. In addition, it must be acknowledged that "prices" are not all identical; actual market prices realized are not identical to ideal prices of several types that can be extrapolated from real prices.

Marx's theory of production prices is still at a far too abstract theoretical level to explain anything resembling original price fluctuations, which is a more serious criticism. In other words, Marx only used examples to illustrate the general outcomes that the competitive process would tend to produce in a capitalist social system. He attempted to determine what governs product prices in the "purest and simplest case." He believed that if this could not be accomplished, then none of the variations from the pure case could be explained. However, he had not provided a model for accurately predicting price fluctuations. In this regard, it is intriguing to examine Michael Porter's writings to determine how Marx's original intent relates to contemporary competitive business practice and how it could be expanded.

Some critics conclude that because Marx fails to "transform" value magnitudes into price magnitudes in a manner consistent with formal logic, he has not demonstrated the existence of value or that it affects prices; therefore, his theory of labor exploitation must be false. Marx's value theory or exploitation theory, however, may not depend on the validity of his specific transformation procedures, and Marxian scholars frequently argue that critics misunderstand what he meant by them. In particular, since, according to Marx, value relations describe the proportionalities between the current average quantities of labor required to produce products, value proportions between products exist quite independently of prices (and irrespective of whether goods are currently priced or not). As the structure of product values changes over time, the structure of product prices is likely to change as well, but product prices will fluctuate above or below product-values and typically respond to shifting value proportions with a time lag.

Essentially, the advantage of distinguishing between values and prices in this context is that it enables us to depict the interaction between shifts in product-values and shifts in product-prices as a dynamic process of real-world business and market behavior, given the reality of different growth rates of supply and demand, i.e. not a study of the conditions for market equilibrium, but a study of the actual process of market equilibrium occurring with a particular socioeconomic system.

Arguably, ideal prices could be substituted for values in this analysis, but Marx argues that product-values exist ontologically regardless of corresponding product-prices, i.e., regardless of whether product-values are actually traded, whereas ideal prices do not exist outside of computations; they are merely a hypothetical description. Product-values refer to empirical quantities of labor performed, which are not hypothetical but rather a physical and social fact. This type of analysis paves the way for an important new Marxian critique of Piero Sraffa's otherwise brilliant capital theory critique.

In Sraffian theory, the value of a commodity "contains" both the average labor directly involved in its production ("direct labor") and the past labor contained in its constituent materials ("indirect labor" or "dated labor").

Some economists and computer scientists, such as Prof. Anwar Shaikh and Dr. Paul Cockshott, argue with statistical evidence that even a "93 percent accurate Ricardian labor theory of value," That is, the only real proofs of Marx theory and its applicability, beyond demonstrating its internal logical consistency, are to be found in the evidence of experience.

Uncertain is whether more academics will accept this challenge to conduct more exhaustive research. In general, economists have preferred to construct abstract mathematical models based on a number of assumptions, as opposed to systematically examining available empirical data for the purpose of developing an empirically based theory of economic life. This is in contrast to business managers, who have a strong empirical theory of how business actually operates, based on their daily experience.

It is not difficult to demonstrate a close positive correlation between the value of net output and the hours of labor required to produce it, given that the payments constituting that value are necessarily proportional to hours worked and paid. Even if it is assumed that gross profits are not proportional to time worked by a certain margin, the total labor-cost involved in the total net output is typically greater than fifty percent of the total net output or gross value added (in the US, labor compensation is nowadays around 55 percent of the value of total net output).

According to the National Income and Product Accounts (NIPA) for 2015, annual labor costs in the United States were approximately $9.7 trillion, while the total operating surplus or gross profit (net of depreciation) was approximately \$4.5 trillion. In other words, total U.S. labor earnings are double the total gross profit receipts generated directly by production. Since total wage costs are based on time-wages, any measure of the net value added (gross labor compensation + gross profits), which Marx referred to as the value product, must necessarily exhibit a strong positive correlation with the total labor hours worked.

Much more difficult to demonstrate statistically is the relationship between prices and values in the actual distribution of net output (a traditional example mentioned, is that while in South Korea workers on average work the most working hours in the world, per capita per year, Korean value-added per capita has been much lower than might be expected; it is not so easy to explain, why this is the case).

An unexpected source, post-Keynesian economics, provides a highly intriguing confirmation of Marx's fundamental idea. Fred Lee, a prominent heterodox "real-world" economist, concluded after amassing an abundance of empirical data on pricing practices that:

Pricing administrators use markup, normal cost, and target rate of return pricing procedures to establish prices that cover costs, hopefully generate a profit, and, most importantly, allow the enterprise to engage in sequential acts of production and transactions.

Marx's theory must be distinguished from subsequent Marxist and Sraffian theories. As Lee emphasizes, "the typical statement made by Sraffians and Marxists that prices equal their production costs (which includes a uniform profit rate) in long-period positions has no conceptual correspondence with the concepts of costs and prices used by business enterprises." Marxists and Sraffians confuse a purely abstract model with empirical reality; as a result, their theories are not grounded in the real world of business operations.

Marx attempted to sketch a redistribution of value in overly simplistic terms, considering the profitability of various production capitals in isolation from the total circuit of capital.

The issue that Ricardo was unable to resolve was how equal-sized capitals could attract remarkably similar profits despite their unequal labor-time expenditures. But this issue can be resolved more credibly if we take competition in the sphere of capital finance, i.e., the sphere of credit, into account. In this sense, David Harvey notes that "the growing power of the credit system in relation to industry also tends to force an equalization of the profit rate (the connection between enterprise profit and the interest rate is now extremely strong)" In actual capitalist competition, a type of price regulation exists, the dynamics of which he explains in detail. Shaikh concurs with Keynes and businesspeople that the relationship between the real rate of interest on capital and the real rate of profit on capital is what matters financially in business (at the micro level of individual firms and at the macro-level of aggregated business results).

According to the statistical calculations of Shaikh and Tsoulfidis, the discrepancies between the various empirical measures of product-values, prices of production, regulating prices, and market prices (using input-output data, labor data, and capital stock data) are, on average, not exceptionally large.

{End Chapter 11}

Chapter 12: Net output

The United Nations System of National Accounts (UNSNA) and the NIPAs, as well as occasionally corporate or governmental accounts, both use the accounting concept of net production. The idea's original purpose was to calculate the overall net increase in a nation's stock of wealth brought about by production over the course of an accounting period. Net output can be defined as "gross production income less the value of the items and services consumed in that production." The theory states that by subtracting intermediate costs from the annual flow of income produced by manufacturing, one may calculate the net new value of the newly manufactured products.

Net output in national accounts is the gross value created over the course of an accounting period when producing companies use labor and capital assets as inputs to produce outputs. Because it includes depreciation costs or the consumption of fixed capital, gross value added is called "gross". The computation is significantly impacted by how incomes and expenses are defined as part of "production"; some are included as "factor income" or "factor expenditure" directly related to production, while others are not.

In order to determine the true value of an enterprise's outputs of products and services, the calculation uses an accounting technique known as "grossing and netting" of those revenues.

According to a normal valuation, this approach must consistently identify and differentiate between costs and revenues as well as between used up materials or services, fixed assets, and new outputs. This is crucial for national accounting since inputs from one enterprise become outputs from another and vice versa; without a consistent process, double counting would occur. Additionally, the "grossing and netting" technique presupposes a definition of the coverage of production as well as a value theory. With that, we can combine many values to get a price for the entire worth of net output.

Typically, it is believed that an aggregate net output's worth is equal to the sum of

labor charges (or compensation of employees), depreciation (or consumption of fixed capital), Government subsidies to producers lower income tax and indirect tax imposts on production, profit (or operating surplus).

Government subsidies received by producing firms are often deducted from indirect taxes paid by them during the same accounting period when computing net output for national accounts.

The Gross Domestic Product, or GDP, of a country's economy is the sum of all net domestic production produced by residents. The productive activity of government organizations and some home income-generating activities are included in this total.

Typically, the term "net output" is used to describe how much a specific economic sector—such as agriculture, manufacturing, business services, etc.—contributes to total value added or GDP over the course of a quarter or an entire year.

The whole value of an industry's outputs, as opposed to just its net output, really comprises the value added by production as well as the value of inputs used up (i.e., intermediate consumption) in producing the total value of outputs. For instance, a vehicle manufacturer adds value to the materials and parts utilized in the production of the car. However, the worth of the finished car also takes into account the materials and supporting operating expenses utilized to create the car, in addition to the value added during production. As a result, the gross output rather than the "net output" (the value-added) is the appropriate measure if we want to determine the overall sale value of the output of the vehicle manufacturer. The right ratio is between labor expenses and the gross output value of the automobiles, for instance, if we wanted to calculate a "unit labor-cost" for the output value of the cars. As a result, the concept of a country's total new net production value, which is determined by subtracting the value of products and services used up from gross expenditures or gross sales income, is distinct from that of a specific industry's net output.

Disaggregated data on the gross and net outputs of various economic sectors and sub-sectors are utilized in input-output analysis to examine the interactions between them. Consequently, for instance, a sector buys inputs from numerous other sectors and sells outputs to numerous other sectors. We can predict the impact of changes in business activity within a sector or group of sectors on the economy as a whole by determining the quantities of inputs and outputs involved.

As previously stated, a value theory, a method of grossing and netting, and strategies for consistently aggregating the prices of transaction volumes are necessary for the computation of net production. Of course, there are other approaches to this, but often a legal framework restricts the number of modifications that are both conceivable and allowed (business accounts have to be audited and so on, to guarantee a fair statement of business operations within the law of the land). However, the method for calculating net output can be disputed.

The standards used for value may be disputed and vary slightly between nations.

The value product, which reflects the additional value created by living labor, is presented as an alternative output metric in Marxian economics.

However, there is also the ecological critique that is occasionally voiced. The claim is that costs and production are only evaluated in terms of price when computing net output. As a result, production inputs and outputs that lack a price are not included in the value. Nevertheless, regardless of whether they might be given a price or converted into a tradeable good, such inputs and outputs can still have economic or human value. The cost of resolving air pollution or fish population depletion in open waters is not factored into the net output of polluters or fishing businesses. As a result, taxes are occasionally imposed. Some people consider "emissions trading," which involves buying and selling the license to pollute, to be a wholly wicked activity. It was inspired by the Kyoto Protocol. Others counter that it demonstrates how competitive markets can address any issues with resource allocation.

{End Chapter 12}

Chapter 13: Productivity model

In economics, productivity is typically defined as the ratio of what is produced (a total output) to what was consumed to produce it (an aggregate input). Productivity and the measurement of production efficiency are closely related. A measurement technique that is applied in practice to quantify productivity is called a productivity model. When there are numerous alternative outputs and inputs, a productivity model must be able to compute Output / Input.

Understanding the similarities and variations between the models' attributes is the basis of the comparison of productivity models. This work is made easier by the fact that the measurement formula for these traits makes it easy to identify them. It is feasible to determine the models that are best for assessing productivity based on the model comparison. The production theory and function serve as one of the criteria for this solution. The model must have the ability to explain the production function.

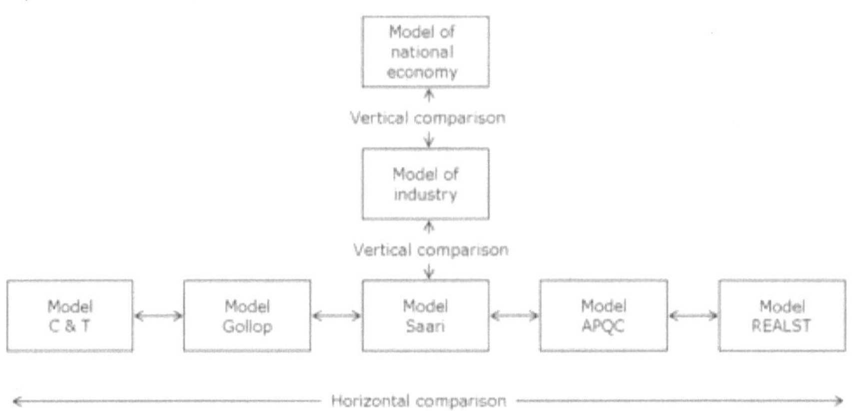

Dimensions of productivity model comparisons (Saari 2006b)

The figure makes the model comparison principle clear. The comparison involves two dimensions. A comparison of various business models is referred to as a horizontal model comparison. A vertical model comparison is a comparison of the levels of business, industry, and the whole national economy or of economic activity.

A shared understanding of the concept of productivity and how it should be modelled and quantified is prevalent at all three levels of the economy, i.e., business, industry, and national economy. The comparison indicates various variances that can be mostly attributed to variations in measuring precision. For the simple reason that measuring data in company are much more exact, it has been able to create the productivity model of business to be more accurate than that of the national economy. (2006) Saari

The models that can be used to measure productivity are numerous. The most difficult part has been systematically comparing the models. It has not been possible to establish the unique and shared qualities of them in pure mathematics in order to comprehend each model independently and in connection to other models. The productivity model, which is a model with configurable properties, can be used to make this kind of comparison. With the properties of the model being examined, an adaptable model can be set, resulting in the identification of both differences and similarities.

The ability to characterize the production function is a quality that sets productivity measurement models apart from all others. The model can be used to measure overall productivity if it can describe the production function. On the other hand, the model is inadequate for the task if it cannot adequately or just partially describe the production function. The production function-based productivity models are a relatively cohesive group with only minor model variances. The differences don't matter much, and the optional solutions can be suggested for legitimate reasons. There are six ways in which productivity measuring methods can differ from one another.

It is first important to look over and make clear the variations in the names of the concepts. The same concepts have been given many names by model creators, which has led to a lot of confusion. It goes without saying that variations in names have no bearing on the reasoning behind modeling.

Because model variables can vary, the model's fundamental logic can also vary. Which variables are employed for the measurement is the issue. The ability of a model to describe the production function is its most crucial quality. If the model includes the productivity and volume production function variables, this condition is met. Only those models are worth comparing more closely that satisfy this condition. (2006) Saari

The order of the variables in the calculation may vary. The calculation is based on the Ceteris paribus principle, which states that all other variables must be held constant while estimating the effects of a change in one variable. The outcomes of the calculations are somewhat influenced by the sequence in which the variables were calculated, but the difference is not very large.

Either cost theory or production theory can serve as the model's theoretical foundation. The production theory-based approach uses input volume to calculate activity volume. In a cost-theory-based model, output volume serves as a proxy for the amount of activity.

There are variations in accounting procedure, or how measurement data are created. Three strategies are used in calculations: ratio accounting, variance accounting, and accounting form. Different accounting methodologies may not necessarily result in different accounting outcomes, but rather in different levels of clarity and understandability. Variance accounting offers the user the most analytical options.

The model's flexibility. Fixed and adjustable versions come in two varieties. They can compare the qualities of the other models because characteristics on an adjustable model can be altered. An immovable model cannot be altered. It maintains the quality that the developer programmed into it.

These models can be divided into three categories based on the variables utilized in the productivity model provided for measuring corporate productivity:

Productivity index models

PPPV models

PPPR models

In 1955, Davis presented a productivity index approach in a book he wrote titled Productivity Accounting.

Based on Davis' model several versions have been developed, yet, The fundamental answer is constant (Kendrick & Creamer, 1965), 1973 Craig & Harris, Hines 1976, Mundel 1983, Sumanth 1979).

Productivity is the sole variable in the index model, It suggests that the production function cannot be described by the model.

Therefore, No more information about the model is provided here.

Profitability is stated as a function of the following variables, collectively referred to as PPPV:

Efficiency = f (Productivity, Prices, Volume)

As a result of the model's connection to the profit and loss statement, profitability is shown as a function of output, sales volume, and unit costs. A production function's variables, productivity and volume, can be used to describe the actual manufacturing process. A shift in unit costs indicates a shift in the production-income distribution.

The term "PPPR" stands for the following function:

Efficiency = f (Productivity, Price Recovery)

Productivity and price recovery are the profitability factors in this strategy. The only variable in the production function is productivity. The model cannot describe the production function since it is missing the volume variable. Since they do not apply to characterizing the production function (Saari 2000), the American models of REALST (Loggerenberg & Cucchiaro 1982, Pineda 1990) and APQC (Kendrick 1984, Brayton 1983, Genesca & Grifell, 1992, Pineda 1990) are not more thoroughly examined here.

CHOISES	Saari	Kurosawa	Gollop	C & T
Variables used in the model	Distribution Productivity Volume	Distribution Productivity Volume	Distribution Productivity Volume	Distribution Productivity Volume
Theory, alternatives, 1. Production function 2. Cost function	Production function	Production function	Cost function	Cost function
Calculation order of variables	1. Distribution 2. Productivity 3. Volume	1. Volume 2. Productivity 3. Distribution	1. Volume 2. Productivity 3. Distribution	1. Volume 2. Productivity 3. Distribution
Accounting technique, alternatives, 1. Variance accounting 2. Ratio accounting 3. Accounting form	All changes, Variance accounting	All changes, Accounting form	Distribution, Variance acc. Productivity, Ratio acc. Volume, Account form	All Changes Accounting, form
Adjustadility, alternatives, 1. Adjustable 2. Fixed	Adjustable	Fixed	Fixed	Fixed

Summary of productivity models (Saari 2006b)

PPPV models calculate profitability as a function of output, volume, and distribution of revenue (unit prices). These models are

Asian Kurosawa (1975)

Temple & French Courbois (1975)

Nordic Saari (1976, 2000, 2004, 2006a, 2006b)

United States Gollop (1979)

The PPPV models' characteristics are shown in the table. The same variables are utilized in all four models to develop formulas for measuring changes in profitability. These elements include production, volume, and the distribution of income (prices). One result is that all models have the same fundamental measuring logic. Because different models provide different results from the same calculation material, the implementation of the measurements varies to some extent.

Even though the profitability and volume variables for the production function were included in the model, the calculation can still be done in accordance with the cost function in practice. Models C & T and Gollop exhibit this as well. Different calculation techniques use either output volume or input volume to calculate the volume of activity. The first solution satisfies the cost function, whereas the second satisfies the production function. It is clear that the algorithm yields various outcomes from the same data. Applying calculations in line with the production function is advised. The quantity and quality of output per unit of input is what is meant by productivity, according to the concept of the production function employed in Saari and Kurosawa's productivity models.

Models' methods of calculation greatly differ from one another. It is more a matter of differences in model clarity and understandability between the models than differences in calculation technique, which does not lead to disparities in calculation outcomes. It is clear from the comparison that the models of Courbois and Temple and Kurosawa are solely founded on mathematical formulas. The aggregates in the loss and profit account are the foundation for the calculation. Therefore, analysis is not appropriate for it. The only foundation of the Saari productivity model is variance accounting, which is well-known from traditional cost accounting. The variance accounting is used for basic variables, such as the quantities and costs of various inputs and outputs. Variance accounting offers the greatest analytical options to the customer. In terms of calculation, the Gollop model is a mixed model. Different computation methods are used to calculate each variable. (2006) Saari

The efficiency model The only model whose attributes can be changed is Saari. Thus, it is a model that can be adjusted. Utilizing this specific feature of this model has made it possible to compare it to other models.

The same concept of productivity as in business must be operationalized in order to measure the productivity of a country or an industry, but the subject of modeling is much broader and the data is more aggregate. The SNA, or System of National Accounts, time series, which has been created and refined over half a century, is the foundation for estimations of total production of a country or an industry. A system known as national accounting uses the UN's SNA 93 principles to measure a country's overall production and income as well as how those resources are employed.

Due to the availability of all fundamental information regarding the quantities and costs of the inputs and outputs used in production, productivity measurement is at its most accurate in the business world. More data must be pooled the more complete the entity is that we want to measure. Combining and aggregating data in productivity measurement invariably results in decreased measurement accuracy.

The amount of total production has the same meaning conceptually in both the national economy and business, although modeling the idea differs due to practical considerations. The whole production of a country's economy is calculated as the value added, but in a firm it is calculated as the total output value. All buy inputs (energy, materials, etc.) and their effects on productivity are disregarded when the output is calculated by the value added. As a result, the national economy's production function is expressed as follows:

Input + Value + Output = f (Capital, Labour)

Production in business is assessed by the gross value of production, which includes all buy inputs such as raw materials, energy, outsourced services, supplies, components, etc. in addition to the producer's own inputs (capital and labor). As a result, it is feasible to quantify overall productivity in business, which implies that all inputs are taken into account in their entirety. It is obvious that business productivity measurement provides a more accurate result since it examines all of the production inputs. (2006) Saari

Recently, the national accounting-based productivity measurement has been under development. The approach, known as KLEMS, takes into account all production inputs. The acronym KLEMS stands for "capital," "labor," "energy," "materials," and "services." All inputs are, in theory, handled equally. This means that the capital input in particular is quantified by capital services rather than the capital stock.

The issue with merging or aggregating the inputs and outputs is solely a measurement issue and is brought on by the fixed grouping of the elements. Data must be fed into fixed items in national accounting, resulting in big output and input items that are not homogeneous as stated in the measures but instead incorporate qualitative variations. Both inputs and products are present in calculations by their own names, representing the fundamental price and amount of the calculation material, but there is no defined grouping of things in the business production model. (2006) Saari

The value of the nation's total output, or GNP, is determined for productivity assessments using fixed prices. According to the fixed price computation approach, prices used to evaluate quantities are kept constant across a specific time period. By using the so-called basic year prices, a fixed price GNP is produced in the computation that complies with national accounting. The evaluation of the output and input numbers does not alter throughout the course of five years because the basic year is typically updated every fifth year. Relative prices will change in proportion to the prices of the preceding basic year when the new basic-year prices are imposed, which will inevitably have an influence on productivity.

The production measurement is inaccurate when using old basic-year pricing. Due to market economics, the relative values of inputs and outputs fluctuate, but the relative prices of the base year are unaffected by these changes. Such structural alterations will be incorrectly assessed. Products with short lifespans lack an evaluation framework since they are created and destroyed between the two fundamental years. If outdated, long-term fixed prices are being employed, it is neglected that good productivity can be obtained through elasticity. This issue does not arise in commercial models because the right pricing are always accessible. (2006) Saari

{End Chapter 13}

Chapter 14: Measurement in economics

Physical measurements, nominal price value measurements, and fixed price value measurements are the types of measurements used in economics. These metrics vary from one another depending on the variables they measure and the variables they do not include in their calculations. Quantity, quality, and distribution are the measurable factors in economics. A more restricted approach is required, yet excluding variables from the measurement process allows for a better focus on a particular variable. The table was created to contrast the fundamental measurements. The measure types are presented in the first column, the variables being measured in the second, and the variables excluded from measurement in the third.

TYPE OF MEASURE	Variables to be measured	Variables excluded
Physical	Quantity	Quality and distribution
Fixed price value	Quantity and quality	Distribution
Nominal price value	Quantity, quality and distribution	None

Comparison of basic measure types (Saari 2006)

Quantity, quality, and distribution are the measurable factors in economics. Quantity measurement in economics is governed by the same principles as physics. Changes in production process quality are referred to as quality variables. When the relative values of several constant-price input and output factors change, qualitative changes occur. The term "distribution" refers to a sequence of occurrences in which the unit prices of inputs and outputs of constant quality change, resulting in a change in the income distribution among individuals taking part in the exchange. The amount of the income distribution's shift is closely correlated with the quantity and price of the inputs and outputs. For instance, productivity improvements are passed on to customers as cheaper product pricing or to employees as increased pay.

A physical measurement can quantify a variable's amount while maintaining its integrity. Utilizing a physical measure assumes that the measurement object's quality has been determined and continues to be homogeneous. The measurement yields data that are difficult to understand if the presumption of unchanged quality is not met. Changes in both quantity and quality have an impact on the outcomes in this instance, however it is unclear in what proportion. Price adjustments have no impact on the measurement results since the values of the things being measured have no connection to the physical measurements. Combining physical measures is typically impossible. They work best for precise measurements that don't change in quality or value. Physical measurements are therefore the ideal for gauging the actual process, which explains why operative management frequently employs them. Capacity, efficiencies, lead times, loads, faults, product and process features, etc. are examples of typical ratios in a genuine process.

Changes in quality and quantity are measured using a fixed-price value measure. Prices are held constant for a minimum of two measuring scenarios, as the name suggests. Because of this, it is easy to distinguish between changes in income distribution and changes in the quality and quantity of a wide range of commodities. Because it is easy to combine several commodities based on their value, fixed-price measures are well suited for extensive measurement. A change in quality in a fixed-price measurement corresponds to a change in the relative quantities and prices of different commodities. The productivity equation and the production function are two of its most well-known uses. The productivity and volume variables of the production function are always expressed as fixed-price ratios, meaning that they have fixed-price values.

Due to their ability to convey the profitability of a company operation, figures are the most often used metrics in business. The nominal price measurement includes quality, quantity, and distribution variables (in form of product prices). No variables are excluded. For estimating profitability and its components as well as the value of reserves, nominal price measures of value are appropriate. The loss and profit statement's return and costs are classic illustrations of nominal prices. Nominal price values are ideal for estimates of fixed price values in short-term assessments where little production income distribution occurs.

{End Chapter 14}

Chapter 15: Factor market

A factor market is a market in economics where production factors are bought and sold. The allocation of factors of production, such as land, labor, and capital, and the distribution of income to the owners of productive resources, such as wages, rents, etc., are governed by factor markets. Derived demand is the demand for productive resources that results from the demand for final goods and services or output. For instance, if consumer demand for new automobiles increases, producers will increase their demand for the productive inputs or resources used to manufacture new automobiles.

Production is the transformation of raw materials into finished goods.

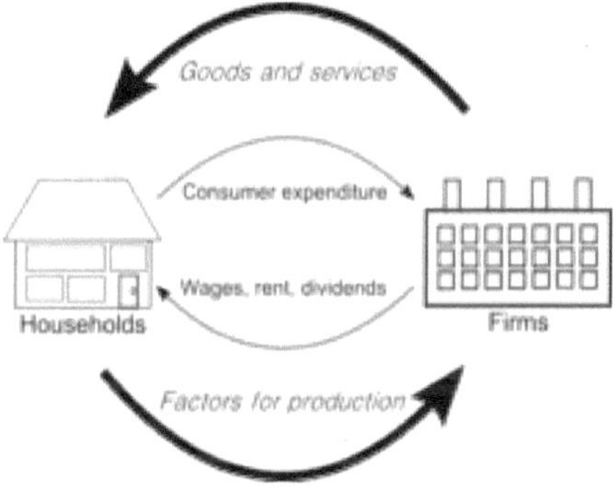

The Circular Flow Diagram

In perfectly competitive markets, businesses are able to "purchase" as many inputs as they require at market price. Because labor is the most essential factor of production, this article will concentrate on the competitive labor market, although the analysis applies to all competitive factor markets. The demand for labor is considered a derived demand, which distinguishes labour markets from the majority of other economic markets. It is important to note that as the number of workers increases, the marginal product of labour decreases, implying that the output process reflects diminishing marginal product. Each additional worker contributes a diminishing amount to output as the number of employed workers rises. The efficient allocation of production factors can account for up to sixty percent of the variation in national productivity levels. In the United States, for instance, relatively competitive factor markets have contributed to the country's economic success. In contrast, certain developing nations may have less developed factor markets, which can hinder their economic development.

Assume that both the product and factor markets have perfectly competitive structures. In both markets, companies act as price takers. The price is determined by the interaction of supply and demand at the market level. As price-takers, the companies can sell as much product as they want at the set price. There are numerous instances in which factor markets have influenced economic outcomes. The effect of labor market regulations on unemployment rates is one example. The research of Bassanini and Duval

A derived demand is the demand for inputs. Changes to either MPL or MR will cause the curve to shift. Changes in (1) the price of the final product or output price, (2) the productivity of the resource, (3) the number of buyers of the resource, and (4) the price of related resources can cause a shift in the curve.

Changes in the output price - The MRPL is the MPL × the output price thus if the price of the output increases due to an increase in demand for the product the value of the marginal product of labor increases at every price and the resource demand curve shifts out.

For example, If the price of the output rises, companies will respond by producing more to meet demand, which will increase the demand for inputs.

Changes in productivity - Changes in productivity have multiple effects on resource demand. For instance, the invention of inexpensive industrial robots may reduce the marginal production of labor, shifting the labor demand curve to the left. This phenomenon is referred to as labor-saving technological development. However, technological development continues to be primarily labor-enhancing.

Variations in the number of buyers of the resource - As with any market, an increase in buyers will cause the demand curve to shift to the right.

Price fluctuations of related resources - Related resources include complementary and substitute resources. A change in the cost of a related resource will impact labor demand. Automobiles, for instance, can be assembled using various combinations of labor and machinery. If the price of machinery decreases, firms will tend to replace labor with machines, reducing the demand for labor. If labor and machinery are complementary resources and the price of machinery falls, then more machinery will be purchased and more workers will be required to operate the new machines, causing the labor demand curve to shift to the right.

As with the product market, a manager must not only understand the direction and magnitude of a change in demand. In other words, the manager must know how much to adjust the use of a resource if its price changes.

Determinants of PERD

The price elasticity of resource demand is the percentage change in resource demand in response to a one percent change in resource price. PERD for a resource is contingent on:

The PED of the output for which the input was used - The greater the product's PED, the greater the resource's PERD. Coca-PED Cola's is relatively high. If the price of Coca-Cola increases, there will be a significant decline in demand for the product. The decline in Coca-Cola demand will reduce the demand for all inputs utilized in the production of Coke.

The significance of factor in the manufacturing process

The number of substitutes for the resource; the greater the PERD, the greater the number of substitutes.

The period - Time to discover additional resources. The greater the PERD, the greater the time to adjust.

The rate of decline of the factor's MPP = The faster the MPP declines, the more elastic the factor's demand.

Resource owners supply the market with resources. Individual supply curves are summed to form the market supply curve. The resource supply curve and the product supply curve are comparable. The market supply curve is upward-sloping and the sum of individual supply curves. It illustrates the relationship between the price of a resource and the quantity of that resource that sellers are willing and able to sell.

The price paid for any factor of production equals that factor's marginal production. The marginal production of any factor is proportional to the quantity of that factor available. Due to diminishing marginal production, the marginal production of a factor in abundant supply is low, resulting in a low price, whereas the marginal production of a factor in scarce supply is high, resulting in a high price. Thus, when the supply of a factor falls, the equilibrium price of that factor rises.

Changes in preferences - More women choose to work rather than stay at home and care for their children, thereby increasing the labor supply.

Availability of alternative opportunities – The supply of labor is contingent on the opportunities offered on other labor markets.

Migration – Another significant source of gaps in the labor supply curve is the movement of workers from one region/nation to another.

The price elasticity of resource supply (PERS) is equal to the percentage change in resource supply caused by a percentage change in resource price.

If a good is produced by a monopoly, the factor demand curve is identical to the MRPL curve. As output rises, both the marginal product of labor and the marginal revenue decline. This is in contrast to a competitive firm, where marginal revenue is constant and the downward slope is solely attributable to the diminishing marginal product of labor. The MRPL curve for a monopoly therefore lies below the MRPL curve for a competitive firm. The implication is that a monopoly or any firm operating in imperfect market conditions will produce less and employ fewer workers than a perfectly competitive firm at a given price.

A monopsony is an economic market structure that consists of a single buyer of a specific good or service in the factor market.

Comparatively to a monopoly, The entities that control the two market structures are the primary difference between the two market structures.

A monopoly is the dominance of a single seller over the market.

A monopsony is the dominance of a single buyer over the market.

In this circumstance, A firm determines the market price it will pay for a factor, as opposed to accepting the market-determined price, In addition, the quantity of the factor to purchase is selected concurrently under the constraint that the price-and-quantity combination is a point on the market's factor supply curve.

Furthermore, Typically, monopsonists are more prevalent in factor markets than in product markets.

A monopsonist is a concern for factor markets due to the fact that, A monopsony has the ability to significantly influence the factor market's prices and quantities, this is due to the firm's market power over a particular factor of production.

Combined with the ability to steer a particular industry in a manner that is advantageous to the monopsolist

The economic market state of oligopsony is characterized by a small number of dominant buyers. Similar to a monopsony, an oligopsony consists of a small number of powerful buyers who purchase the majority of goods and services. Monopsonies and oligopsonies are market conditions in which a single firm or a small number of firms have substantial market power in their respective factor market. It has been debated whether firms with substantial market power can benefit industries within the factor market.

{End Chapter 15}

Chapter 16: Technological theory of social production

In the technological theory of social production, the increase in output, measured in monetary units, is proportional to advances in technological labor and energy consumption. Based on classical political economy and neoclassical economics, this theory appears to be a generalization of the known economic models, such as the neoclassical model of economic growth and the input-output model.

The major characteristics of social production is its output Y

, This is the value produced per unit of time, whose basic origins are production factors, What are some common aspects of manufacturing processes?.

In standard political economy (Smith),, Marx, Ricardo), it is human efforts (labour) L

, They are quantified in terms of working hours.

Neoclassical practice adds capital K

, What is the estimated cost of production equipment?, This is the total worth of all energy-converting machinery and data processing equipment, plus structures to contain and transport them, including residential real estate, When capital is seen in a broader context.

early speculations presumed, that output Y

can be considered a function of labour L

and capital K

, as innovative elements of production, $Y = Y(K, L).$

This relationship formalized the neoclassical political economy idea of capital substitution for labor.

There are numerous possible implementations of the above function.

The next significant development in the understanding of economic growth occurred in the middle of the previous century.

To include technical advancement into the theory, It is regarded to be the ultimate cause of economic progress in industrialized nations over the past several centuries, It was suggested that conceptions of arguments in the production function be modified such that they are not considered capital and labor expenses, but services of the capital K'

and work L'

, so that

$$Y = Y(K', L').$$

The quantity $K' = A_K(t)K$

and $L' = A_L(t)L$

are capital and labour services which are connected with measured quantities of capital stock K

and labour L

, but are somewhat dissimilar to them.

That is to say, A time dependence of the production function must be assumed (so-called exogenous technological advancement).

This method describes empirical data using two production factors and an empirical variable referred to as total factor productivity.

$$P = A_K(t)K$$

Suggesting that capital service can be considered as an independent variable, whereas labour service

$$L' = L$$

is regarded just as labour, One arrived at the development of technical theory, in which, taking also capital stock K into account, production of value Y can be considered as a function of the three production factors

$$Y = Y(K, L, P)$$

This function is likewise comparable to the preceding expression, Capital as a variable performed two unique roles: capital stock as the value of industrial equipment, and capital service as a worker replacement.

The only thing which is done is a separation of the two roles of capital: we consider capital stock K to be the means of attracting labour L and capital service P, to the performance.

It was shown also that capital service P

, as one of the three production factors, refers to the substitution of industrial equipment (energy delivered to animate production equipment).

In one sector, the theory was regarded an approximation of the industrial system, Including some mention of a multisector strategy.

The production expansion, characterised by changes of the accumulated value K

, requires additional labour L

and substitutive work P

, so that balance equations can be written for the production factor dynamics.

The first terms in the right side of these relations describe the increase in the quantities caused by gross investments I

accumulated in a material form of production equipment.

Equations (1) present the quality of investment, which is comprised of the technological characteristics of manufacturing equipment: coefficients of labor and energy demand, which can be altered in both the three-dimensional, λ

and ε

, dimensionalless (with a bar on top) shapes, $\bar{\lambda} = \lambda K / L$

and $\bar{\varepsilon} = \varepsilon K / P.$

The second terms on the right side of equations (1) reflect the decrease in the corresponding quantities due to the removal of a part of the production equipment from service with the depreciation coefficient μ

, which is assumed to be equal for all variables, ensure the equipment's technological qualities do not alter after installation, if not, the dynamic equations assume a more complicated form.

Production function, as function of independent variables: labour L

, capital K

and substitutive work P

, must fulfill certain requirements, which contribute to its shape.

Taking into account that substitutive work P

and labour L

inputs are substitutes to each other and capital K

has to be considered to be a complement to work (L

and P

) of the production equipment, Our case's production function can be described as:

where Y_0

, L_0

and P_0

correspond to output, labour and replacement work in the base year.

The index α

is connected with technological characteristics of production equipment

After differentiating relations (2), one obtains the output growth rate equation.

The initial terms on the right side of the equation represent the contribution of the growth rate of labor and substitution work to the growth rate of output, the latter - a contribution directly attributable to improvements in the production system.

The productivity of the capital stock ξ

and the index α

in equation (2) are parameters of the production system itself, as well as their derivatives are related to the characteristics of the industrial system.

In the multi-sector approach (input-output model), technical index changes are connected to aggregate sectoral technology change and the difference in growth rates between sectors.

The actual investments are based on the premise that the production system attempts to consume all available production elements. In any case, real growth rates do not surpass prospective growth rates, presented as functions of time.

Consequently, based on equation (1), one should write for investments.

The three lines of this relationship define three kinds of economic development for which different formulas are used to calculate actual growth rates. The first line of (5) holds true if there are insufficient investments, an abundance of labor, energy, and raw resources. The second line holds true when there is a dearth of labor, a surplus of investment, energy, and raw materials. Last line of equations holds true if there is an absence of energy, an abundance of investment, labor, and raw resources.

In the first approximation, one can derive the technological coefficient equations under the assumption that technological coefficients have inclinations to change such that the production system attempts to utilize all available production components.

where T

is time of crossover from one technological situation to another, when external parameters $\tilde{\nu}$

and $\tilde{\eta}$

change.

It is determined by the inherent processes of technological attraction.

The aforementioned relationships provide a framework for describing economic development, It can be utilized in the event, if supply of production factors is adequate, determined by their rates of potential growth $\tilde{\nu}$

for labour and $\tilde{\eta}$

for substitutive work, are given.

The first number is associated with population size, in fact, One can estimate that almost half of the whole population is employed.

The availability of substitute employment is a variable quantity.

It is determined by fundamental scientific findings, by research, by project's means, And by the actualization of all human imagination regarding the utilization of energy in lieu of labor for manufacturing.

The availability of production factors should be endogenous in population evolution problems, when population dynamics and the store of knowledge are taken into account.

Scientific and technological advancement can be reduced to processes of innovation introduction, It is the replacement of instruments in succession, materials, designs, Adaptations and other objects that are, from this or that perspective, more ideal.

Among all replacement procedures,, The process of replacing human labor with machine labor, with the help of natural forces, plays a starring role.

Substitution of human labor with machine labor is a unique replacement process that effects labor productivity as the ratio of output value to labor expenditures.

Productivity of labour depends on the ratio of substitutive work to workers' efforts P/L

and, in accordance (2), can also be stated as

Here, output should be measured in value units of constant purchasing capacity, representing a 'physical' output measurement.

The growth rate of labor productivity is stated by four numbers:

The labour requirement $\bar{\lambda}$

appears to be the most important quantity, It determines the shift in labor productivity.

If $\bar{\lambda} = 1$

, Variations in technology are nonexistent, constant productivity of labor, And every increment of output is directly proportional to an increase in human effort.

Human endeavours are, certainly, the primary driving force, but, under condition of $\bar{\lambda} < 1$

the workers' efforts partially are replaced with work of the machines movable by outer energy sources, and the labour product growth rises.

This is an overview of the impact of scientific and technical advancement, This naturally fits into a depiction of human advancement.

Increase in labor productivity cannot be comprehended apart from the phenomenon that accompanies the development of production: the attraction of natural energy sources (animals, wind, water, coal, oil, and others) for the execution of work that substitutes the efforts of humans in production. The development of machine technology appears to boost labor productivity through substitution. Increasing amounts of energy are consumed by human cultures due to technological advancements.

The idea can be used to describe the "stylized" facts of economic growth, specifically the exponential growth of output and production factors. In such relatively tranquil phases of development, the growth rates of production components can be assumed to be constant, resulting in exponential growth according to equation (1).

To generate an expression for output, one turns to relations (2) and (8), per which the output can be expressed as follows:

This relationship describes the well-known fact that the growth rate of output and capital are equal. Given the rough estimation of the problem's parameters, the discrepancy between the growth rates of capital and output appears to be rather inaccurate. However, the difference can be explained by differentiating the growth rates of sector outputs.

The rate of output increase can be divided into two sections, while on the average a fraction of the rate $(1 - \alpha)\nu$

is connected with growth of expenditures of labour, and the other part $\alpha\eta$

—with growth of substitutive work.

The hypothesis predicts, that going forward, when $\nu \rightarrow 0$

and energy conversion efficiency approaches thermodynamic limits, the growth rate of output approaches to the growth rate of consumption of total amount of energy carrier multiplied by the technological coefficient α

.

Capital is the means by which production elements are attracted to the manufacturing process, Increased use of manufacturing components correlates with capital growth.

One can formally separate the growth rate of capital δ

in the growth rate of output to get the expression for conventional Solow residual (total factor productivity) in neoclassical theory of economic growth as

{End Chapter 16}

Chapter 17: Fei–Ranis model of economic growth

John C. H. Fei and Gustav Ranis created the Fei-Ranis model of economic growth, which may be seen as an expansion of the Lewis model and is a dualistic model in developmental economics or welfare economics. It is often referred to as the model of surplus labor.

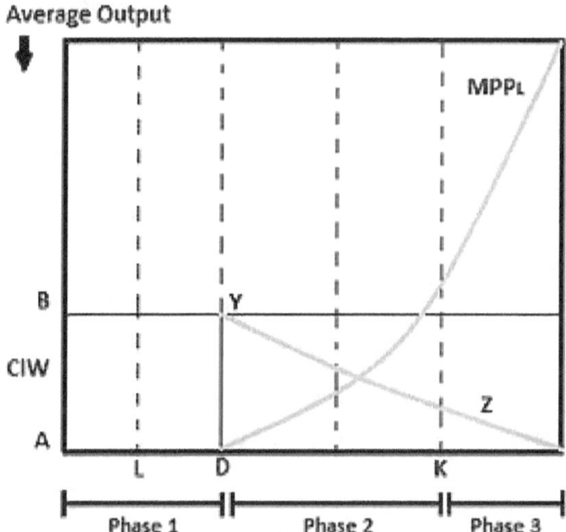

Depiction of Phase1, The dual economy model's Phases 2 and 3 using average output.

The Lewis model's undercutting of the contribution of agriculture to the expansion of the industrial sector was one of its main flaws. In addition, he did not recognise that the rise in labor productivity ought to occur before the division of labor between the two sectors. However, the Fei-Ranis dual economy model of three growth stages took these two concepts into consideration. The agricultural labor force's elasticity is infinite in Phase 1 of the Fei-Ranis model, which causes it to experience hidden unemployment. Additionally, labor's marginal product is zero. The Lewis model is comparable to this stage. Step 2 of the model sees an increase in agricultural productivity, which fuels faster industrial growth and lays the groundwork for phase 3. Agricultural surplus may exist in Phase 2 as an increasing average product (AP) that is higher than the marginal product (MP) but not at the same level as the subsistence wage.

With the aid of the left-hand figure, we can observe that

Phase 1 : AL(from figure) $= MP = 0$ and AB(from figure) $= AP$

Fei and Ranis claim that the agricultural sector may relocate AD quantity of labor (see figure) without any output loss. Consequently, it is extra labor.

Phase2 : $AP > MP$

Industrial labor increases from zero to a value equal to AD when MP starts to rise. BYZ displays the AP of agricultural labor, and we can see that this curve deviates to the left after AD. This decrease in AP can be linked to the fact that as agricultural workers move from the agricultural sector to the industrial sector, the real wage of industrial workers declines due to the lack of food supply, since fewer workers are now employed in the food industry. The level of profits and the magnitude of the surplus that could have been reinvested for further industrialization both decline as real wages rise. But as long as there is a surplus, growth can be accelerated without slowing the pace of modernization. The moving of the MP curve outward can be used as a visual representation of this reinvestment of surplus. AK provides the level of covert unemployment in Phase 2. This enables the agriculture sector to reduce its workforce by certain percentage till

$MP = $ Real wages $= AB = $ Constant institutional wages (CIW)

Phase 3 starts at K in the Figure, which is the moment of commercialisation. Without any covert unemployment, this is the time where the economy entirely commercializes. Phase 3's labor supply curve is steeper, and both sectors begin competing equally for labor.

Phase3 : MP > CIW

The amount of labor that is transferred and the duration of that transfer depend on:

the expansion of agricultural surplus and the expansion of industrial capital stock, both of which are reliant on the expansion of industrial profits; The nature of industry technical advancement and its bias; the population's rate of growth.

Consequently, the three core concepts in this model are:

Growth in the agricultural and industrial sectors is equally vital; Growth in the agricultural and industrial sectors is equal; The economy won't be able to escape the Malthusian population trap until the rate of labor migration from the agricultural to the industrial sectors outpaces the rate of population growth.

Fei and Ranis emphasized the interdependence of business and agriculture and claimed that strong connectivity between the two will promote and hasten development. The industrial and agricultural sectors can be connected if agricultural workers hunt for industrial employment and industrialists hire more people by using larger capital goods stocks and labor-intensive equipment. Additionally, the surplus owner will probably choose the productivity from which future savings might be directed if he invests in the industrial sector of a known location that is adjacent to the soil. They used the 19th-century dualistic economy of Japan as an illustration and claimed that the existence of a decentralized rural industry that was frequently tied to urban output increased connectivity between the two sectors of Japan. According to them, a limited number of entrepreneurs with access to land and authority to make decisions who employ industrial capital and consumer products for agricultural operations are responsible for achieving economic success in dualistic economies of developing nations.

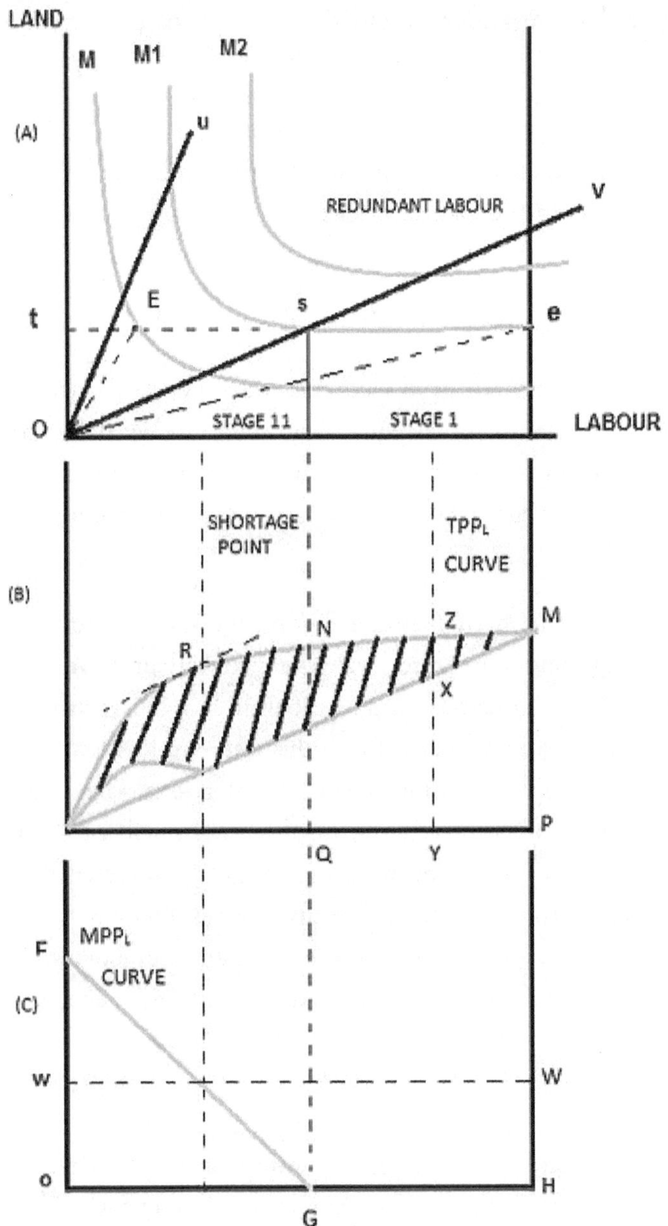

Land-Labor Production Function

In (A), measuring land along its vertical axis, and employment on a horizontal axis.

In terms of two ridge lines, Ou and Ov, and M shows the production contour lines, M1 and M2.

The region of factor substitutability is defined by the space bounded by the ridge lines, or the area where variables are freely interchangeable.

Let's examine the consequences of this.

If the labor figure represents all the labor employed in the agriculture industry,, the intersection of the ridge line Ov with the production curve M1 at point s renders M1 perfectly horizontal below Ov.

The manufacturing line's horizontal behavior suggests that factor substitutability is not universal outside of this region, Once land is fixed and labor is expanded, output ceases and labor becomes unnecessary.

If Ot is the entire amount of land used for agriculture, then ts is the maximum amount of labor that may be used without it being redundant, and es is the amount of agricultural labor that is redundant. Fei and Ranis created the idea of labor utilization ratio as a result, which they describe as the number of productive labor units per unit of land that can be engaged (without redundancy). Figure on the left, labor utilization ratio

$$R = \frac{ts}{Ot}$$

This, graphically, corresponds to the ridge line's inverse slope Ov.

The endowment ratio, a metric for the relative availability of the two variables of production, was also developed by Fei and Ranis. The endowment ratio in the illustration is determined by if Ot represents agricultural land and tE represents agricultural labor.

$$S = \frac{tE}{Ot}$$

which is the same as OE's inverted slope. E provides the precise point of endowment.

Last but not least, Fei and Ranis created the idea of the non-redundancy coefficient T, which is calculated by

$$T = \frac{ts}{te}$$

These three ideas assisted them in establishing a connection between T and, R and S.

If ::
$$T = \frac{ts}{te},$$

then

$$T = \frac{ts/Ot}{te/Ot} = \frac{R}{S}, \text{ or } T = \frac{R}{S}$$

This mathematical relationship demonstrates that the non-redundancy coefficient is inversely related to the endowment ratio and directly proportionate to the labor utilization ratio.

(B) displays the total physical productivity of labor (TPP_L) curve.

The rate of the curve's growth is diminishing, as additional labor units are combined with a fixed amount of land.

Located at N, This point N fits the curve's horizontal contour and coincides with point G in (C), which shows the marginal productivity of labor (MPP_L) curve, in addition, with point s on the ridge line (A).

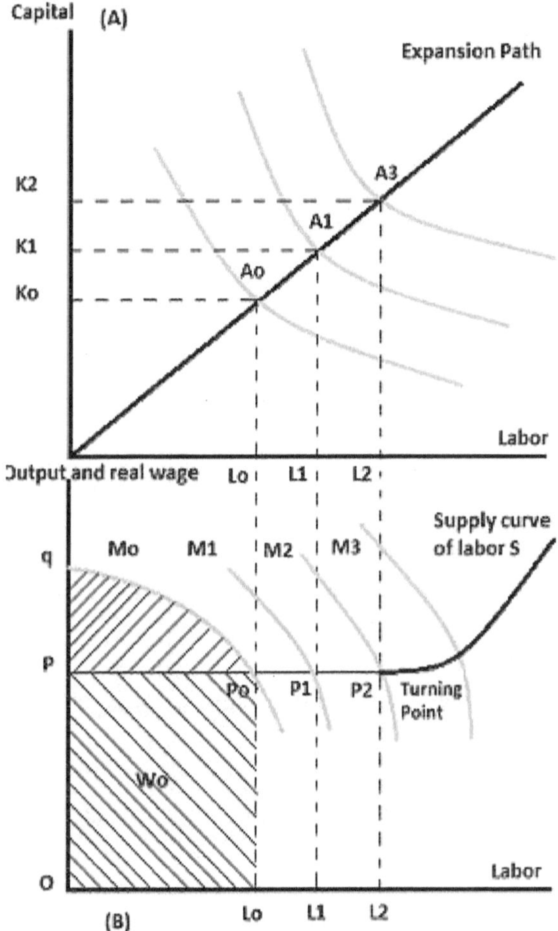

Capital-Labor Production Function

similar to the farming industry, In the industrial sector, Fei and Ranis presumptively observe continuous returns to scale.

However, Capital and labor are the primary production-related components.

On the right side of the graph (A), On a graph of the production functions, labor is plotted along the horizontal axis and capital is plotted along the vertical axis.

The expansion path of the industrial sector is given by the line $OA_0A_1A_2$.

As capital increases from K_0 to K_1 to K_2 and labor increases from L_0 to L_1 and L_2, the industrial output represented by the production contour A_0, A_1 and A_3 increases accordingly.

In line with this model, The agriculture sector is the industrial sector's main source of manpower, due to the agricultural labor force's redundancy.

(B) displays the industrial sector S's labor supply curve.

PP_2 represents the straight line part of the curve and is a measure of the redundant agricultural labor force on a graph with industrial labor force on the horizontal axis and output/real wage on the vertical axis.

due to the excess of agricultural workers, the real wages remain constant but once the curve starts sloping upwards from point P_2, The increasing slope suggests that more labor would only be available if real wages increased in tandem.

MPPL curves corresponding to their respective capital and labor levels have been drawn as M_0, M_1, M_2 and M_3.

When capital stock rises from K_0 to K_1, the marginal physical productivity of labor rises from M_0 to M_1.

When capital stock is K_0, the MPPL curve cuts the labor supply curve at equilibrium point P_0.

In this moment, the total real wage income is W_0 and is represented by the shaded area POL_0P_0.

λ is the equilibrium profit and is represented by the shaded area qPP_0.

Due to the exceedingly low income levels of the workers, they barely save from that income and hence industrial profits (π_0) become the prime source of investment funds in the industrial sector.

$$K_t = K_o + S_o + \Pi_o$$

Here, K_t gives the total supply of investment funds (given that rural savings are represented by S_o)

Due to an increase in the overall supply of investment money, total industrial activity grows, which increases industrial employment.

In general, agricultural surplus is defined as agricultural output that is greater than the societal demands for it and can either be exported or kept for later use.

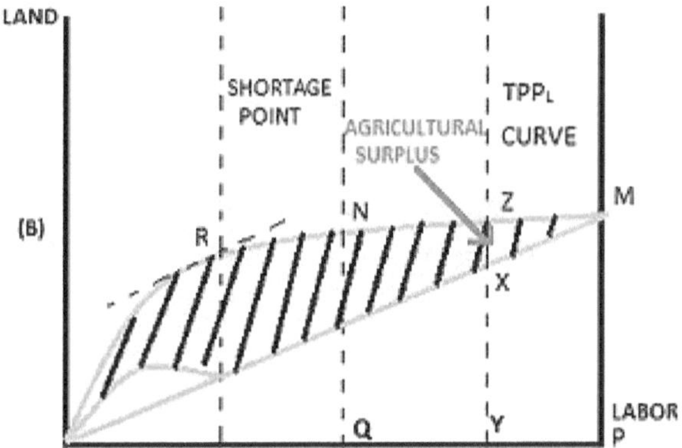

Agricultural surplus in the dual economy of Fei and Ranis

To comprehend how agricultural surpluses are created, We must take a look at the agricultural sector's graph (B).

A portion of the previous graph is replicated in the figure on the left, with some modifications to clarify the idea of agricultural surplus.

We first derive the average physical productivity of the total agricultural labor force (APP$_L$).

The constant institutional wage hypothesis, put out by Fei and Ranis, claims that it is equivalent to the real pay.

In terms of value, it is also equivalent to the proportion of all agricultural output to all agricultural population.

Utilizing this connection, we can obtain APP$_L$ = MP/OP.

This corresponds to the slope of line OM visually, , which is depicted by the line WW in (C).

Look at the graph's point Y, which is located just to the left of P. The labor force remaining in the industrial sector is represented by the point Y if a portion of the redundant agricultural labor force (PQ) is eliminated from the overall agricultural labor force (OP) and incorporated into it. Now, YZ represents the output created by the remaining labor force, and XY provides the real income of this workforce. The entire agricultural surplus of the economy is calculated as the difference between the two terms. It is crucial to realize that this excess is the result of labor being redistributed in a way that the industrial sector can use it. This might be interpreted as the use of untapped rural savings for the development of the industrial sector. Due to this allocation of surplus labor and the resulting agricultural surplus, we can understand how the agricultural sector contributed to the growth of the industrial sector.

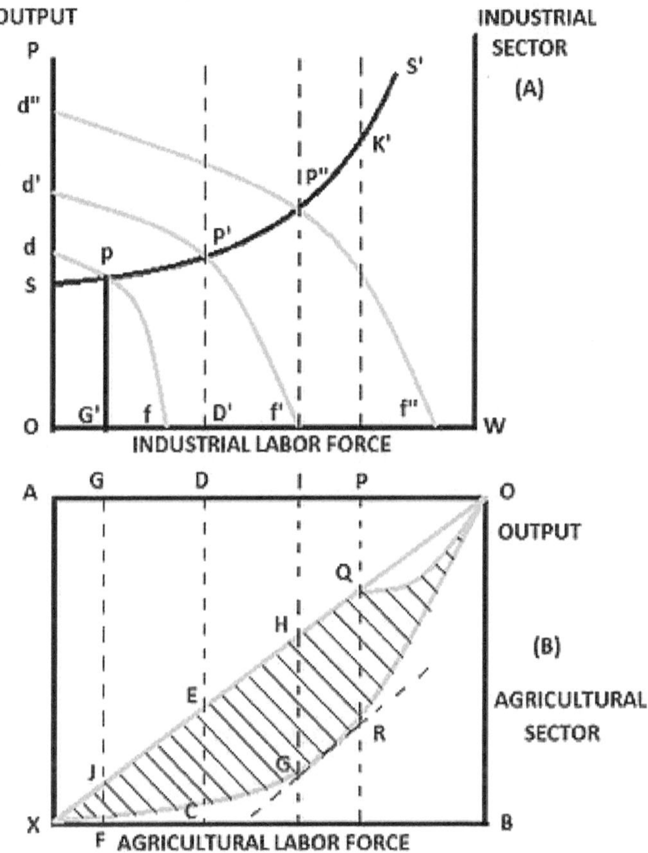

Integration of agricultural and industrial sectors to explain use of agricultural surplus as wage fund in a dual economy.

The agricultural surplus is a key component of the wage fund. The graph on the right, which combines the industrial sector graph with an inverted agricultural sector graph with the agricultural sector's origin located in the upper-right corner, can assist illustrate its significance. The graph is now seen differently as a result of the origin's inversion. The output numbers are read vertically downward from O, while the labor force values are read from the left of 0. This inversion is only being done for convenience's sake. The point of commercialization is located at point R, where the tangent to the line ORX runs parallel to OX, as previously explained (See Section on Basics of the model).

The full labor pool is present in the agricultural sector before a portion of the redundant labor force is absorbed into the industrial sector. The residual labor in the agricultural sector is then represented by OG' once the AG quantity of labor force (let's say) has been absorbed by the industrial sector. However, how is the amount of labor absorbed into the industrial sector decided? The labor supply curve for SS' and numerous labor demand curves for df, d'f, and d"f are shown in (A). The equilibrium employment point G' is determined by where the demand-supply curves cross when the labor demand is df. Therefore, OG stands for the amount of labor that has been absorbed by the industrial sector. The only labor left in the agriculture industry in that circumstance is OG. This OG quantity of labor results in an output of GF, of which GJ is the labor spent by agriculture, and JF is the surplus produced by agriculture at that employment level. When the agricultural sector's unproductive labor force is absorbed by the industrial sector, it simultaneously becomes productive and produces the OG'Pd production depicted in the graph, earning a total pay income of OG'PS.

The same people who went for the industrial sector need the agricultural surplus JF produced for consumption. As a result, agriculture successfully offers both the labor force needed for productive activities abroad and the necessary pay budget.

Agriculture is neglected in the Lewis model, which is why it is criticized. Fei-Ranis model takes a step further and asserts that the expansion of the industrial sector depends heavily on agriculture. In reality, it claims that the amount of the overall agricultural surplus and the sum of industrial sector earnings determine the pace of expansion of the industrial sector. Therefore, the rate of expansion of the industrial economy will be greater the more surplus there is, the more excess is invested productively, and the more industrial profits are made. Fei and Ranis believe that the ideal shift occurs when investment funds from surplus and industrial profits are sufficiently large to buy industrial capital goods like plants and machinery. The model focuses on the shifting of the focal point of progress from the agricultural to the industrial sector. Employment opportunities must be created in order to use these capital assets. Therefore, Fei and Ranis' prerequisite for a successful transformation is that

Rate of employment opportunities and capital stock growth > population growth rate

The agricultural sector loses workers as an impoverished nation transitions to its industrial phase of growth. The economy of a country grows more quickly the more reallocation there is. The idea of labor reallocation is supported economically by the need for greater economic growth. Engel's Law, which stipulates that the proportion of income spent on food falls with an increase in an individual's income level, even while there is a rise in the actual expenditure on food, is the foundation of labor reallocation. For instance, if agriculture employs 90% of the total population in the economy in question, only 10% of the people would be employed in the industrial sector. As agricultural production rises, just 35% of the population can continue to ensure a sufficient food supply for the remainder of the population. As a result, 65% of the population is currently employed in the industrial sector. A larger labor supply for the industrial sector would be appreciated under the current circumstances because the growth of industrial products is dependent on the rate of per capita income whereas the growth of agricultural goods is merely dependent on the rate of population growth. In fact, as consumers start to prefer industrial goods relative to agrarian goods, this labor reallocation becomes inevitable.

Fei and Ranis were quick to point out, however, that, in accordance with the discussion of Engel's Law, the need for labor reallocation must be more closely related to the requirement to create more capital investment products than to the notion of industrial consumer goods. This is due to the fact that the idea that there is a large demand for industrial goods looks implausible given how low the real wage in the agriculture sector is and how this lowers the demand for industrial goods. In addition, low and generally stable wage rates will result in low and constant wage rates in the industrial sector. This suggests that the rate of increase in demand for industrial goods will not be as high as that predicted by Engel's Law.

Due to the slow-paced development in consumer spending power during the economic process, dualistic economies adopt a natural austerity strategy that places a greater emphasis on the production of capital goods than consumer goods. Private entrepreneurs are turned off by the lengthy gestation time that comes with capital goods investments. This implies that, especially in the early phases of growth, the government must intervene and play a significant role in order to facilitate growth. Additionally, the government constructs roads, railways, bridges, educational institutions, healthcare facilities, and other infrastructure to reduce social and economic costs.

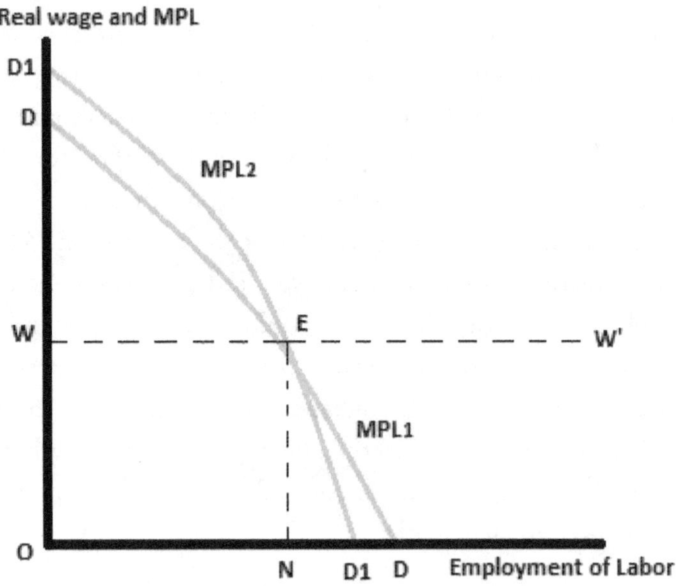

Graph showing growth without development

According to the Fei-Ranis model, it is possible that as technology advances and manufacturing methods shift to ones that require less labor, the economy will flourish and earnings will rise without any real economic improvement. With the aid of the graph in this section, this can be discussed in detail.

The graph shows two MPL lines that are plotted, with employment of labor on the horizontal axis, real pay and MPL on the vertical axis. OW stands for the subsistence wage level, which is the lowest salary at which an employee (and his family) might live comfortably. Since there is no limit to the supply of labor at the subsistence wage level, the line WW' that runs parallel to the X-axis is thought to be indefinitely elastic. The wage bill is represented by the square area OWEN, and the surplus or profits are represented by the square area DWE. If the MPL curve shifts, this excess or profit could rise.

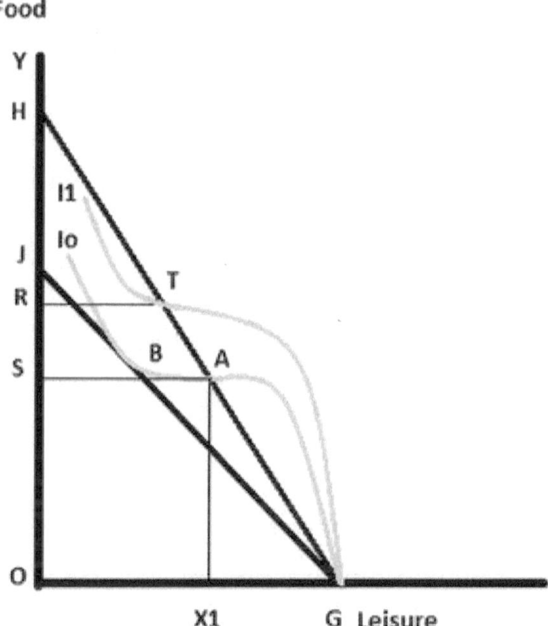

Food-Leisure Graph

The Fei-Ranis model of economic growth has drawn criticism for a variety of reasons, but if it is adopted, it will have significant theoretical and policy implications for the efforts of developing nations to advance as well as for the ongoing contentious claims regarding the balanced vs. unbalanced growth debate.

It has been said that Fei and Ranis lacked a thorough knowledge of the weak economic climate that prevailed in underdeveloped nations. They would have discovered that the prevailing agricultural backwardness was caused by the institutional structure, specifically the feudal system that predominated, if they had carefully examined the nature and reasons of it.

Ranis and Fei state, "It has been claimed that in an aggregate production function, money is not a straightforward replacement for physical capital. At some point in the economic cycle, there are reasons to think that the relationship between money and physical capital may be complementary, to the point where credit regulations may be crucial in removing obstacles to the expansion of agriculture and industry." This suggests that they are ignoring the importance of money and prices during the development process. They fail to make the important distinction between family labor and wage labor, which is necessary to assess the costs of dualistic development in an underdeveloped economy.

Fei and Ranis assume that MPPL is zero during the early phases of economic development, which has been criticized by Harry T.Oshima and some others on the grounds that MPPL of labor is zero only if the agricultural population is very large, and if it is really massive, Some of that workforce will move to urban areas in quest of employment.

In the near future, This segment of the labor force that moved to the cities is still unemployed, however, with time, it either becomes absorbed by the unorganized sector, else it goes back to the villages and makes an effort to cultivate additional marginal land there.

Additionally, they have ignored seasonal unemployment, which is temporary and results from seasonal changes in labor demand.

To better comprehend this, When referencing this section's graph,, This places leisure on the horizontal axis and food on the vertical axis.

OS stands for the minimum level of dietary intake, is the amount of food that agricultural workers must consume in order to survive.

I0 and I1 between the two commodities of food and leisure (of the agriculturists).

The initial letter is G, so that OG stands for the most labor and the labor input is measured from the right to the left.

From A, the transformation curve SAG declines, It shows that the same amount of land is being used for more leisure.

At A, the marginal transformation between food and leisure and MPL = 0 and the indifference curve I_0 is also tangent to the transformation curve at this point.

The point of leisure satiation is at hand.

Take the example of a worker who transitions from the agriculture to the industrial sectors. In that situation, the remaining laborers would split up the remaining land, changing the transformation curve from SAG to RTG. MPL at point T would be 0 and APL would remain the same as it was at point A. (assuming constant returns to scale). The curve RTG must be flat at point T in order to maintain the same level of output if MPL = 0 is taken as the point at which agriculturalists live on a subsistence level. That, however, would imply either that leisure is sated or that leisure is a lesser good, which are both extreme circumstances. Therefore, it may be inferred that, in typical circumstances, the output would decrease as labor moved into the industrial sector but the per capita output remained constant. This is due to the fact that a decline in per capita output would result in consumption that is lower than the level necessary for subsistence, and the amount of labor input per person would either increase or decrease.

In their 1968 publication, Berry and Soligo critiqued this model for its MPL=0 assumption and for assuming that the transfer of labor from the agricultural sector results in a phase-one output that is unaltered. They demonstrate that until the following circumstances occur, the production changes and may be subject to different land tenure regimes:

1. The list of lesser goods includes leisure. 2. There is satiation from leisure. 3. Food and leisure are perfectly interchangeable, and the marginal rate of substitution is constant across all real income levels.

The choice of satisfying oneself with leisure now becomes invalid if MPL is more than zero, and it also becomes invalid if MPL is equal to zero. Therefore, leisure as a lesser benefit is the only viable option left.

They have omitted to acknowledge the necessity of capital while highlighting the significance of high agricultural production and the generation of surplus for economic development. Although it is crucial to produce excess, it is also crucial to keep it alive through technological advancement, which is made possible by capital accumulation. However, the Fei-Ranis model only takes into account labor and output as components of production.

The empirical question of whether MPL = 0 is at hand. Because food production is primarily seasonal in developing nations, MPL would almost certainly be more than zero, especially under favorable meteorological conditions, like when harvesting or sowing.

Fei and Ranis base their assumptions on a tight model, therefore there is no foreign trade in the economy, which is highly implausible because food or raw materials cannot be imported. If we use Japan as an example once more, the nation bought low-cost agricultural products from other nations, which improved the nation's terms of trade.

The hesitant expansionary growth of subsistence agriculture can be linked to the slow increase in productivity of the industrial sector in developing nations. This shows that surplus growth becomes a more essential factor than surplus reinvestment, which is in line with Jorgenson's theory from 1961, which stressed the importance of surplus generation and persistence.

There is no differentiation between work done for family and work done for pay, nor has stagnation been taken into account. Additionally, neither the self-sustaining growth mechanism nor the investment function are explained. Agricultural and industrial trade agreements, foreign exchange, money, and price are completely ignored.

{End Chapter 17}

Chapter 18: Cambridge capital controversy

The Cambridge capital debate, often known as "the capital controversy," is sometimes referred to as "the capital controversy." The term derives from the location of the principals involved in the controversy: Joan Robinson and Piero Sraffa of the University of Cambridge in England and Paul Samuelson and Robert Solow of the Massachusetts Institute of Technology in Cambridge, Massachusetts, United States dominated the dispute.

The English side is commonly referred to as "post-Keynesian," but some refer to it as "neo-Ricardian," while the Massachusetts side is referred to as "neoclassical.".

The vast majority of the argument is mathematical, however a few key aspects can be explained by reference to the aggregation problem. The criticism of neoclassical capital theory can be summed up by stating that the theory suffers from the fallacy of composition, i.e., we cannot apply microeconomic notions to the production of the entire society. Economists have not reached a consensus on the resolution of the dispute, in particular the scope of its ramifications.

If the real economic growth rate falls below the natural rate, then the unemployment rate will rise; if it climbs beyond the natural rate, then the unemployment rate will decline. Therefore, the natural rate of growth must be the growth rate that maintains the unemployment rate constant.

If the natural growth rate is not exogenously determined, but rather is endogenous to demand or the actual growth rate, this has two implications. The natural rate is viewed as strictly exogenous; it is shaped by the increase of the labor force and labor productivity, without recognizing or assuming that either could be demand-endogenous. In addition, the idea lacked any fiscal or other economic mechanism that might align the required rate of growth with the natural rate of growth, i.e., for society to reach full or greater utilization of its resources.

Central to the dispute between neoclassical and Keynesian/post-Keynesian economists is the question of whether the natural growth rate is exogenous or endogenous to demand (and whether input growth generates output growth, or vice versa). The latter group thinks that growth is essentially demand-driven because both labor force expansion and labor productivity growth respond to home and overseas demand pressure. Post-Keynesians assert that their view does not imply that demand growth determines supply growth without limit; rather, they assert that there is not a single, full-employment growth path and that, in many countries, demand constraints (related to excessive inflation and balance of payments issues) tend to emerge well before supply constraints are reached.

Roy Harrod, in his seminal paper, was a pioneer, Robert Solow developed the model separately and independently

Post-Keynesian economists including Nicholas Kaldor, Luigi Pasinetti, Richard Kahn, and Joan Robinson offered an alternative growth model. Adjustments to the income distribution are made in their method to bring the required growth rate into line with the natural growth rate. The rate of profits is the quotient of the rate of growth and the ratio of the savings rate out of profits, despite the fact that Kaldor and Pasinetti varied in their justifications. The name for this equation is the Cambridge equation. As in Keynes, investment is considered an independent variable, and savings adjust to investment.

The inability of the Harrod–Domar model to align the warranted growth rate with the natural growth rate sparked the growth debate in the mid-1950s, a dispute that "involved some of the brightest minds in the economics profession for nearly two decades." The neoclassical and Neo-Keynesian sides were represented by Paul Samuelson, Robert Solow, and Franco Modigliani, who taught at the Massachusetts Institute of Technology (MIT) in Cambridge, Massachusetts, while the Keynesian and Post-Keynesian sides were represented by Nicholas Kaldor, Joan Robinson, Luigi Pasinetti, Piero Sraffa, and Richard Kahn, who taught primarily at the University of Cambridge in England. The shared name of the two locations spawned the phrases "the two Cambridges debate" and "the Cambridge capital controversy."

In general, both groups accepted the natural rate of growth as a given. The vast majority of the discussion focussed on the potential processes by which the mandated growth rate may be made to converge on the natural rate, resulting in a long-term equilibrium growth path. The Cambridge team from the United States worked on adjusting the capital/output ratio through capital-labor substitution if capital and labor grew at different rates. The English Cambridge team focused on adjusting the saving ratio through changes in the distribution of income between wages and profits, based on the notion that the inclination to save from earnings is greater than from wages.

Much of the intensity of the disagreement stemmed from the fact that the technical criticisms of marginal productivity theory were linked to broader ideological considerations. John Bates Clark, a renowned neoclassical economist, viewed the equilibrium rate of profit (which serves to define the income of owners of capital goods) as a market price set by technology and the relative proportions in which "factors of production" are utilized. Profits are the compensation for the productive contributions of capital; therefore, the regular operations of the system under competitive conditions result in the payment of profits to the owners of capital. Clark wrote in response to the "indictment that hovers over society" that it exploits labor:

The goal of this work [his 1899 'Distribution of Wealth'] is to demonstrate that the distribution of a society's income is governed by a natural law, and that if this rule operated without friction, every agent of production would receive the amount of wealth that agent generates. It is asserted that the rates of pay that result from freely negotiated transactions between individual men tend to equal the proportion of the product of industry that is attributable to the labor itself, and that interest tends to equal the proportion of the product that is attributable to capita.

In turn, these earnings are viewed as rewards for saving, i.e. refraining from current consumption, which leads to the production of capital goods. Later,

John Maynard Keynes and his school claimed that saving did not necessarily result in the purchase of tangible capital assets. Therefore, according to this viewpoint, profit gain is a reward for people who place a high value on future revenue and are willing to forego current satisfaction. However, strictly speaking, modern neoclassical theory does not assert that the income of capital or labor is "earned" in a moral or ethical sense.

Even if the means of production "earning" a return based on their marginal product, this does not entail that their owners (i.e., capitalists) created the marginal product and should be compensated. According to Sraffians, the profit rate is not a price, and it is unclear whether it is established in a market. Specifically, it only partially represents the shortage of production means relative to their demand. While the prices of various types of means of production are prices, the profit rate can be viewed in Marxist terms as a reflection of the social and economic power that owning the means of production grants to a minority in order to exploit the majority of workers and earn profit. However, not all Sraffa followers interpret his theory of production and capital in this Marxist manner. Nor do all Marxists adopt the Sraffian paradigm; in fact, authors such as Michael Lebowitz and Frank Roosevelt are strongly dismissive of Sraffian interpretations, except as a technical critique of the neoclassical perspective. Marxian economists such as Michael Albert and Robin Hahnel believe that the Sraffian theory of prices, wages, and profits is preferable to Marx's own theory.

In neoclassical economics, for instance, a production function is frequently assumed,

$$Q = Af(K, L)$$

where Q represents, A is the technology-representing factor, K represents the total value of capital items, L represents the labor input.

The price of the homogeneous output is taken as the numéraire, so that the value of each capital good is considered equivalent to output.

Various types of labor are expected to be reduced to a single unit, typically unskilled work.

Both inputs contribute positively to output, with declining marginal yields.

In some of the neoclassical school's more intricate models of general equilibrium, labor and capital are supposed to be heterogeneous and quantified in physical units. In most versions of neoclassical growth theory, however (such as in the Solow growth model), it is assumed that the function applies to the entire economy. This approach depicts an economy as a single enormous factory rather than a collection of numerous diverse workplaces.

This perspective generates a central premise in neoclassical economics textbooks, namely, that the revenue produced by each "factor of production" (primarily labor and "capital") is equal to its marginal product. With perfect product and input markets, it is believed that the salary (divided by the price of the product) equals the marginal physical output of labor. The rate of profit (often mistaken with the rate of interest, i.e. the cost of borrowing funds) is expected to equal the marginal physical product of capital. (For brevity, "capital goods" is abbreviated as "capital.") A second fundamental tenet is that a change in the price of a factor of production will result in a change in the usage of that factor; a rise in the profit rate (related with falling wages) will result in a greater use of that factor in production. The law of diminishing marginal returns states that greater use of this input will result in a lower marginal product, all else being equal. Since a firm receives less from adding a unit of capital goods than it did from the previous unit, the profit rate must increase to encourage the employment of this additional unit, assuming profit maximization.

Piero Sraffa and Joan Robinson, whose research sparked the Cambridge dispute, noted that applying this model of income distribution to capital presented a measurement issue. Capitalist income (total profit or property income) is defined as the rate of profit multiplied by the amount of capital, however the measurement of "amount of capital" requires the addition of various tangible items, such as the number of trucks and lasers. Thus, just as it is impossible to add disparate "apples and oranges," we cannot simply add basic units of "capital." Robinson contended that there is no such thing as "leets," an inherent component of each capital commodity that can be added up apart from the pricing of those commodities.

Neoclassical economists assumed there was no actual issue in this situation. Inflation-adjusted sum of the monetary values of all capital items. But Sraffa noted that this financial measure of the amount of capital is somewhat affected by the profit rate. This is problematic since, according to neoclassical theory, this rate of profit should be dictated by the amount of capital employed. The argument is circular in nature. A declining profit rate has a direct impact on the amount of capital; it does not merely result in a larger utilization of capital.

Consider, for the sake of simplicity, that the existing capital consists of 10 trucks and 5 lasers. Each truck is manufactured and sold for $50,000, while each laser costs $30,000. Therefore, the worth of our capital is (price)*(quantity) = 10*$50,000 + 5*$30,000 = $650,000 = K.

As said, this K can alter as the profit rate increases. Define the cost of manufacturing for the two types of capital goods to demonstrate this. Follow the pricing rule employed by Classical economics for manufactured things, where price is determined by explicit manufacturing costs, for each item:

P = (labor cost per unit) plus (capital cost per unit) multiplied by P. (1 + r)

Here, P is the item's price and r is the profit margin. Assume that the factory owners are compensated in proportion to the amount of capital they invested in manufacturing (with the proportion being determined by the profit rate). Assume that the labor cost per unit in each sector equals W. (and does not change). r and W are supposed to be equalized across sectors due to competition, i.e. the mobility of capital and labor.

Notably, this classical understanding of pricing differs from the common neoclassical "supply and demand" perspective. It refers to price determination in the long run. It can be reconciled with neoclassical economics by assuming continuous returns to scale in production.

Additionally, this formulation does not consider the profit rate to be a price set by supply and demand. It is more consistent with neoclassical notions of "normal" earnings. These are the profits that capital owners must earn in order to remain competitive in their industry. Third, whereas neoclassical economics considers that the "normal" rate of profit is determined by aggregate output (as mentioned previously), this formulation assumes that the rate of profit is given exogenously. Because the entire neoclassical theory of profit-rate determination is being questioned: if we can go from the marginal product of capital to the profit rate, we should also be able to move in the opposite direction. In any case, few, if any, Cambridge Controversy participants attacked the Sraffian critique on these grounds.

Return to the pricing formula listed above. As in the real world, the capital intensity of production (cost of capital per unit) varies between sectors that produce various types of capital goods. Assume that producing trucks requires twice as much capital per unit of output as producing lasers, so that the capital cost per unit is \$20,000 for trucks (T) and \$10,000 for lasers (L), with the initial assumption that these coefficients will not change. Then, P_T = W + \$20,000*(1 + r)

P_L = W + \$10,000*(1 + r)

When W = \$10,000 and r = 1 = 100% (an extreme example used to illustrate the computations), then P_T = \$50,000 and P_L = \$30,000, as assumed.

As above, K = \$650,000.

Now, supposing r becomes zero (another extreme case).

Then P_T = \$30,000 and P_L = \$20,000, Thus, the value of the capital equals 10 times \$30,000 plus 5 times \$20,000, or \$400,000.

Therefore, the value of K fluctuates with the profit rate.

The exact consequence relies on the proportional "capital intensity" of the two sectors, unlike a general inflation or deflation that affects both prices by the same percentage.

This outcome is unaffected by the fact that the capital cost per unit for both items would fluctuate when the two prices change (contrary to the assumption made above). Neither does it alter if the pay rate or labor cost per unit (W) vary.

As with many inflation adjustments, it is also possible to aggregate capital by utilizing the first set of prices and disregarding the second. This does not work, however, because the variation of the profit rate is believed to occur at a precise point in time and in strictly mathematical terms, and not as part of a historical process. The point is that if neoclassical theories fail to operate at a particular moment (in statics), they cannot manage the more complex challenges of dynamics. This critique of the neoclassical perspective is primarily about highlighting the theory's significant technical faults than proposing an alternative.

In general, this debate indicates that the distribution of income (and r) contributes to the determination of the measured amount of capital, as opposed to being completely decided by this amount. In addition, it states that physical capital is heterogeneous and cannot be accumulated in the same manner as financial capital. For the latter, all units are measured in monetary terms, allowing for easy addition. Even yet, the cost of a sum of financial capital will vary with interest rates.

By reducing all machines to a sum of dated labor from different years, Sraffa proposed an aggregation method (inspired in part by Marxian economics) for calculating the amount of capital. A machine produced in the year 2000 can be treated as the labor and commodity inputs used to produce it in 1999 (multiplied by the profit rate); and the commodity inputs in 1999 can be further reduced to the labor inputs that made them in 1998 plus the commodity inputs (multiplied by the profit rate again); and so on, until the non-labor component was reduced to a negligible (but non-zero) amount. Then, the dated labor value of a vehicle may be added to the dated labor value of a laser.

However, Sraffa pointed out that this precise measuring technique still involved the profit rate: the amount of capital was dependent on the profit rate. This reversed the direction of causality assumed by neoclassical economics between profit rate and capital stock. In addition, Sraffa demonstrated that a change in the rate of profit would affect the measured amount of capital in highly nonlinear ways: an increase in the rate of profit could initially increase the perceived value of the truck more than that of the laser, but this effect would be reversed at higher rates of profit. Refer to "Resetting" below. Further, the study suggests that a more intensive use of a factor of production, including factors other than capital, may be associated with a higher rather than a lower price for that factor.

According to Cambridge, England, critics, this approach poses a significant challenge to the neoclassical picture of prices as measures of scarcity and the straightforward neoclassical version of the principle of substitution, particularly in factor markets.

The Classical pricing formulae are not required to comprehend the aggregation problem in a different approach. Consider a decline in r, the return on capital (corresponding to a rise in w, the wage rate, given that initial levels of capital and technology stay constant). This results in a change in the distribution of income, the demand for various capital products, and consequently their pricing. This results in a change in K's value (as discussed above). As the neoclassical model of growth and distribution assumes, the rate of return on K (i.e., r) is not independent of K's size. The direction of causality is both from K to r and r to K. This issue is sometimes compared to the Sonnenschein-Mantel-Debreu conclusions (e.g., Mas-Colell, 1989) in general equilibrium theory, which demonstrate that representative agent models cannot be theoretically justified under any circumstances (see Kirman, 1992 for an explanation of the Sonnenschein-Mantel-Debreu results as an aggregation problem). This indicates that not just K is prone to aggregation difficulties, but also L.

Many neoclassical economists assume that both individual enterprises (or sectors) and the overall economy conform to the Cobb–Douglas production function with constant returns on scale. In other words, the output of every sector I is specified by the equation:

$$Y_i = A_i . K_i^a . L_i^{1-a}$$

A is a constant (representing technology and the like), K is considered to represent the stock of capital goods (which is measurable), and L is the quantity of labor input. The coefficient an is intended to represent the sector's I technology. (Its subscript is omitted for simplicity.)

We cannot say that this Cobb–Douglas production function for sector I plus one for sector j (plus one for sector k, etc.) equals a Cobb–Douglas production function for the economy as a whole unless we impose very tight mathematical limits (with K and L being the sum of all of the different sectoral values). For the aggregate of Cobb–Douglas production functions to equal a Cobb–Douglas, all of the sectors' production functions must have the same A and a values.

Reswitching indicates that there is no simple (monotonic) correlation between the type of the production techniques employed and the profit rate. For instance, a production technique may be cost-minimizing at low and high profit rates, whereas another technique is cost-minimizing at intermediate profit rates.

Reswitching suggests the prospect of capital reversal, which is correlated with high interest rates (or profit rates) and capital-intensive processes. Thus, reswitching requires the rejection of a simple (monotonic) non-increasing relationship between capital intensity and the profit rate, also known as the interest rate. Profit-seeking enterprises, for instance, can switch from one set of strategies (A) to another (B) and then back to A as interest rates decline. This topic pertains to either a macroeconomic or a microeconomic production process, and so extends beyond the aggregation issues addressed previously.

The eminent neoclassical economist Paul A. Samuelson outlines the reswitching controversy in a 1966 paper:

"The phenomena of returning at a very low interest rate to a set of tactics that seemed possible only at a very high interest rate involves more than esoteric challenges.".

It demonstrates that Jevons's simple account was a lie, Böhm-Bawerk, According to Wicksell and other neoclassical authors,, As the interest rate reduces as a result of foregoing present expenditure in favor of future consumption, the rate of inflation rises, The statement "technology must grow more 'circular,''mechanized,' and 'productive' cannot be generally true." (A Conclusion, Quarterly Journal of Economics, volume. 80, 1966, p. 568.)

Samuelson provides an illustration involving both the Sraffian concept of new products made with labor employing capital goods represented by dead or "dated labor" (as opposed to machines having an independent role) and the "Austrian" concept of "roundaboutness" — supposedly a physical measure of capital intensity.

In lieu of assuming a neoclassical production function as a given, Samuelson follows the Sraffian tradition of deriving a production function from various means of producing a product. The proposed approaches feature distinct combinations of inputs. Given an externally set wage or profit rate, Samuelson demonstrates how profit maximization (cost minimization) identifies the optimal method of production. Through the use of a "surrogate production function," Samuelson ultimately rejects his previously held belief that heterogeneous capital might be considered as a single capital good, homogeneous with the consumption good.

Consider the "Austrian" approach of Samuelson. In his example, there are two approaches, A and B, that use labor at distinct times (−1, −2, and −3, signifying years in the past) to produce output of 1 unit at the later time 0 using labor at different times (−1, −2, and −3). (the present).

Then, using this example (and subsequent debate), Samuelson proves, according to Austrian statements, that it is difficult to determine the relative "circularity" of the two procedures as in this example. He demonstrates that a profit-maximizing business will utilize approach A when the profit rate is above 100 percent, technique B when the profit rate is between 50 and 100 percent, and strategy A again when the interest rate is below 50 percent. Extreme interest rates are used, but the phenomena of reswitching can be demonstrated using cases with more moderate interest rates.

The second table depicts three potential interest rates and the resulting total accumulated labor expenses for the two strategies. Since the advantages of both techniques are identical, we can simply compare their costs. The costs at time 0 are computed using traditional economic methodology, assuming that each unit of labor costs \$w to employ:

$$Cost = (1+i)w.\,L_{-1} + (1+i)^2w.\,L_{-2} + (1+i)^3w.\,L_{-3}+\ldots+(1+i)^nw.\,L_{-n}$$

where L_{-n} is the amount of labor input in time n previous to time 0.

The findings in boldface represent the less expensive technique, demonstrating switching. At either the macroeconomic or microeconomic level of aggregation, there is no straightforward (monotonic) relationship between the interest rate and the "capital intensity" or indirectness of output.

Obviously, the two competing schools reach different conclusions about this argument. It is advantageous to cite some of these.

Here are the opinions of various Cambridge critics::

"The neoclassical concepts of input substitution and capital or labor scarcity are rendered meaningless by capital reversing. It threatens the neoclassical theory of capital and the concept of input demand curves at both the national and industry levels. It also jeopardizes neoclassical theories of output and employment determination, as well as Wicksellian monetary theories, because stability is compromised. Thus, the implications for neoclassical analysis are severe. Capital reversal is commonly believed to influence primarily aggregate neoclassical theory of the textbook form, and thus macroeconomic theory based on aggregate production functions. However, when neoclassical general equilibrium models are extended to long-run equilibria, stability proofs need the absence of capital reversals (Schefold 1997). Capital reversal would influence all neoclassical production models in this regard." (Lavoisier, 2000)

"These findings destroy the general validity of Heckscher-Ohlin-Samuelson international trade theory (as demonstrated by authors such as Sergio Parrinello, Stanley Metcalfe, Ian Steedman, and Lynn Mainwaring), of the Hicksian neutrality of technical progress concept (as demonstrated by Steedman), of neoclassical tax incidence theory (as demonstrated by

Steedman and Metcalfe), and of the Pigouvian taxation theory applied in environmental economic (2000) Gehrke and Lager

Christopher Bliss, a neoclassical economist, provides commentary:

"...what can be termed the existential side of capital theory has not garnered much attention over the past quarter-century.".

A small band of 'true believers' has kept up the assault on capital theory orthodoxy until today, At least one of my co-editors is a member of their organization.

I will refer to this loosely linked school as the Anglo-Italian theorists.

No simple moniker is perfect, However, the one I've chosen suggests at the very least that Piero Sraffa and Joan Robinson were influential, in particular, are fundamentally important.

Even in that circumstance, A scent of necrophilia pervades the air.

If one asks, what new ideas have emerged from Anglo-Italian thought in the past two decades?, One creates an awkward social circumstance.

This is because it is unclear whether anything novel has resulted from the old, bitter debates.

In the meantime, mainstream theory has moved in numerous directions. The focus has turned away from general equilibrium-style (high-dimensional) models and towards simplified, primarily one-good models. Models of dynamic optimization in the style of Ramsey have essentially supplanted the fixed-saving-coefficient method. The numerous consumers that Stiglitz introduced into neoclassical growth models did not thrive. Typically, the representative agent is now the driver of the model. The exogenous technical progress of Harrod and the majority of writers on growth from any school in the 1960s and after has been joined by numerous models that make technical development endogenous in one of a variety of ways.

Can outdated concerns about capital be dusted off and applied to contemporary models? If this were possible, one would expect that its contribution would be more constructive than the approach of mutually assured annihilation that dominated some debates in the 1960s. Clearly, richer models produce richer possibilities. When optimization drives model solutions, proportions are not maintained. However, we know that when all agents optimize, many-agent models can have numerous equilibria. There may be productive routes in that direction.

Old contributions that involve utilizing capital as a club to attack marginal theory should be buried. All optimums imply some type of marginal conditions. These circumstances are a component of the solution as a whole. Neither they nor the quantities they entail are preceding the total solution. It reflects poorly on economists and their intellectual acuity that this was not always clear." 2005, from Bliss

In his 1975 book Capital Theory and the Distribution of Income, Bliss demonstrated that in general equilibrium, relative scarcity and relative pricing are unrelated. Nonetheless, each factor's return remains equal to its disaggregated marginal production.

The high level of abstraction and idealization that occurs in the development of economic models for topics such as capital and economic growth contributed to this discussion. The initial neoclassical models of aggregate growth developed by Robert Solow and Trevor Swan were simplistic, with uncomplicated results and conclusions that implied predictions about the actual, empirical world. The adherents of Robinson and Sraffa contended that more complex mathematical models showed that for the Solow–Swan model to convey anything about the reality, key unrealistic assumptions (which Solow and Swan had overlooked) must be true.

To pick an example that did not garner much attention during the argument (since it was shared by both sides), the Solow–Swan model presupposes 'full employment' of all resources and continuous equilibrium. Contrary to Keynesian economics, under these models saving determines investment (rather than vice versa). It was quite impossible to do anything other than 'criticize' Solow and Swan due to the fact that their criticism was likewise based totally on the same type of erroneous assumptions. In other words, Sraffian models were consciously detached from empirical fact. And, as is typical in discussions, it was much simpler to dismantle neoclassical theory than to build a comprehensive alternative that can help us comprehend the reality.

In short, the Cambridge Controversy resulted in a shift from an unrealistic dependence on unsaid or unknown assumptions to a clear awareness of the necessity to make such assumptions. However, this left the Sraffians in a position where the unreal assumptions hindered the majority of empirical applications and further theoretical development. It is therefore not unexpected that Bliss asks, "What new notion has emerged from Anglo-Italian thought in the past two decades?"

Even though Sraffa, Robinson, and others have argued against its underpinnings, the Solow–Swan growth model based on a single-valued aggregate stock of capital goods has remained a cornerstone of neoclassical macroeconomics and growth theory. It also serves as the foundation for the "new growth theory." In some instances, the use of an aggregate production function is supported by an appeal to instrumentalist technique and the requirement for simplicity in empirical study.

Neoclassical thinkers, such as Bliss (mentioned below), have usually accepted the "Anglo-Italian" critique of the simple neoclassical model and have moved on to apply the "more general" political-economic vision of neoclassical economics to new challenges. Some theorists, such as Bliss, Edwin Burmeister, and Frank Hahn, felt that microeconomics and intertemporal general equilibrium models are the best way to provide rigorous neoclassical theory.

The critics, including Pierangelo Garegnani (2008), Fabio Petri (2009), and Bertram Schefold (2005), have consistently claimed that such models are not practically applicable and that the capital-theoretical difficulties reemerge in such models under a different guise. The abstract character of these models has made it more difficult to highlight these issues as clearly as they do in long-term models.

Since Samuelson was one of the most prominent neoclassical defenders of the notion that heterogeneous capital could be treated as a single capital good, his article (discussed above) demonstrated conclusively that results from simplified models with a single capital good do not necessarily apply to more general models. Thus, he predominantly employs multisectoral models of the Leontief-Sraffian tradition as opposed to the neoclassical aggregate model.

Most neoclassicals just disregard the dispute, and many are unaware of its existence. In fact, the vast majority of graduate economics programs in the United States do not teach it:

"It is crucial to note, for the record, that significant debate participants freely recognized their errors. Errors were eliminated from the seventh edition of Economics by Samuelson. Levhari and Samuelson issued a paper with the introduction, "We desire to make it obvious that the nonreswitching theorem linked with us is demonstrably untrue." We appreciate Dr. Pasinetti...' (1966, Levhari and Samuelson). I collaborated with Leland Yeager to issue a message recognizing his previous error and attempting to reconcile the conflict between our theoretical ideas. (1978, Burmeister and Yeager).

Levhari was incorrect, Samuelson was wrong, Solow was wrong, MIT was wrong, and consequently neoclassical economics was wrong. Consequently, some economists have abandoned neoclassical economics in favor of their own classical economics modifications. In contrast, mainstream economics in the United States continues as if the dispute never occurred. In macroeconomics textbooks, 'capital' is discussed as if it were a well-defined notion, when it is not, especially in a world with only one capital good (or under other unrealistically restrictive conditions). The challenges of heterogeneous capital goods have also been neglected by the "rational expectations revolution" and almost all econometric research. (1900's Burmeister)

{End Chapter 18}

Chapter 19: Socially necessary labour time

Marx's critique of political economy holds that it is socially necessary labor time that controls the market value of goods traded and, as a result, restrains producers' efforts to reduce labor costs. They are not "guided" by it because it can only be known after the fact and is therefore not available for planning ahead.

Marx's exchange value is conceptualized as a percentage (or "aliquot part") of society's labor-time, in contrast to the classical labour theory of value developed by Adam Smith and David Ricardo, which viewed individual labor hours as the basis for value.

Marx did not describe this idea in words that were mathematically precise, allowing for flexibility in its application to relate average levels of labor productivity to societal demands that present themselves as commercially viable market demand for commodities in particular circumstances. Furthermore, despite the fact that it is axiomatic that socially necessary labor input determines commodity values, precise numerical calculation of such an input in relation to the value of a specific commodity, i.e. the empirical regulation of the values of different types of commodities, is incredibly challenging because of the constantly changing social, physical, or technological circumstances affecting the labor process.

Labor costs for generating outputs and market demand for those outputs constantly adjust to one another in a market economy. As the total market demand for their products expands and contracts, businesses with varied levels of productivity and unit costs compete with one another in this complicated process. Marx examines how a commodity's market value (or "regulating price") may be established under various demand and productivity situations in the third volume of Das Kapital.

A certain amount of new value is created in a certain amount of time, but the final determination of whether and how this new value will be realized in monetary terms and divided as income and reinvestment will not be made until after goods have been sold at a certain market price. When a commodity's market is oversupplied, more labor has been put into producing it than was socially necessary, which lowers its exchange value. A commodity's exchange value increases if the market is undersupplied, which means that less labor was used to produce it than was socially necessary.

The simplest way to define socially necessary labor time is the amount of time it takes a worker with average ability and productivity to produce a given good using instruments with average potential for productivity. This "average unit labor cost" is calculated based on working hours.

If a worker produces a commodity on average in one hour while a worker with lower skill levels produces the same commodity in four hours, then the less skilled worker has only contributed one hour's worth of value in terms of socially essential labor time over those four hours. Unskilled labor only contributes a fourth of what the average worker does in one hour to society.

However, the creation of any good or service typically includes both labor and certain capital products, such as tools and materials, that have already been produced. The quantity of labor needed in this way is referred to as the direct labor input into the commodity. However, in the past, labor and other capital goods were used to manufacture the necessary capital goods, and so on and so forth for these other capital goods. The total quantity of labor that was a direct input into this line of historically produced capital goods is referred to as the indirect labor input into the commodity. The entire labor input into the commodity, also known as the total embodied labor in it or its direct and indirect labour contents, is obtained by adding together the direct and indirect labor inputs.

Marx, however, refers particularly to the whole amount of labor-time that is currently, on average, needed to produce an output when he uses the phrase "socially necessary labor." The value of the output is determined by the current labor cost. Therefore, Marx's exchange value in a mature market refers to the typical amount of live labor required to manufacture a good under the current economic climate. The quality of labor, the quality of machinery, the quality of distribution, and the volumes of labor, machinery, and sales in the branch are all constantly changing, thus predicting "present" requirements is mostly an exercise in approximation and depends on the scales used.

When selling their products at the current market pricing, producers who manufacture goods at labor costs below the social average make an additional profit, while those who do so at labor costs above the average suffer a corresponding loss. Therefore, there is a continuing motivation to increase labor force productivity in order to decrease labor expenses.

This can be accomplished by increasing exploitation, cutting costs, and using improved equipment. The long-term result is that producing a commodity requires progressively less labor. Because these costs are almost never within an organization's control, businesses typically are powerless to significantly reduce their fixed input costs. However, they can always attempt to lower their labor costs.

Therefore, "socially essential labor" refers to at least three different types of economic interactions:

between a producer's individual productivity and the branch's average productivity; between the branch of production's products and social demands represented by economically viable demand; and

between a producer's output and the output of the entire branch (that can be sold).

To put it another way, we must discern between

Particular that a commodity is a bearer of exchange value, the amount of labor required to produce a given amount of a commodity determines the output's total value; The amount of labor time deemed socially necessary to produce the proper amount of a good, that is, the amount of a good that, at its production price, satisfies the effective demand for it, defines the correspondence between the total amount of a good produced as use-values and the effective demand for those use-values.

The difference between real supply and effective demand, which determines the unit value of commodities and, consequently, their production price, is determined by the latter. This difference then causes the difference between market price and production price.

Economic value, often known as exchange value, is regarded by Marxist value theory as a property of labor-products and commodities that results from social relations of production in the capitalist mode of production. Value is therefore entirely a social attribute of goods. A specific amount of social labor makes up the core of a commodity's worth.

To put it another way, social relationships between members of an organized society are necessary for the existence of exchange value. The phrase "socially necessary labor time" captures this crucial "relatedness" of value; rather than simply being labor that is performed, it is labor that is evaluated in connection to social demands.

Although it distinguishes Marx from other political economists, this point is frequently missed in discussions of Marx's value theory. In later editions and the Afterword to the Second German Edition, Marx exhorts readers to pay close attention to the mediations between the Ricardian category and the one his own theory sought to establish. Marx was aware that the casual reader might mistakenly treat his category as interchangeable with its Ricardian predecessor. Marx did not intend for his idea of value to represent an equilibrium price. Instead of assuming market equilibrium, he seeks to explain how the process of supply and demand convergence actually works, or why supply and demand collide at a specific price point when a sale is made in a particular market.

Many critics found Marx's conception of value from the standpoint of society as a whole to be obscure. In a letter to his friend Dr. Louis Kugelmann, Marx made an effort to respond to them:

"All that blather about having to demonstrate the concept of worth stems from a total lack of understanding of the topic at hand as well as the scientific process. Every child is aware that a country would perish if it stopped functioning—not for a year, but merely for a week. Every youngster is also aware that distinct and quantifiably determined masses of the total labor of society are needed to produce the masses of goods corresponding to various wants. It goes without saying that a specific type of social production cannot possible eliminate the necessity of the distribution of social labor in specific proportions; it can only alter the manner in which it manifests itself. No natural rule can be abolished. Only the manner in which these rules assert themselves can change under historically distinct conditions. In a state of society where the interconnection of social labor is expressed in the private exchange of the individual products of labor, the form in which this proportional distribution of labor asserts itself is precisely the exchange value of these products. "Where science comes in is to show how the law of value asserts itself."

Marxian economics has a disagreement over whether product values generated and traded just correspond to current average production costs or whether they also take into account direct and indirect labor (or the value of current average replacement costs).

For instance, Marx is charged by Mirowski (1989) of vacillating between a field theory (labor time currently required by society) and a substance theory of value (embodied labour-time). This type of critique results from the conflation of the task of calculating the exchange value added with the overall labor process (adding use to a product, which under capitalism translates to adding value to a commodity). The basic process attaches labor time to a product, and as long as the commodity performs as intended, the quantity of labor time is irrelevant—in a sense, an abstract unknown—and can be stated in a variety of ways, such as "embodied in," "attached to," "related with," etc. Focusing on the social, mutable nature of socially essential labor and explicitly acknowledging that the quantities are 'current,' that is, constantly changing, are both necessary when attempting to quantify the amount of labor time related with commodities. The amount of value can only be calculated numerically based on a single point in time at which values are realized concurrently at particular prices since today's value is different from yesterday's and tomorrow's.

Marx's theory is therefore best understood as a field theory, but for the reasons already mentioned, it is difficult, if not certainly impossible, to mathematically represent the determination of value by socially necessary labor time.

{End Chapter 19}

Chapter 20: Surplus value

Marxian economic theory, The difference between the amount raised from the sale of a product and the cost to manufacture it is the surplus value. i.e. The amount raised through product sales minus the cost of materials, plants and manpower.

The origin of the concept is Ricardian socialism, William Thompson first coined the term "surplus value" in 1824; however, It was not differentiated consistently from the related concepts of surplus labor and surplus product.

Karl Marx subsequently developed and popularized the concept.

Marx's formulation is the standard interpretation and primary foundation for subsequent developments, though how much of Marx's concept is original and distinct from the Ricardian concept is disputed (see § Origin).

Marx's term is "Mehrwert" (German), which literally means added value (sales revenue minus the cost of materials used up), and is cognizant with English "more valuable".

It is a central concept in the political economy critique of Karl Marx. Value-added is traditionally equal to the sum of gross wage income and gross profit income. Marx, on the other hand, uses the term Mehrwert to refer to the yield, profit, or return on production capital invested, i.e., the amount of the capital's value increase. Therefore, Marx's use of Mehrwert has always been rendered as "surplus value" to differentiate it from "value added." According to Marx's theory, surplus value corresponds to the new value created by workers in excess of their own labor costs, which is appropriated by capitalists as profit when products are sold. Marx believed that the enormous growth in wealth and population from the 19th century onwards was primarily the result of a competitive drive to extract maximum surplus-value from the employment of labor, resulting in an equally enormous growth in productivity and capital resources. To the extent that the economic surplus is increasingly convertible into money and expressed in money, wealth accumulation on a larger and larger scale is possible (see capital accumulation and surplus product). The notion is closely associated with producer surplus.

In the 18th century, during the Age of Enlightenment, French physiocrats were already writing about the surplus value extracted from labor by "the employer, the owner, and all exploiters" despite using the term net product. Adam Smith, who also used the term "net product," continued to develop the concept of surplus value, while his successors, the Ricardian socialists, began using the term "surplus value" decades after its coinage by William Thompson in 1824.

Here, there are two measures of the value of this use: the measure of the laborer and the measure of the capitalist. The measure of the laborer is the contribution of such sums as would replace the waste and value of the capital by the time it would be consumed, with such additional compensation to the capital's owner and manager as would allow him to live in the same level of comfort as the more actively employed productive laborers. The measure of the capitalist, on the other hand, would be the additional value produced by the same quantity of labor due to the use of machinery or other capital, with the entire surplus value being enjoyed by the capitalist as a reward for his superior intelligence and skill in accumulating and advancing to the laborers his capital or the use of it.

— William Thompson, *An Inquiry into the Principles of the Distribution of Wealth (1824)*, p.

128 (2nd ed.), *emphasis added*

William Godwin and Charles Hall are also credited as the concept's early developers. In Marxian economics, the terms "surplus labor" and "surplus produce" (in Marx's terminology, surplus product) have distinct meanings: surplus labor produces surplus product, which has surplus value. Some authors, including Anton Menger, consider Marx to have completely borrowed from Thompson:

... Marx is completely influenced by the earlier English socialists, and especially by William Thompson.... The entire theory of surplus value, its conception, its name, and the estimates of its amounts are taken from Thompson's writings.

Compare Marx, Das Kapital, English translation, 1887, pages 156, 194, and 289, with Thompson, Distribution of Wealth, pages 163 and 125 of the second edition. Godwin, Hall, and especially W. Thompson are the true founders of the theory of surplus value.

— Anton Menger, *The Right to the Whole Produce of Labour (1886)*, p. 101

This claim of priority has been vigorously contested, most notably in an article by Friedrich Engels, completed by Karl Kautsky, and published anonymously in 1887 in response to and criticism of Menger's The Right to the Whole Produce of Labour, arguing that the only similarity is the term "surplus value".

Marx's original contribution is his explanation of how surplus value is created.

— John Spargo, *Socialism (1906)*

In the 1830s and 1840s, Johann Karl Rodbertus developed a theory of surplus value, notably in Zur Erkenntnis unserer staatswirthschaftlichen Zustände (Toward an appreciation of our economic circumstances, 1842), and claimed precedence over Marx, to have specifically "shown practically the same as Marx", only more concisely and explicitly, "the source of the capitalists' surplus value".

The debate, advocating for Marx's priority, is described in the Introduction to Capital, Volume II authored by Engels.

Following earlier developments in his 1840s writings, Marx first elaborated his theory of surplus value in 1857–58 drafts of A Contribution to the Critique of Political Economy (1859). It is the topic of his 1862–1863 manuscript Theories of Surplus Value, which was subsequently published as Capital, Volume IV, and is also discussed in Capital, Volume I. (1867).

Friedrich Engels expressed as follows the difficulty of explaining the source of surplus value::

"Where does this surplus value originate? It cannot result from either the buyer purchasing the goods below their value or the seller selling them above their value. In both instances, the gains and losses of each individual cancel each other out, as each individual acts as buyer and seller in turn. Even though cheating can enrich one person at the expense of another, it cannot increase the total amount possessed by both parties, and thus cannot increase the total value in circulation. (...) This problem must be solved, and it must be solved in a purely economic manner, excluding all cheating and the use of force — the problem being: how is it possible to continually sell for more than one has purchased, even if equal values are always exchanged for equal values?"

Marx's solution consisted of first differentiating between labor-time worked and labor power, and then between absolute surplus value and relative surplus value. A worker who is sufficiently productive can generate an output value that exceeds his hiring cost. Despite the fact that his salary appears to be based on hours worked, in an economic sense, it does not reflect the full value of what he produces. Effectively, the worker does not sell labor, but rather his ability to work.

Consider a worker who is hired for an hourly wage of $10. Once a worker is employed by a capitalist, the capitalist can have him operate a machine that produces $10 worth of work every 15 minutes. Each hour, the capitalist receives $40 worth of labor but pays the worker only $10, pocketing the remaining $30 in gross income. After deducting fixed and variable operating costs of (say) $20 (leather, machine depreciation, etc.), the capitalist is left with $10. Thus, for a capital expenditure of $30, the capitalist receives a surplus value of $10; his capital has not only been replaced, but also increased by $10.

This "simple" exploitation characterizes the capitalist's acquisition of absolute surplus value. This benefit cannot be captured directly by the worker because he has no claim to the means of production (e.g., the boot-making machine) or its products, and his ability to bargain over wages is constrained by laws and supply/demand for wage labor. This form of exploitation was well understood by pre-Marxist Socialists and left-wing followers of Ricardo, such as Proudhon, as well as by early labor organizers, who sought to unite workers in unions capable of collective bargaining to gain a share of profits and limit the length of the working day.

The creation of relative surplus value does not occur in a single enterprise or location of production. It derives from the total relationship between multiple enterprises and multiple branches of industry when the required labor-time of production is decreased, resulting in a change in the value of labor-power. When new technology or business practices increase the productivity of labor a capitalist already employs, or when the commodities necessary for workers' subsistence fall in value, the amount of socially necessary labor-time is decreased, the value of labor-power is decreased, and a relative surplus value is realized as profit for the capitalist, thereby increasing the overall general rate of surplus value in the total economy.

I refer to the surplus value produced by extending the working day as absolute surplus value. On the other hand, I refer to relative surplus-value as the surplus-value resulting from the reduction of necessary labor-time and the corresponding change in the lengths of the two components of the working day.

In order to cause a decline in the value of labor,, Increases in labor productivity must target those industrial sectors whose products determine the value of labor-power, and therefore either belong to the category of customary means of subsistence;, or are capable of substituting for those means.

However, the value of a commodity is established, not only by the amount of labor that the worker directly contributes to that commodity, however also by the labor contained within the means of production.

For instance, the value of a pair of boots depends not only on the cobbler's labour, but also on the leather's value, wax, thread, &c.

Hence, An increase in the productiveness of labor also contributes to a decline in the value of labor, ...and by a corresponding depreciation of goods in those industries that provide the tools of labor and the raw materials, that constitute the material components of the constant capital required to produce life's necessities.

— *Marx, Capital Vol. 1, ch. 12, "The Concept of Relative Surplus-Value"*

Marx refers to the mass or volume of surplus-value. Total surplus-value in an economy is roughly equal to the sum of net distributed and undistributed profit, net interest, net rents, net tax on production, and various net receipts associated with royalties, licensing, leasing, etc (see also value product). Obviously, the manner in which generic profit income is grossed and netted in social accounting may differ somewhat from that of a specific business (see also Operating surplus).

Marx's own discussion focuses primarily on profit, interest, and rent, largely ignoring taxation and royalty-type fees, which were very small proportional components of the national income during his lifetime. However, over the past 150 years, the role of the state in almost every country's economy has increased. Around 1850, the average share of government spending in GDP (See also Government spending) in advanced capitalist economies was around 5 percent; in 1870, it was slightly above 8 percent; on the eve of World War I, it was just under 10 percent; just prior to the outbreak of World War II, it was around 20 percent; by 1950, it was nearly 30 percent; and today, the average is between 35 and 40 percent. (for instance, see Alan Turner Peacock, "The growth of public expenditure," in Encyclopedia of Public Choice, Springer, 2003, pp. 594–597).

Surplus-value can be viewed in five different ways:

As a component of the new value product, which Marx defines as the sum of labor costs relative to capitalistically productive labor (variable capital) and surplus-value. In production, workers produce a value equal to their wages plus an additional value, the surplus-value, according to his argument. In addition, they transfer a portion of the value of fixed assets and raw materials to the new product, which is equal to economic depreciation (consumption of fixed capital) and intermediate goods consumed (constant capital inputs). Labor costs and surplus value are the monetary valuations of what Marx refers to as the necessary product and the surplus product, also known as paid labor and unpaid labor.

In addition, surplus value can be viewed as a flow of net income appropriated by the owners of capital by virtue of asset ownership, which includes both distributed personal income and undistributed business income. This will include both income directly from production and property income for the entire economy.

Surplus-value can be viewed as the source of a society's accumulation fund or investment fund; a portion of it is re-invested, but a portion is appropriated as personal income and used for consumption by the owners of capital assets (see capital accumulation); in exceptional cases, a portion of it may also be hoarded. In this context, surplus value can also be measured as the increase in the stock value of capital assets during an accounting period prior to distribution.

Surplus-value can be viewed as a social relation of production or as the monetary valuation of surplus-labour – a sort of "index" of the power balance between social classes or nations in the process of dividing the social product.

In a developed capitalist economy, surplus value can also be viewed as an indicator of the level of social productivity attained by the working population, i.e. the net amount of value the working population can produce with its labor in excess of its own consumption needs.

Marx believed that the long-term historical trend would be for disparities in the rates of surplus value between enterprises and economic sectors to level off, as he explains in two places in Volume 3 of Capital:

"If capitals that mobilize unequal quantities of living labour produce unequal amounts of surplus-value, this assumes that the level of exploitation of labour, or the rate of surplus-value, is the same, at least to some extent, or that the distinctions that exist here are balanced by real or imagined (conventional) grounds of compensation. This presupposes competition among workers and an equalization brought about by their constant migration between production spheres. Assume a general rate of surplus value of this type, as a tendency, like all economic laws, as a theoretical simplification; however, this is in practice an actual premise of the capitalist mode of production, even if inhibited to varying degrees by practical frictions that produce more or less significant local differences, such as the settlement laws for agricultural laborers in England. We assume in theory that the laws of the capitalist mode of production evolve in their purest form. In reality, this is only an approximation; however, the more the capitalist mode of production is developed and the fewer remnants of earlier economic conditions it incorporates, the more accurate this approximation becomes."

– Capital, volume 3, chapter 10, Pelican edition, page 275.

Consequently, he assumed a uniform surplus value rate in his models of surplus value distribution under competitive conditions.

Marx asserts, both in Das Kapital and in preparatory manuscripts such as the Grundrisse and Results of the immediate process of production, that commerce by stages transforms a non-capitalist production process into a capitalist production process by fully integrating it into markets, so that all inputs and outputs become marketed goods or services. According to Marx, when this process is complete, the entirety of production is simultaneously a labor process that creates use-values and a valorisation process that creates new value, and more specifically a surplus-value appropriated as net income (see also capital accumulation).

Marx argues that in this situation, the entire purpose of production is the growth of capital, i.e., the production of output is contingent on capital accumulation. Eventually, capital will be withdrawn from production if it becomes unprofitable.

The implication is that the primary driving force of capitalism is the quest to maximize the appropriation of surplus value that increases the capital stock. Thus, the driving force behind efforts to conserve resources and labor would be to achieve the greatest possible increase in income and capital assets ("business growth") and to provide a stable or rising return on investment.

According to Marx, absolute surplus value is generated by increasing the number of hours worked per worker during a given accounting period. Marx focuses primarily on the length of the working day or week, whereas the modern concern is the number of hours worked per year.

As productivity increased in many parts of the world, the workweek decreased from 60 hours to 50, 40, or 35 hours.

Principally, relative surplus value is obtained by:

If wages fall below the ability of workers to purchase their means of subsistence, they will be unable to reproduce and capitalists will be unable to find sufficient labor force.

reducing the cost of wage-goods through a variety of means in order to curb wage increases.

Mechanisation and rationalisation increase the productivity and intensity of labor in general, resulting in a greater output per hour worked.

According to Marx, the attempt to extract ever-increasing surplus-value from labor, on the one hand, and the resistance to this exploitation, on the other, are at the heart of the conflict between social classes, which is sometimes muted or concealed, but sometimes erupts into open class warfare and class struggle.

Marx made a clear distinction between value and price, in part because he makes a clear distinction between the production of surplus-value and the realization of profit income (see also value-form). Producing output with surplus value (valorization) is possible, but selling that output (realization) is not at all an automatic process.

It is uncertain, until payment from sales is received, how much of the surplus value produced will be realized as profit from sales. Consequently, the magnitude of profit realized in the form of money and the magnitude of surplus-value produced in the form of goods can vary considerably, depending on market price fluctuations and the vagaries of supply and demand. This insight is the foundation of Marx's theory of market value, prices of production, and the tendency of competition to level out the profit rates of different businesses.

Marx examined in great detail, in his published and unpublished manuscripts, a variety of factors that could affect the production and realization of surplus value. This, he believed, was essential for comprehending the dynamics and dimensions of capitalist competition, including not only business competition but also competition between capitalists and workers and competition among workers themselves. However, his analysis did not go much further than specifying some of the process's overall outcomes.

His main conclusion, however, is that employers will seek to maximize the productivity of labor and minimise the use of labor in order to reduce their unit costs and maximize their net returns from sales at current market prices; at a given prevailing market price for a given output, every decrease in costs and increase in productivity and sales turnover will increase profit income for that output. The primary technique is mechanisation, which increases the fixed capital expenditure in investment.

In turn, this causes the unit-values of commodities to decline over time, as well as a decline in the average rate of profit in the sphere of production, culminating in a crisis of capital accumulation, in which a sharp reduction in productive investments combines with mass unemployment, followed by an intensive rationalisation process of takeovers, mergers, and fusions aimed at restoring profitability.

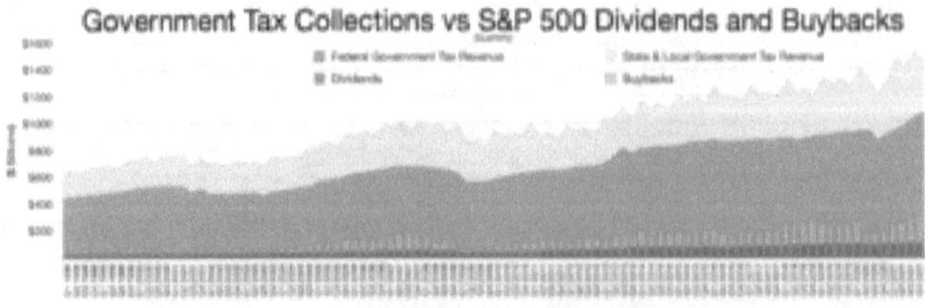

S&P 500 dividends and buybacks vs.

Federal and State tax revenue State tax income Federal tax income S&P 500 Stock repurchase S&P 500 Stock Dividends

In general, business leaders and investors oppose any attempts to reduce total profit volume, particularly those involving government taxation. If all else is equal, the lower taxes are, the greater the amount of profit that can be distributed to private investors. At the beginning of the capitalist era, tax revolts acted as a powerful impetus for the bourgeoisie to seize state power from the feudal aristocracy.

In reality, a significant portion of tax dollars are also redistributed to the private sector through government contracts and subsidies. Due to the fact that what is a cost to some capitalists is a source of profit to others, there may be internal conflict regarding taxes. Marx never analyzed this in detail; however, the concept of surplus value will primarily apply to taxes on gross income (personal and business income from production) and on the exchange of goods and services. Infrequently, estate duty contains a surplus value component, despite the possibility of estate transfer profits.

Marx appears to have viewed taxation imposts as a "form" that concealed true product values. Ernest Mandel, in his 1960 treatise Marxist Economic Theory, refers to (indirect) taxes as "arbitrary additions to commodity prices," apparently echoing this view. This, however, is somewhat of a misnomer, as it disregards the fact that taxes become an integral part of the production cost structure. In his later treatise on late capitalism, Mandel astonishingly makes no mention of the significance of taxation, a glaring omission from the perspective of the real world of contemporary capitalism, where taxes can amount to a third or even half of GDP (see E. Mandel, Late Capitalism. London: Verso, 1975). In the United Kingdom, for example, 75 percent of all tax revenue is derived from just three taxes. In reality, 75% of the country's GDP is derived from income tax, national insurance, and value-added tax.

Marx's Das Kapital focuses primarily on the surplus value created by production and its distribution. Thus, he intended to explain the "origin of national wealth" given a capitalist mode of production. In any real economy, however, a distinction must be made between the primary and secondary capital circuits. In some measure, national accounts also accomplish this.

The primary circuit refers to the incomes and goods distributed as a result of productive activity (reflected by GDP). Secondary circuits refer to trade, transfers, and transactions that occur outside this sphere and can also generate incomes; these incomes may also involve the realization of a surplus value or profit.

Marx's contention that no net additions to value can be created through acts of exchange is accurate; economic value is a property of labor-products (previous or newly created). Nonetheless, trading activity outside the realm of production can obviously also generate a surplus-value, which represents a transfer of value from one individual, nation, or institution to another.

A simple illustration would be if someone sold a used asset for a profit. Despite the fact that this transaction is not recorded in gross product measurements (since it is not new production), a surplus-value is obtained from it. Another illustration would be capital gains from the sale of real estate. Marx sometimes refers to this type of profit as profit upon alienation, where alienation is used in the legal sense and not the sociological sense. By implication, the total surplus-values realized as income in a country would be understated if we only considered surplus-values newly created in production. This is evident when comparing census estimates of income and expenditure to GDP figures.

This is another reason why surplus-value produced and surplus-value realized are distinct concepts, despite the fact that this distinction is largely overlooked in the economics literature. But when the real growth of production stagnates and a growing portion of capital shifts out of the realm of production in search of surplus-value from other transactions, it becomes of paramount importance.

Marxian economists such as Samir Amin conclude that surplus-value realized from commercial trade (representing to a large extent a transfer of value by intermediaries between producers and consumers) grows faster than surplus-value realized directly from production due to the fact that the volume of world trade is growing significantly faster than GDP.

Consequently, if we took the final price of a good (the cost to the final consumer) and analyzed the cost structure of that good, we might discover that, over time, the direct producers earn less and the intermediaries between producers and consumers (traders) earn more. In other words, control over the access to a good, asset, or resource as such may become an increasingly crucial factor in creating surplus value. In the worst-case scenario, this constitutes parasitism or extortion. This analysis illustrates a key characteristic of surplus value, namely that it is only accumulated by capital owners in inefficient markets, as only inefficient markets — i.e., those with low levels of transparency and competition — have sufficient profit margins to facilitate capital accumulation. Ironically, profitable – meaning inefficient – markets have trouble meeting the definition of a free market because a free market is in part defined as an efficient market: one in which goods or services are exchanged without coercion or fraud, or in other words, with competition (to prevent monopolistic coercion) and transparency (to prevent fraud).

Marx attempted to measure the rate of surplus-value in monetary units for the first time in chapter 9 of Das Kapital, utilizing factory data from a spinning mill provided by Friedrich Engels (though Marx credits "a Manchester spinner"). Marx examines in detail, in both published and unpublished manuscripts, variables affecting the rate and mass of surplus-value.

Marx, according to some Marxian economists, believed that the possibility of measuring surplus value depends on publicly available data. We can develop statistical indicators of trends without conflating data with the actual phenomenon they represent or postulating "perfect measurements or perfect data" in an empiricist fashion.

Since early studies by Marxian economists such as Eugen Varga, Charles Bettelheim, Joseph Gillmann, Edward Wolff, and Shane Mage, numerous attempts have been made by Marxian economists to measure the trend in surplus-value using national accounts data. Probably the most convincing contemporary effort is that of Anwar Shaikh and Ahmet Tonak.

Reworking the components of the official measures of gross output and capital outlays to approximate Marxian categories in order to estimate empirically the trends in the ratios considered important in the Marxian explanation of capital accumulation and economic growth: the rate of surplus-value, the organic composition of capital, the rate of profit, the rate of increase in the capital stock, and the rate of reinvestment of realised profits.

The Marxian mathematicians Emmanuel Farjoun and Moshé Machover argue that "even if the rate of surplus value has changed by 10–20% over a hundred years, "The real mystery is why it has changed so little" (1983), p. 192).

The response to this inquiry must be, in part, be looked for in artifacts (statistical distortion effects) of data collection methods.

Ultimately, mathematical extrapolations are based on the available data, However, this information may be incomplete and not a "complete picture.".

Paul A. Baran, for instance, substitutes the concept of "economic surplus" for Marx's surplus value in neo-Marxist thought. Paul Baran and Paul Sweezy define the economic surplus in a joint work as "the difference between what a society produces and its production costs" (Monopoly Capitalism, New York 1966, p. 9). How the costs are valued and which costs are considered are crucial factors. Piero Sraffa also refers to a "physical surplus" with a similar meaning, which is calculated based on the price relationship between physical inputs and outputs.

In these theories, surplus product and surplus value are equated, whereas value and price are identical; however, the distribution of the surplus tends to be theoretically separated from its production, whereas Marx insists that the distribution of wealth is governed by the social conditions under which it is produced, particularly by property relations that grant entitlement to products, incomes, and assets (see also relations of production).

In Volume 3 of Capital, Marx insists vehemently that:

"The specific economic form in which unpaid surplus labor is pumped out of direct producers determines the relationship between rulers and ruled, as it emerges directly from production and in turn reacts to it. This, however, is the basis for the entire formation of the economic community that emerges from the production relations themselves, as well as its particular political form. It is always the direct relationship of the owners of the conditions of production to the direct producers – a relationship always naturally corresponding to a specific stage of the methods of labor and, therefore, its social productivity – that reveals the deepest secret, the hidden basis of the entire social structure, and with it the political form of the relation of sovereignty and dependence, or, in short, the corresponding specific form of the state. This does not prevent the same economic basis – the same in terms of its fundamental conditions – from displaying innumerable variations and gradations in appearance, which can only be ascertained by analyzing the empirically given conditions."

This is a substantial – if abstract – thesis on the fundamental social relationships involved in giving and receiving, taking and receiving in human society and their effects on the distribution of labor and wealth. It provides a starting point for investigating the issue of social order and social change. Nonetheless, this is only the beginning of the story, which would include all "variations and gradations.".

Lester Thurow provides a textbook example of an alternative interpretation to Marx's. In a capitalist society, profits and losses take center stage, he argues. However, he asks, what explains profits?

Thurow identifies five reasons for profitability:

Profit is the capitalists' reward for delaying their own personal gratification.

Some profits are a reward for taking risks.

Some profits are the result of organizational skill, initiative, and entrepreneurial spirit.

Some profits are economic rents – a firm with a monopoly on the production of a particular good or service can charge a higher price than it would in a competitive market and thus earn above-average returns.

Some profits are attributable to market imperfections; they result when goods are exchanged at a premium to their competitive equilibrium price.

Thurow does not provide an objective explanation of profits, but rather a moral justification for profits, i.e., as a legitimate entitlement or claim, in exchange for the provision of capital.

He adds, "Attempts have been made to organize productive societies without the profit motive (...) but since the industrial revolution, there have been virtually no successful economies that have not utilized the profit motive." Again, the issue is one of moral judgment, contingent upon your definition of success. Some profit-driven societies were destroyed; profit is not a guarantee of success, although it has strongly stimulated economic growth.

Thurow continues, "When it comes to the actual measurement of profits, complex accounting issues arise." Why? Because, after deducting costs from gross income, "it is difficult to determine precisely how much must be reinvested to maintain the capital stock's size." Thurow implies that the tax agency is the ultimate arbiter of profit volume because it determines depreciation allowances and other costs that capitalists may deduct annually when calculating taxable gross income.

Clearly, this theory is very different from Marx's. The purpose of business, according to Thurow's theory, is to maintain the capital stock. In Marx's theory, competition, desire, and market fluctuations generate the drive and pressure to increase the capital stock; the sole purpose of capitalist production is capital accumulation, or the maximization of net income through business expansion. Marx argues that there is no proof that the profit accruing to capitalist owners is quantitatively related to the "productive contribution" of the capital they own. In practice, there is no standard procedure within a capitalist firm for calculating this "productive contribution" and distributing residual income accordingly.

Profit, according to Thurow's theory, is primarily "something that happens" when costs are subtracted from sales, or a justly earned income. Marx argues that increasing profits is, at least in the long run, the "bottom line" of business conduct: the pursuit of additional surplus-value and the resulting incomes are what drives capitalist development (in modern language, "creating maximum shareholder value").

Marx observes that this pursuit always involves a power relationship between different social classes and nations, as individuals attempt to force others to pay for costs as much as possible while maximizing their own entitlement or claims to income from economic activity. The inevitable clash of economic interests implies that the battle for surplus value will always involve an irreducible moral dimension; the entire process rests on a complex system of negotiations, dealing, and bargaining in which justifications for claims to wealth are asserted, typically within a legal framework and occasionally through wars. Marx argues that beneath it all was an exploitative relationship.

Marx argued that this was the primary reason why the real sources of surplus-value were obscured by ideology and why political economy merited a critique. Simply put, economics was incapable of theorizing capitalism as a social system, at least not without moral biases interfering with the definition of its conceptual distinctions. Therefore, even the simplest economic concepts were frequently contradictory. But market trade could function normally even if the theory of markets were false; all that was required was a legally binding accounting system. On this point, Marx would have likely agreed with the Austrian School of economics; no knowledge of "markets in general" is necessary to participate in markets.

{End Chapter 20}

Chapter 21: Macroeconomics

Using interest rates, taxes, and government spending to regulate economic growth and stability are all examples of the kinds of macroeconomic decisions that macroeconomists study.

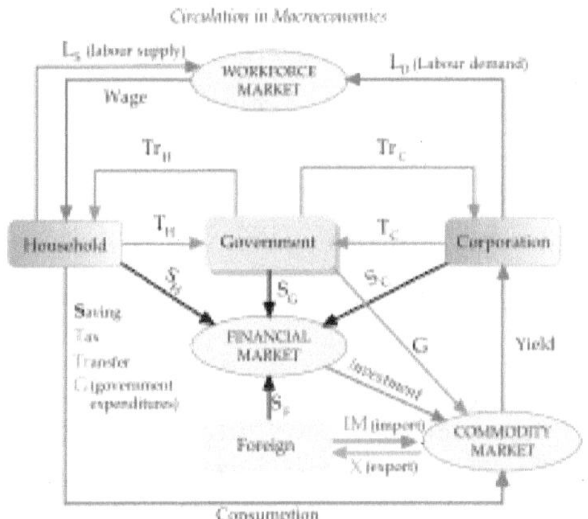

(Production and national income) Macroeconomics takes a big-picture view of the entire economy, Including Role Analysis,, connection between, corporations, households and national governments, and the various commercial arenas, markets like those for financial instruments and labor.

However, Its models rarely account for the consumption of natural resources or the release of waste products like greenhouse gases.

Gross Domestic Product (GDP), unemployment (including unemployment rates), national income, price indices, output, consumption, inflation, saving, investment, energy, international trade, and international finance are all things that macroeconomists study.

The two broadest subdisciplines of economics are macroeconomics and microeconomics.

Business cycle theory and monetary theory eventually merged to form macroeconomics. Prior to World War II, the quantity theory of money held sway. There were various iterations, including one based on Irving Fisher's research:

$$M \cdot V = P \cdot Q$$

According to the conventional interpretation of the quantity theory, if the money supply (M) were to increase, prices would rise proportionally because the velocity of money (V) and the output of goods (Q) would remain unchanged (P). In the early twentieth century, the classical theory of economics predominated, and with it came the quantity theory of money.

One of the earliest books from the Austrian School to address macroeconomic issues was Ludwig von Mises's Theory of Money and Credit (1912).

John Maynard Keynes is widely credited as the father of modern macroeconomics. Classical economists struggled during the Great Depression to justify why so many products went unsold and so many people lost their jobs. Prices and wages would fall until the market cleared and all goods and labor were sold, according to classical economic theory. To explain why markets might not clear, Keynes proposed a novel economic theory that came to be known as Keynesian economics (also known as Keynesianism or Keynesian theory) in the latter half of the 20th century.

Although Keynes explained this phenomenon in terms of liquidity preferences, it led to the breakdown of the quantity theory in his theory. A small drop in consumption or investment, Keynes argued, could have a significant impact on the economy as a whole due to the multiplier effect. Keynes also discussed the impact of fear and greed on the economy.

The role of money demand was added by Milton Friedman to the updated quantity theory of money. He contended that explanations focused on aggregate demand were superfluous because the role of money in the economy was sufficient. But Friedman was skeptical of the government's ability to "fine-tune" the economy with monetary policy, despite his claim that it was more effective than fiscal policy. He preferred less frequent intervention and more steady growth in the money supply. Friedman and Phelps were proven correct when the oil shocks of the 1970s led to soaring unemployment and price increases. The early 1980s saw a heyday for monetarism. Central banks struggled to implement the monetarist recommendation of targeting money supply rather than interest rates, and thus monetarism fell out of favor. When central banks manufactured recessions to curb inflation, monetarism lost political support.

The Keynesian school was also met with opposition from new classical macroeconomics. Robert Lucas's introduction of rational expectations to macroeconomics was a major step forward for new classical thought. Adaptive expectations, where agents are assumed to consider recent past when making expectations about the future, had been widely used by economists prior to Lucas. Agents are thought to be more intelligent under rational expectations. The average inflation rate over the past few years has been around 2%, but consumers won't blindly assume that will continue. Instead, they'll consider the state of the economy and monetary policy right now. By including rational expectations in their models, new classical economists demonstrated the limits of monetary policy.

The criticism Lucas made of Keynesian empirical models was also significant. He contended that no matter what the underlying model generating the data was, a forecasting model based on empirical relationships would always yield the same results. He argued for economically sound models that would, in theory, retain their structural validity even as economies evolved. Real business cycle (RB C) models of the macro economy were developed by new classical economists in response to Lucas's criticism.

In response to the new classical school, new Keynesian economists embraced rational expectations and prioritized the development of micro-founded models that could withstand the Lucas critique. In their pioneering work, Stanley Fischer and John B. Taylor demonstrated the efficacy of monetary policy even in rational expectations models with wage contracts. Olivier Blanchard, Julio Rotemberg, Greg Mankiw, David Romer, and Michael Woodford, among other new Keynesian economists, built on this work and showed other examples of inflexible prices and wages resulting in real effects of monetary and fiscal policy.

It was assumed in both classical and new classical models that monetary policy would only have an effect on prices and that prices would be able to adjust perfectly. Due to imperfect competition, prices and wages are sticky and resistant to monetary policy's ability to lower or raise them. New Keynesian models have explored these causes.

Economists had arrived at a general agreement by the late 1990s. Dynamic stochastic general equilibrium (DSGE) models were developed by fusing the nominal rigidity of new Keynesian theory with rational expectations and the RBC methodology. The new neoclassical synthesis refers to the integration of ideas from various theoretical traditions. These models have become an integral part of modern macroeconomics, and are used by a growing number of central banks.

In part as a reaction to new classical economics, new Keynesian economics aims to give Keynesian economics microeconomic grounding by demonstrating how imperfect markets can justify demand management.

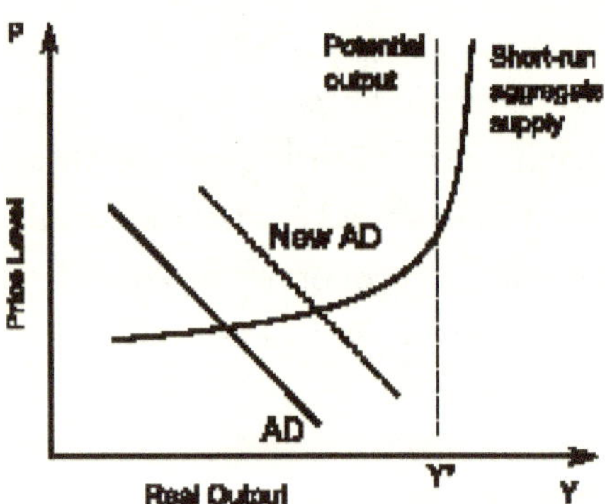

A traditional AS–AD diagram showing shift in AD and the AS curve becoming inelastic beyond potential output

The AD-AS model has largely replaced other macroeconomic models in introductory courses. Any increase in AD will result in higher prices rather than higher output because the economy can't produce more than its potential output.

Inflation is just one example of the many macroeconomic phenomena that can be modeled using the AD-AS diagram. Aggregate demand (AD) and its associated AD curve are sensitive to changes in non-price level factors or determinants. When consumer demand is greater than available resources, demand-pull inflation sets in and the AD curve moves upward, leading to higher prices. Cost-push inflation happens when costs in the economy rise, pushing prices up along the AS curve.

Macro economics also deals with study of GDP(gross domestic product)employment, inflation.

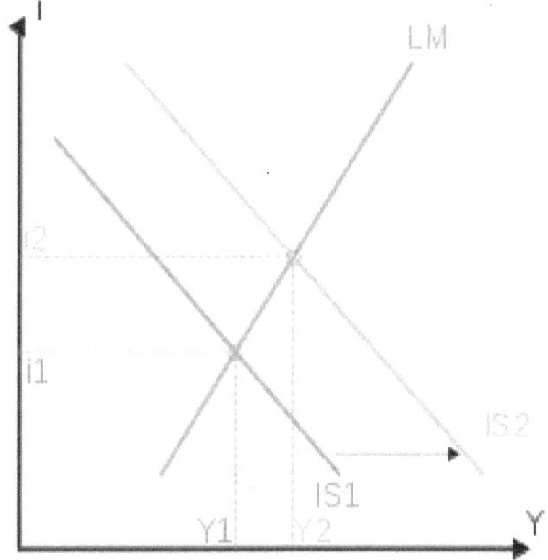

In this example of an IS/LM chart, There is a rightward shift in the IS curve, increasing I interest rates and (ii) "real" economic growth (GDP), or Y).

The IS-LM model serves as the basis for total market demand (itself discussed above). It provides an answer to the question, "At what price level is the maximum quantity demanded of a good?" To maintain monetary and goods market equilibrium, this model demonstrates the optimal interest rate and output levels.

Robert Solow's neoclassical growth model is widely used in economics textbooks as an explanation for long-term economic expansion. and without relying on uncontrollable and unexplained technological advancement, thereby fixing the central problem with Solow's theory of economic growth.

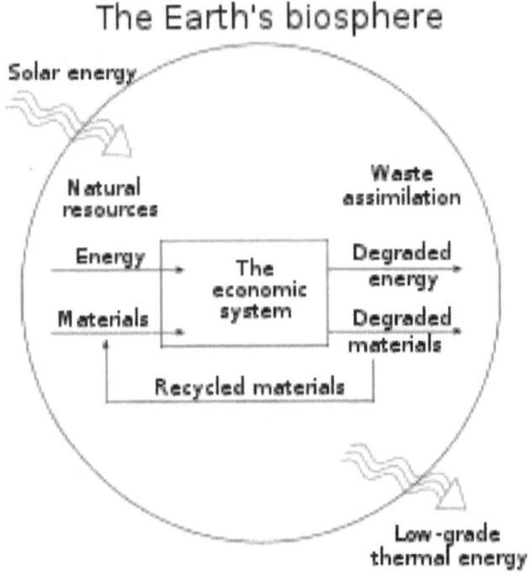

Natural resources flow through the economy and end up as waste and pollution.

When it comes to ecological economics' macro models,, The economy is a part of the ecological system.

Assumed herein, In ecological economics, the circular flow of income is replaced by a more complex flow diagram that takes solar energy into account, which maintains environmental services and natural resources that are converted into economic output.

Once consumed, The economy loses natural resources through pollution and waste.

The term "environment's source function" is used to describe the capacity of a given setting to supply goods and resources, and this capacity is diminished as resources are used up or tainted by pollution.

When waste production exceeds the limit of the "sink function," the environment can no longer absorb and neutralize the waste and pollution that has been produced, long-term damage occurs, Pollutants affect human health and the health of the ecosystem.

Despite the breadth of macroeconomics, the field can be broken down into three main subfields. Most macroeconomic theories draw connections between the three economic phenomena of output, unemployment, and inflation. These issues are crucial to workers, consumers, and producers even outside the realm of macroeconomics.

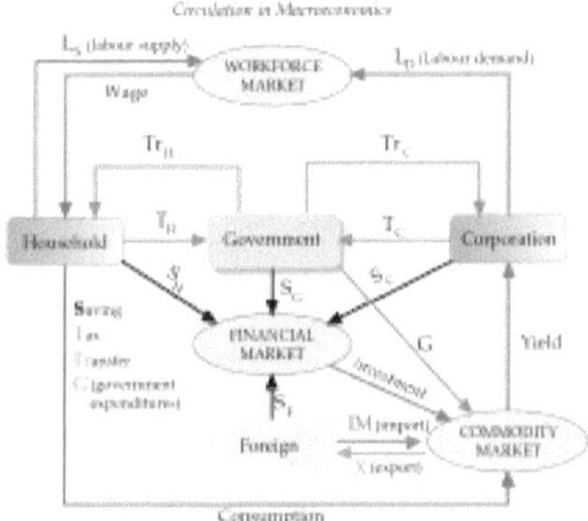

Circulation in macroeconomics

The output of a nation is the sum of all of its manufactured goods and services over a specific time frame. Every item made and sold brings in the same amount of money. GDP per person is used as a proxy for the economy's overall output. The two terms, output and income, are often used interchangeably because of their similar connotations. The value of the economy's final goods and services, or the value added across the board, can be used as a proxy for output.

Gross domestic product (GDP) or another national account is commonly used to quantify macroeconomic output. Long-term productivity gains are of interest to economists, so their research focuses on economic growth. Increases in economic output are the result of a variety of factors, including technological progress, the accumulation of machinery and other capital, and improvements in education and human capital. However, productivity is not always steadily rising. Recessions are temporary drops in output brought on by the business cycle. Macroeconomic policies that reduce the likelihood of recessions and boost long-term growth are the holy grail of the economics profession.

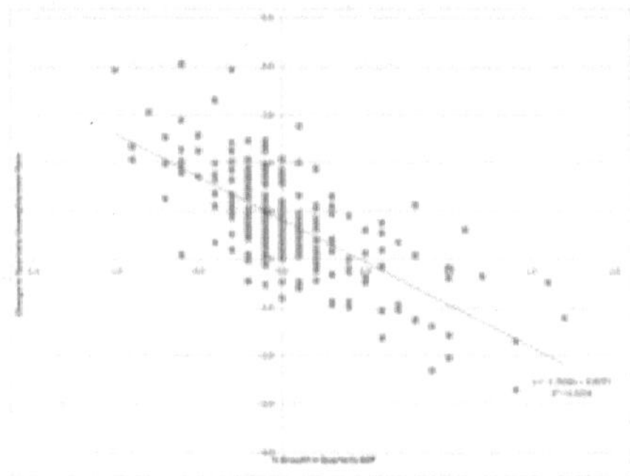

A chart using US data showing the relationship between economic growth and unemployment expressed by Okun's law.

Evidence of cyclical unemployment can be seen in the correlation.

When the economy improves, the unemployment rate drops.

The unemployment rate, or the share of the workforce that is unemployed, is a key indicator of the extent to which an economy is suffering from joblessness. Only people who are actively seeking employment are counted in the unemployment rate for the labor force. Excluded are the retired, the students, and those who are disheartened from looking for work due to a lack of opportunities.

There are a few distinct categories of unemployment, each of which is associated with a unique set of factors.

According to the traditional explanation for unemployment, wages must be too high for businesses to hire additional staff. There are newer economic theories that propose higher wages reduce unemployment by boosting consumer demand and thus the economy as a whole. These more modern explanations for unemployment blame a lack of consumer demand for labor's end product and claim that higher wages only lead to joblessness in markets with extremely slim profit margins and where consumers simply cannot afford a price hike.

According to the classical theory of unemployment, frictional unemployment takes place when there are jobs that are a good fit for a given worker, but that worker remains unemployed because it takes too long to find that job.

The term "structural unemployment" is used to describe a wide range of factors that can contribute to joblessness.

While some forms of joblessness are possible in any economy, cyclical unemployment develops whenever growth slows. The empirical connection between unemployment and economic expansion is represented by Okun's law.

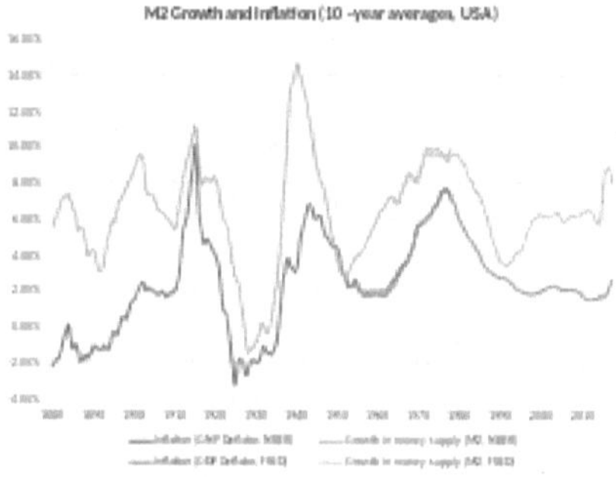

Changes in the ten-year moving averages of price level and growth in money supply (using the measure of M2, money in circulation (which includes currency and deposits in most bank accounts) in the United States from 1880 to 2016.

Over the course of time, A strong connection can be seen between the two series.

Inflation refers to a widespread rise in prices throughout a country's economy. Deflation is defined as a period of falling prices. Economists use price indexes to track these shifts. When economic growth accelerates too rapidly, inflation can result. Deflation is another consequence of a faltering economy.

Monetary policy is one tool used by a country's central bank to keep prices stable. Inflation can be tamed, so the theory goes, if interest rates are made higher or the money supply is made smaller. Inflation can increase unpredictability and have other undesirable effects. The economy may suffer as a result of deflation. To shield economies from the potentially disastrous effects of price fluctuations, central banks actively work to maintain price stability.

Several variables can contribute to a shift in the general level of prices. The money supply is directly linked to the price level, according to the quantity theory of money. Most economists think this connection is responsible for explaining price trends over the long term. Although monetary factors may play a role in short-term price fluctuations, shifts in aggregate demand and supply are also important. Deflation, for instance, can occur when demand drops off, as it often does during recessions. When aggregate supply drops due to a negative supply shock like the oil crisis, inflation can result.

Fiscal policy and monetary policy are the usual methods used to implement macroeconomic policy. The goal of both types of policy is to maintain economic stability, which can be defined as an increase in GDP commensurate with full employment.

Monetary policy is put into action by central banks, which regulate the money supply in various ways. In expansionary monetary policy, central banks increase the money supply by issuing new currency to purchase bonds (or other assets), while in contractionary monetary policy, banks sell bonds and remove funds from circulation to raise interest rates. In practice, policies rarely involve manipulating the money supply.

To keep an interest rate at a set level, central banks constantly adjust the money supply. Some of them are more concerned with controlling inflation than they are with stabilizing interest rates. Typically, central banks aim for high output without unleashing monetary policies that lead to significant inflation.

In a liquidity trap, conventional monetary policy may not work. Traditional methods of monetary easing by the central bank are ineffective when interest rates and inflation are very close to zero.

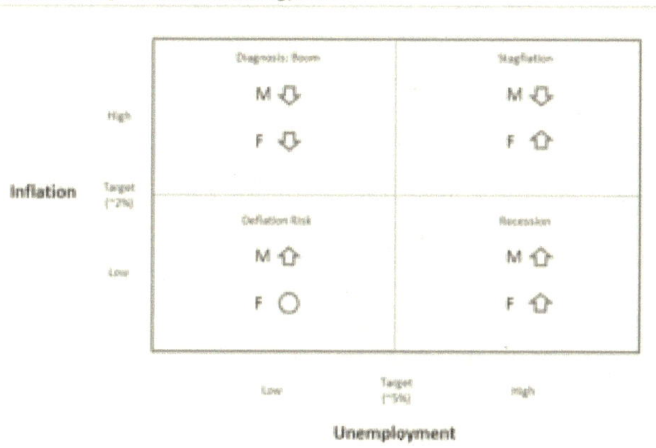

An example of intervention strategy under different conditions

Unconventional monetary policy, such as quantitative easing, can be used by central banks to boost output. Central banks can engage in quantitative easing by purchasing a wide variety of assets, including but not limited to government bonds, corporate bonds, stocks, and other securities. This means that a wider range of assets, not just government bonds, can benefit from reduced interest rates. The Federal Reserve of the United States recently tried an unconventional monetary policy with their Operation Twist. The Federal Reserve was unable to reduce short-term interest rates, so it opted to reduce long-term rates by purchasing long-term bonds and selling short-term bonds, effectively flattening the yield curve.

Distinguishing Macroeconomics from Microeconomics

Furthermore, economists think about two different factors. In its broadest sense, macroeconomics examines how economies function as wholes. It looks into things like employment, GDP, and inflation, which can be used in news articles and policy debates. The study of supply and demand in localized commodity and service markets is the focus of "small-scale microeconomics.".

Macroeconomics examines national economies and the aggregate phenomena that emerge from the interplay of national and international markets. Microeconomics examines the effects of supply and demand on a single market to answer questions like "why are oil and car prices rising?" The function of government in fostering economic expansion or regulating prices is a common topic of study in macroeconomics. Macroeconomics often deals with the global scale because of the interconnectedness of markets around the world through trade, investment, and capital movements. However, microeconomics is not always restricted to domestic concerns. The global oil market is a good example of how single markets are not always restricted to a single country.

The macro/micro divide is institutionalized in economics from the first-year "principles of economics" course all the way through graduate school. Both macro and micro specializations are common among economists. The American Economic Association has recently released a number of brand new academic journals. Microeconomics is the first. Separate from microeconomics is a field called macroeconomics.

Microeconomics, which focuses on the actions of individuals and small businesses, is split into subfields that study things like consumer demand theory and production theory (also called the theory of the firm), as well as related topics like how markets work, the state of the economy, and the impact of imperfect information. General equilibrium, which considers the interaction of multiple markets at once, is also considered a branch of microeconomics at its most theoretical level. The vast majority of economists focus on studying small-scale economic phenomena. It covers topics like how minimum wages, taxes, price supports, or monopolies affect specific markets, and is therefore rife with principles that can be applied in the real world. It is applied in many different fields, including business, economics, industrial organization and market structure, economics of labor, economics of public finance, and economics of social welfare. Establishing a new business is just one of many endeavors that can benefit from microeconomic analysis.

Macroeconomics is more complex and difficult to grasp. It explains the interrelationships among massive, abstract quantities like national income, savings, and inflation rates. Traditional subfields include studying long-term national economic growth, analyzing short-term deviations from equilibrium, and developing policies to stabilize the national economy (i.e., reduce volatility in growth and prices). Both the government (via taxation and spending) and the central bank (via monetary policy) are capable of taking such actions.

Government spending and taxation are two tools of fiscal policy used to shape the economy. Spending, taxation, and debt are all examples of such instruments.

If the economy isn't meeting its full potential, for instance, the government can increase spending to put idle resources to use. The output gap need not be fully compensated for by government spending. Government spending has a greater impact due to the multiplier effect. For instance, when the government subsidizes a bridge project, it not only increases output by the value of the bridge itself, but also reduces the output gap by allowing bridge workers to increase their consumption and investment.

Fiscal policy's impact can be dampened by crowding out. The private sector has less access to resources because of government spending projects. When public expenditures are used to replace private sector output rather than boosting total economic output, crowding out occurs. Government spending that drives up interest rates and dampens investment is another example of crowding out. When the economy is in a slump, many resources are sitting idle, and interest rates are low, proponents of fiscal stimulus argue that crowding out is not a problem.

Automatic stabilizers can be used to implement fiscal policy. When compared to discretionary fiscal policy, the policy lags experienced by automatic stabilizers are negligible. Conventional fiscal mechanisms are used by automatic stabilizers, but they go into effect as soon as the economy starts to decline. For example, in a progressive income tax system, the effective tax rate goes down as unemployment benefits go up.

There are two main reasons why economists prefer monetary policy over fiscal policy. To begin, governments are not responsible for implementing fiscal policy, but rather independent central banks. Central banks that operate independently are less likely to be influenced by political considerations.

{End Chapter 21}

Epilogue

As we conclude our journey through "Economic Production," we hope that this book has left an indelible mark on your understanding of the vital role production plays in our economic and social landscapes. This epilogue serves as both a reflection on our shared exploration and an invitation to continue the pursuit of knowledge and inquiry into the ever-evolving world of economics.

Throughout this book, you've delved into the core principles of economic production, from its foundations in the production process to its profound influence on economic growth. You've navigated through intricate theories and concepts that underpin the very essence of our economies. Whether you are a student, a professional, or simply a curious mind, we trust that this journey has broadened your horizons and provided you with a deeper appreciation for the complexities of economic production.

The world of economics is dynamic and ever-changing, driven by innovation, technology, and the collective efforts of individuals and institutions. We encourage you to continue your exploration of this fascinating field, to keep asking questions, and to seek new insights that challenge existing paradigms and shape the future. Your curiosity and engagement are the driving forces behind the evolution of economic thought.

Our epilogue is not an ending but a beginning. It is an invitation to join us in the ongoing discourse on economic production, to apply the knowledge you've gained to real-world situations, and to contribute to the betterment of our economic systems and society as a whole. The challenges and opportunities of the future are waiting for your insights and contributions.

In closing, we express our gratitude for accompanying us on this intellectual journey through "Economic Production." We hope that this book has sparked your passion for economics and has provided you with the tools to make informed decisions, whether in your studies, your career, or your personal life. We look forward to your continued engagement in the fascinating world of economic production and invite you to be part of the ongoing dialogue that shapes our economic future.

With that, we bid you farewell but not adieu. We hope you will return to these pages whenever you seek to deepen your understanding of economic production or to explore new horizons in economics. As you close this book, remember that your journey in the world of economics is far from over. The future awaits, filled with opportunities for growth, innovation, and discovery. Thank you for being a part of this intellectual adventure, and we look forward to crossing paths again in the world of economic thought.

Appendix

One Billion Knowledgeable

We are living in a society dominated by change. The technological, economical, and social evolution has shaped people's way of living and thinking. The globalized markets, the technical revolutions are transforming the modern economy into a "knowledge-based society", in which new ways of organizing the work are governing the world, demanding a perpetual buildup of competences, a rapid spread of high-performance technologies, solid knowledge and increasing responsibilities.

In the society of the future, knowledge will play the key part in the way of life specific to this knowledge-based society. Introducing in the knowledge is a prerequisite of national cultural success, as much as it is also a prerequisite of economic competitiveness. The real knowledge-based society, as an expression of the globalized society, tries to connect the needs of human nature, ever growing and more and more diversified, with its own regeneration, coming up with ways of developing the inexhaustible resources – the human intelligence, the innovative spirit, the associative creativeness, etc.

The Problem: Ignorance is the Root of all Evil

The problem I am trying to solve is "Ignorance", which is having or showing a lack of necessary knowledge or understanding of what is happening around.

Ignorance + Poverty = Crime

Ignorance + Richness = Corruption

Ignorance + Freedom = Chaos

Ignorance + Authority = Tyranny

Ignorance + Religion = Terrorism

But if you replace 'Ignorance' with 'Knowledge':

Knowledge + Poverty = Satisfaction

Knowledge + Richness = Creativity

Knowledge + Freedom = Happiness

Knowledge + Authority = Justice

Knowledge + Religion = Integrity

So, I once asked myself a question, If I could change only ONE aspect of the world to make it a better place, what would that be? I reached a conclusion that it would make the people more knowledgeable. I felt like this aspect could have the power to social change for a better world.

Ignorance may not be the root of all evil. Evil can be committed with many different types of agendas. BUT ignorance is definitely a good answer as to why evil remains, and sometimes ignorance is the direct root cause.

Most people believe knowledge is power and that success depends on how much a person knows. Knowledge is power, but knowledge without action can be useless; we gain knowledge by acting; without action, knowledge is useless, and knowledge is not necessarily understanding.

Imagine you have a bucket. If every time you tried to fill this bucket, 90% of the water leaked out, you probably would not fill this bucket until the leak is fixed. All the reading you do is like filling a bucket which leaks 90% of the water. You only retain 10% of what you read maybe after 24-hour period. Knowledge is power, but you are wasting time acquiring it if you retain very little of it. This is the key finding behind the study that produced the learning pyramid.

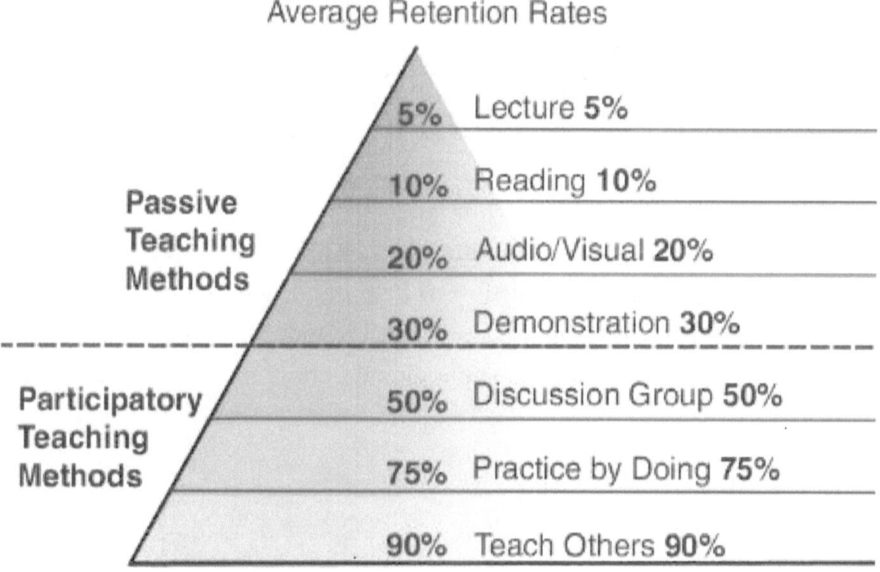

Figure 6: The Pyramid Learning

The Solution: 1BK Community

So, if people are knowledgeable and can retain their knowledge by reading, listening, and watching, and ultimately to teach others to become more knowledgeable; we will drain out most of the roots of the evil in this world.

This mission may be the most important of our time. Together we can make this happen. This mission is my attempt to fulfill the task of changing only ONE aspect of the world to try to make it a better place.

Sharing knowledge has a great positive impact, so I took an ambitious mission: To help one billion people become more knowledgeable. #1BK is a community, I ask you to join, so together we can create a large global community to make the world better place, to fight ignorance by making you, more knowledgeable, deeply aware, well informed, broadly learned, and wonderfully cultivated so people are drawn to you for their own enlightenment.

The spirit of the One Billion Knowledgeable movement is to give ideas a practical, and useful form in the life of the world nations and the people. So, I took on an ambitious mission to help one billion people to be more knowledgeable, a One Billion Knowledgeable movement that I ask you to join so that together we can create a global community of knowledgeable persons.

The Approach: 1BK Factory

Attracting 'knowledge producers' for average subjects and sophisticated ones and help them to produce knowledge in every possible format; and in every possible language, translating to 100+ languages; and in every possible channel; e-books and audio books marketplaces. This will save their time and effort, to focus on more knowledge.

Attracting 'knowledge contributors' to contribute to many tasks, translation, narration, and illustration.

The platform is a must to govern the process between producers, contributors, and 'Knowledge Consumers'; and offers incentives for producing more than consuming knowledge.

The cycle will continue, and every person can be a producer, contributor, or consumer.

If every member can convince 10 people to join, surely, the community will reach 1 billion in 10 years.

Building the 'Knowledge Factory' by software, automation, and systems, to produce knowledge content in every language and in every format, and distribute to many channels, and to have an online presence, such as website, and social media to be in every language, with a local community in every city.

The Action: 1BK Moonshot

When humans launched a craft to the space to put a man on the moon, they did not know they will succeed, but, surely, had enough passion for it. A moonshot is committing to solving a problem before you know you can make it happen. #1BK is a moonshot, and together we can make it happen.

Encouraging knowledge consumers to become knowledge producers, and knowledge contributors, and earn more funds in the e-wallet.

Join the movement at www.OneBillionKnowledge.com[1] by following three simple steps:

Step 1: Make knowledge your priority and recognize that being knowledgeable is your birthright and invest in your knowledge by exploring the One Billion Knowledgeable resources to develop your passion for knowledge.

Step 2: Participate by promoting and improving the knowledge of the One Billion Knowledgeable initiative and creating new knowledge in all fields, in all formats, and in all languages, simple enough for ordinary people to become familiar, and detailed enough to make experienced professional more enlightened.

Step 3: Share the message, pay it forward, tell ten people about the message that you have learned on www.OneBillionKnowledge.com[2], who will tell ten people, who will tell ten people, and in less than ten years, the community will have one billion knowledgeable.

This mission may be the most important of our time, and it is not crazy, together we can make this happen. I am going to tell the world that my priority is to be knowledgeable, and I am going to have the compassion inside me to make others more knowledgeable as this One Billion Knowledgeable mission is at the most pivotal time of humanity because we need the

---

1. http://www.OneBillionKnowledge.com

2. http://www.OneBillionKnowledge.com

knowledgeable persons to see things differently, to change things to the better, push the human race forward, and lead the world to the enlightenment.

About the Author

Fouad Sabry is the former Regional Head of Business Development for Applications at HP in Southern Europe, Middle East, and Africa (SEMEA). Fouad has received his B.Sc. of Computer Systems and Automatic Control in 1996, dual master's degrees from University of Melbourne (UoM) in Australia, Master of Business Administration (MBA) in 2008, and Master of Management in Information Technology (MMIT) in 2010.

Fouad has more than 25 years of experience in Information Technology and Telecommunications fields, working in local, regional, and international companies, such as Vodafone and IBM in Middle East and Africa (MEA) region.

Fouad joined HP Middle East (ME), based in Dubai, United Arab Emirates (UAE) in 2013 and helped develop the software business in tens of markets across Southern Europe, Middle East, and Africa (SEMEA) regions.

Currently, Fouad is an entrepreneur, author, futurist, focused on Emerging Technologies, and Industry Solutions, and founder of one billion knowledge (1BK) initiative.

Where to Find the Author Online

Website: OneBillionKnowledge.com[1]

Twitter: @fouadsabry[2]

Facebook: facebook.com/OfficialFouadSabry[3]

LinkedIn: linkedin.com/in/fouadsabry/[4]

Blog: medium.com/@fouadsabry

---

1. http://www.onebillionknowledge.com/

2. http://www.twitter.com/fouadsabry

3. http://www.facebook.com/OfficialFouadSabry

4. http://www.linkedin.com/in/fouadsabry/